CRIMINOLOGY BOOK TWO

for the WJEC Level 3 Applied Diploma

Rob Webb
Annie Townend

NAPIER PRESS **Criminology**

Published by Napier Press Limited
admin@napierpress.com
www.criminology.uk.net

Second edition © Napier Press Limited 2021
First edition published in 2019 by Napier Press Limited

ISBN-13: 9781838271510
ISBN-10: 1838271511

Rob Webb and Annie Townend assert their moral right to be identified as the authors of this work.

British Library Cataloguing in Publication Data
A catalogue record for this book is available from the British Library.

Design by Global Blended Learning
Cover design by Promo Design

Printed sustainably in the UK by Pureprint. This publication has been printed on Amadeus Silk, an FSC® certified paper from responsible sources. This ensures that there is an audited chain of custody from the tree in the well managed forest through to the finished document in the printing factory.

Endorsement statement by WJEC
This material has been endorsed by WJEC and offers high quality support for the delivery of WJEC qualifications. While this material has been through a WJEC quality assurance process, all responsibility for the content remains with the publisher. WJEC bears no responsibility for the example answers to questions taken from its past question papers which are contained in this publication or any judgments on marking bands. WJEC examination questions are used under licence from WJEC CBAC Ltd.

All rights reserved. No part of this publication may be reprinted, reproduced, transmitted or utilised in any form or by any means now known or hereafter invented, including electronic, mechanical, photocopying, recording or otherwise, or placed in any information storage and retrieval system, without prior permission in writing from the Publisher or a licence permitting restricted copying in the United Kingdom issued by the Copyright Licensing Agency Ltd, 5th Floor, Shackleton House, 4 Battle Bridge Lane, London SE1 2HX.

NOTICE TO TEACHERS IN THE U.K.
It is illegal to reproduce any part of this book in material form (including photocopying and electronic storage) except with the written permission of Napier Press Ltd or under the terms of the licence issued to your employer by the Copyright Licensing Agency Ltd.
It is illegal to reproduce any part of this work for publication or sale.

The publishers gratefully recognise the permissions granted to reproduce copyright material in this book. Every effort has been made to contact the holders of copyright material, but if any have been inadvertently overlooked the publishers will be pleased to make the necessary arrangements at the first opportunity.

Napier Press Ltd does not warrant that any website mentioned in this title or mentioned in the activities referred to in this title will remain live, will be error free, that defects will be corrected, nor that the website and the server that makes it available are free of viruses or bugs. Napier Press Ltd bears no responsibility for the content of third-party websites. Factual information given in this work is to the publisher's knowledge and belief correct at the time of printing.

For online support for Criminology teachers and students using this book, including schemes of work, activities and student workbooks. Go to www.criminology.uk.net

Contents

Introduction 4

Unit 3 Crime Scene to Courtroom

Learning Outcome 1 Understand the process of criminal investigations
Topic 1.1 Evaluate the effectiveness of the roles of personnel involved in criminal investigations 8
Topic 1.2 Assess the usefulness of investigative techniques in criminal investigations 14
Topic 1.3 Explain how evidence is processed 25
Topic 1.4 Examine the rights of individuals in criminal investigations 31

Learning Outcome 2 Understand the process for prosecution of suspects
Topic 2.1 Explain the requirements of the Crown Prosecution Service for the prosecution of suspects 37
Topic 2.2 Describe trial processes 41
Topic 2.3 Understand rules in relation to the use of evidence in criminal cases 47
Topic 2.4 Assess key influences affecting the outcomes of criminal cases 52
Topic 2.5 Discuss the use of laypeople in criminal cases 60

Learning Outcome 3 Be able to review criminal cases
Topic 3.1 Examine information for validity 68
Topic 3.2 Draw conclusions from information 77
Preparing for the Unit 3 controlled assessment 84

Unit 4 Crime and Punishment

Learning Outcome 1 Understand the criminal justice system in England and Wales
Topic 1.1 Describe processes used for law making 87
Topic 1.2 Describe the organisation of the criminal justice system in England and Wales 93
Topic 1.3 Describe models of criminal justice 97

Learning Outcome 2 Understand the role of punishment in a criminal justice system
Topic 2.1 Explain forms of social control 102
Topic 2.2 Discuss the aims of punishment 107
Topic 2.3 Assess how forms of punishment meet the aims of punishment 114

Learning Outcome 3 Understand measures used in social control
Topic 3.1 Explain the role of agencies in social control 122
Topic 3.2 Describe the contribution of agencies to achieving social control 133
Topic 3.3 Examine the limitations of agencies in achieving social control 144
Topic 3.4 Evaluate the effectiveness of agencies in achieving social control 153
Preparing for the Unit 4 exam 166

References 170
Index 1/1

Introduction

Welcome to your *Criminology Book Two*!

This is a brief introduction to give you a quick overview. You probably want to get on with the criminology, but it's worth spending a few minutes first to get to know the key features of your book and how you will be assessed.

Your book's features

If you leaf through your book, you will see some of its main features, including the following.

Topics The book's Units are divided into self-contained Topics, each covering one of the assessment criteria that you need to study.

Getting started Each Topic begins with a short activity to get you thinking about that Topic and to link it back to what you have already learned. Some are to be done with a partner or in a small group and others are for you to do on your own.

Activities Within the Topics you will find a wide variety of Activities to develop your knowledge, understanding and skills. Most of these are online (you'll see links to our website). Some are media-based, others are research or discussion-based, and most are to be done in pairs or groups.

Boxes These contain additional information linked to the main text.

Case studies These involve real-life cases and crime situations for you to consider.

Questions You will find questions to get you reflecting on what you have read.

Controlled Assessment Preparation At the end of every Unit 3 Topic, a special section outlines what you need to do to prepare for the controlled assessment. You will find a description of what the controlled assessment involves below.

Now Test Yourself At the end of every Unit 4 Topic, you will find one or more practice questions like those you will see in the Unit 4 exam. These will either have Advice on how to tackle the question, or a student's answer that scored in the top mark band, plus the marker's comments.

Studying Level 3 Criminology

This book – *Criminology Book Two* – is designed to help you achieve the WJEC Level 3 Applied Diploma in Criminology.

There are four units in the Diploma. You will already have done Units 1 and 2 in your first year. These are covered in *Criminology Book One*.

For the Diploma, you must also pass Units 3 and 4. These are covered in this book.

These are the Units you will study in your second year:
- **Unit 3 Crime scene to courtroom**
- **Unit 4 Crime and punishment**

Learning Outcomes

Each unit is divided into Learning Outcomes. These state what you should know, understand and be able to do as a result of completing the Unit. There are three Learning Outcomes for Unit 3 and three for Unit 4.

Assessment Criteria

Each Learning Outcome is divided into Assessment Criteria. There are eleven of these for Unit 3 and ten for Unit 4. They state what you must be able to do in order to show that you have achieved the Learning Outcomes.

In this book, each Assessment Criterion is covered in a separate Topic. For example, Assessment Criterion AC1.1 is covered by Topic 1.1 and so on.

If you look at the Contents page of this book, you will see the Learning Outcomes for Units 3 and 4 and underneath each one, the relevant Assessment Criteria (these are listed as Topics).

How you will be assessed

In the second year of the Diploma course, you will take a controlled assessment and an external exam. The details of these are as follows.

Unit 3: the controlled assessment

- Unit 3 is assessed using a controlled assessment. Just like in a traditional exam, you work alone.
- But unlike in a traditional exam, you are allowed to take all your notes, handouts, file etc. into the exam room with you.
- The controlled assessment is 8 hours.
- You cannot use the internet and you won't be allowed to access your own electronic files and documents.
- Your teacher will decide when your class will take the controlled assessment.
- The controlled assessment will be marked by your teacher. A sample of the marked work will then be sent to WJEC, the exam board, to check that it has been marked at the correct standard.
- The assessment includes a brief – a scenario describing a situation involving a crime. You have to complete a set of tasks linked to the brief.

Unit 4: the external exam

- Unit 4 is examined by a traditional exam of 1 hour 30 minutes, set and marked by examiners outside your school or college.
- There are three questions each worth 25 marks – a total of 75 marks.
- Each question is sub-divided into part questions. Some of these will be shorter (1 to 4 marks) and others will be longer (6 or 9 marks).
- Each question begins with stimulus material such as a crime scenario. Some of the part questions will relate to this.
- You sit the exam in the summer term. It will assess all three Learning Outcomes.

Unit 4 and synoptic assessment

Synoptic assessment involves making links between what you learn in different Units, and you will find that some of the questions in the Unit 4 exam may require you to use material from Units 1, 2 and 3.

Grades and re-sits

Both units are graded from A to E. The Diploma is graded from A* to E.

For Unit 3, you are allowed one re-sit opportunity. If you re-sit, you must submit a new assessment.

For Unit 4, you are allowed two re-sit opportunities. The higher grade will count towards your final overall grade.

Further guidance on assessment

You will find further guidance on the controlled assessment at the end of Unit 3 and on the exam at the end of Unit 4.

The Diploma units and how they are assessed are summarised below.

Year	Unit	Assessment	Qualification
1	Unit 1 Changing awareness of crime	Controlled assessment 2 parts: 3 hours + 5 hours	25% of the Diploma (50% of the Certificate)
1	Unit 2 Criminological theories	Exam 1 hour 30 minutes	25% of the Diploma (50% of the Certificate)
2	Unit 3 Crime scene to courtroom	Controlled assessment 8 hours	25% of the Diploma
2	Unit 4 Crime and punishment	Exam 1 hour 30 minutes	25% of the Diploma

Crime Scene to Courtroom

UNIT 3

Overview

This Unit takes you on a journey through the criminal justice system. We begin with the initial investigation that takes place once a crime is discovered and then we move through the different stages of arrest, prosecution and conviction of the offender, and finally to any appeal.

We begin by looking at the roles of the different personnel involved once a crime is detected, including police officers, crime scene investigators and forensics specialists. We examine the different techniques investigators use to gather evidence, including forensic laboratory analysis, surveillance, interviewing and offender profiling. Once the evidence against a suspect has been collected, the Crown Prosecution Service has to decide whether to prosecute them. We consider how they reach their decision.

Next we look at the rights of suspects who are arrested, charged and tried, and the safeguards that aim to ensure they receive a fair trial. These safeguards include important rules about what kind of evidence is permitted in court. For example, hearsay evidence and confessions obtained by threatening the suspect are ruled out.

Criminal trials may be held in a magistrates' court or – for more serious offences – before a jury in the Crown Court. We examine the role that ordinary citizens (laypeople) play as magistrates and jurors, including the factors that may influence a jury's verdict. For example, are jurors swayed by what they see on social media about the case they are trying?

Miscarriages of justice occur when an innocent person is convicted of a crime or when the trial itself was so unfair that we cannot be sure the defendant is guilty. In such cases, the court's verdict is unsafe and it may be overturned on appeal. When you have completed this Unit, you will be in a position to review criminal cases, evaluate the evidence and the trial process, and decide for yourself whether the verdict reached by a court is safe and just.

TOPIC 1.1

Evaluate the effectiveness of the roles of personnel involved in criminal investigations

Getting Started

Working in small groups, imagine you are a member of the public at the scene of a suspicious death. What would you do and what do you think the procedure would be to deal with this scene? You could consider the following:

1. What is your first action?
2. Who would you expect to arrive at the scene?
3. What would the personnel who attend the scene be doing?

The key personnel in criminal investigations

In this Topic, we look at the key personnel involved in investigating crimes and the roles they perform, and we examine the strengths and limitations of each of them.

The following personnel are the ones most closely involved in criminal investigations:

- **Police officers** are usually first on the crime scene and they secure it for investigation. Police detectives lead the investigation into the crime.
- **Crime scene investigators** gather and preserve evidence from crime scenes for use in investigations.
- **Forensic scientists** examine, analyse and interpret crime scene evidence using their specialist knowledge and skills.
- **Forensic pathologists** specialise in establishing the causes of suspicious deaths.
- **The Crown Prosecution Service** makes the decision about whether to charge and prosecute a suspect.

Police officers

A police officer is usually the first person called to a crime scene and they have a vital role at the start of the investigation. Officers need to safeguard the public and attend to anyone seriously injured at the scene, for example by calling an emergency ambulance. If possible, they need to arrest the suspect, though in many cases they will have left the scene.

However, as far as the investigation is concerned, the police officer's key job is to secure the crime scene in order to conserve the evidence. As far as possible they should avoid contaminating the scene by moving furniture, opening doors etc.

ACTIVITY Media

Police officers

Go to www.criminology.uk.net

The 'golden hour' is the name sometimes given to the period immediately after a crime is discovered, when officers must act quickly to preserve the scene. It is also important to take initial statements from witnesses and victims while events are still fresh in their minds.

Police detectives are officers who manage a range of criminal investigations, particularly those involving complex or serious crimes. They work within specialist departments such as the CID (criminal investigations department), fraud, drugs and firearms squads, child protection department and Special Branch.

Police forces also have other specialist units, such as traffic and mounted police, air support and underwater search teams, and dog handler units.

Limitations

The police have been criticised for sometimes failing to secure crime scenes and preserve evidence, and more generally for failure to investigate certain crimes, for example domestic abuse or hate crimes such as racist attacks.

Such failures can be due to incompetence in handling evidence or discriminatory attitudes of individual officers. It can also be due to system-level failings such as the institutional racism in the Metropolitan Police that was identified in the Macpherson Report into their investigation of the murder of Stephen Lawrence. Among other matters, the report criticised the force for its scene of crime procedures and for the failure to give first aid to Stephen at the scene.

> **Question**
> In what ways might institutional racism affect the way the police deal with a crime scene?

Crime scene investigators

Crime scene investigators or CSIs are also known in some police forces as scenes of crime officers (SOCOs). They are usually civilians rather than police officers. CSIs undergo specialist training and many have a science degree. The largest forces employ dozens of CSIs, who provide a 24/7 on-call service.

The CSI's role is to collect and process evidence from crime scenes, as well as from post mortems and accidents. A key responsibility is to preserve evidence in an uncontaminated condition, since contamination means that it will be inadmissible in court. Their main activities include the following.

- Taking charge of the crime scene, liaising with police to find out what evidence is required from the scene and deciding how best to obtain it.
- Photographing crime scenes, items and people, such as tyre marks, shoeprints, weapons, injuries, victims and suspects.
- Recovering physical or biological evidence from crime scenes, including fingerprints, gunshot and explosives residue, clothing fibres, hairs, bodily fluids and DNA.
- Packaging, storing and documenting the material recovered from crime scenes.
- Attending post mortem examinations of suspicious deaths.
- Advising police investigators on the physical evidence, photography and samples for laboratory analysis.
- Giving evidence in court.

Strengths

- CSIs may gather evidence that conclusively links suspects to crime scenes and victims.
- The evidence may also prove conclusively that a suspect is in fact innocent, e.g. when their fingerprints do not match those found by the CSI at the crime scene.

Limitations

- The work requires specialist skills (such as forensic photography), as well as patience, meticulous care and attention to detail. Failure to collect and record evidence correctly, or allowing it to become contaminated, can lead to a guilty person going free or an innocent one being convicted.
- The forensic samples that CSIs handle may put their health or safety at risk. These include blood and other body fluids, hazardous chemicals, explosives and incendiary devices, firearms and ammunition, knives and hypodermic syringes.
- The work may be stressful and emotionally demanding. This can lead to burn-out and people leaving the profession, resulting in staff shortages.

Forensic scientists and specialists

Forensic science involves applying scientific knowledge to crime and the legal system. Forensic scientists use their scientific knowledge and expertise to analyse and interpret evidence that has been recovered from the crime scene. For example, they may analyse samples of blood or other bodily fluids to extract DNA and then compare these with a 'control sample' taken from a suspect to see if they match. They then produce a report of their findings and interpretations for the court.

Forensic scientists generally specialise in particular areas, such as DNA analysis. Other specialisms include the analysis of fires (in arson investigations), toxicology (poisons and drugs), computing, psychology and forensic anthropology, which may involve analysis of human remains found in mass graves, for example as a result of war crimes.

Strengths

- The special expertise of forensic scientists may be able to identify and interpret evidence that proves a suspect's guilt or innocence.
- Their expertise may be essential in complex cases where the criminal also has specialist knowledge or skills.

CSIs in a taped-off crime scene examine a hammer used in an attack.

Limitations

- Forensic scientists are highly qualified and their services are expensive.
- Contamination of evidence can occur when it is being examined by scientists, as in the case of Adam Scott, who spent five months on remand in 2011-12 charged with rape. His DNA sample, originally taken by police as a result of a spitting incident in Exeter, became mixed up with genetic material taken from a rape victim in Manchester.
- Forensic experts may disagree. For example, experts called by the defence may contradict those called by the prosecution. The court lacks specialist knowledge and may be unable to evaluate which side is right.
- If an expert deliberately or accidentally misleads the court, this can result in a miscarriage of justice. At the trial of Sally Clark in 1999 for the murder of her two baby sons, an expert witness, the paediatrician Professor Sir Roy Meadow, told the jury that the chance that both deaths were accidental was one in 73 million. Experts now believe that the risk could be as low as one in 100. Sally Clark was convicted and only freed on appeal after three years in jail.

ACTIVITY — Media

Forensic scientists

Go to www.criminology.uk.net

Pathologists

Pathologists are medical doctors who specialise in studying the causes of disease and death, including the examination of dead bodies and body tissues in post mortem examinations (also called autopsies). Where homicide is suspected, Home Office-registered forensic pathologists provide a 24/7 service to assist the police and coroner in establishing the probable cause of death.

At the post mortem, the pathologist first makes a detailed external examination of the body for signs of foul play. Depending on the case, they may also examine internal organs and take tissue samples for laboratory analysis. They can also advise police on how to recover the body from the crime scene to avoid vital trace evidence being lost.

Before the body is released for burial or cremation, a 'defence' post mortem may be carried out on behalf of the defendant in the case, conducted by a different pathologist. Once all the test results are collected, the pathologist produces a report for the coroner and a witness statement for the police. He or she may also be asked to advise police and prosecutors throughout their investigation and to give evidence in court.

Strengths

- The key strength that the pathologist brings to an investigation is that they can often provide conclusive scientific evidence as to the cause and time of death. This may prove decisive in establishing the guilt or innocence of a suspect.

Limitations

- There are only about 35 Home Office-registered forensic pathologists in England and Wales – partly because it is a highly specialised role involving up to seven years further training after first qualifying as a doctor. The shortage of suitably qualified pathologists can delay investigations.
- As highly trained specialists, pathologists are very well paid and forensic pathology services can be an expensive part of a criminal investigation.

- The work demands close attention to detail and sound judgement. Mistakes can cause miscarriages of justice and result in the wrong person serving a life sentence for murder. For example, Sally Clark was wrongly jailed for the murder of her two baby sons partly as a result of the Home Office pathologist Alan Williams failing to disclose information to her defence lawyers. As a result, they remained unaware that Williams had found lethal levels of bacterial infection which could have been the cause of death.

ACTIVITY / Media

Pathologists   Go to www.criminology.uk.net

The Crown Prosecution Service

The Crown Prosecution Service (CPS) is an independent prosecution service operating across England and Wales in 14 regional offices. It uses a panel of over 2,000 solicitors and barristers along with other staff to handle around half a million criminal cases each year.

The CPS has several functions in relation to criminal cases:

- It advises the police on cases for possible prosecution and reviews cases that they submit to it to decide whether to prosecute. Most of this is done through CPS Direct, an on-call advice service that police can access 24/7.
- It makes decisions about prosecuting cases by applying tests to see if there is sufficient evidence for a realistic prospect of conviction and to decide whether prosecution would be in the public interest. (We examine these tests in more detail in Topic 2.1.)
- In all more serious cases, such as rape or murder, it is the CPS that decides whether the police will charge the suspect. Where the decision is made to prosecute, the CPS decides what the charge will be.
- It prepares cases for court hearings, collecting evidence from the police and disclosing material to the defence.
- It presents the prosecution case in court, using its own Crown Prosecutors, as well as self-employed barristers for more complicated cases.
- It has specialist divisions dealing with prosecutions that require specialist knowledge, such as serious organised crime, terrorism and complex frauds.

Strengths

- Before the CPS was set up in 1986, the police were responsible for investigating, charging and prosecuting cases. Combining these roles led to the risk of bias. Because the CPS independently assesses the evidence and decides whether or not to prosecute, it prevents the police from using the prosecution system to victimise particular individuals.
- Having a national organisation responsible for prosecutions means justice is more equal – there is more consistency between different parts of the country in deciding whether to prosecute cases.

Limitations

- The CPS has the power to reject a police request to prosecute someone – for example because the evidence police have gathered is inadequate. This can result in a difficult relationship at times. However, it means that prosecutions are less likely to fail due to inadequate investigation by the police.
- The CPS has sometimes made serious errors, for example in not reviewing the evidence thoroughly before prosecuting. This has resulted in prosecutions failing, such as the murder of Damilola Taylor, where the case collapsed after the evidence of a key witness was dismissed when she was shown to have lied. The CPS had failed to check her account prior to trial.

- Funding and staffing cuts in recent years have meant a growing burden of cases.

> **Question**
> In what ways does the CPS depend on the work of other personnel involved in criminal investigations? Give examples.

Other investigative agencies

While most crime is investigated by local police forces, other agencies are also involved, especially in the case of major, complex or specialised crimes. These agencies include the following.

- **The National Crime Agency** (NCA) The NCA was formerly known as the Serious and Organised Crime Agency (Soca). It has teams dealing with areas such as organised crime, smuggling and people trafficking, economic crime, child exploitation and online protection, and cybercrime.
- **HM Revenue and Customs** investigates and prosecutes tax evasion and other tax frauds.
- **Specialist police forces** such as the British Transport Police, the Civil Nuclear Constabulary and the Border Force are responsible for policing specific locations such as the railways, nuclear power plants and ports of entry to the UK.

CONTROLLED ASSESSMENT PREPARATION

What you have to do

Using your notes from Topic 1.1, give a clear and detailed evaluation of the effectiveness of the roles of the following personnel involved in criminal investigations:

- police officers/detectives
- crime scene investigators
- forensic specialists
- forensic scientists
- pathologists
- the Crown Prosecution Service
- other investigative agencies, e.g. National Crime Agency (formerly called Soca), HM Revenue and Customs.

You should have an understanding of the roles and you should consider their effectiveness in relation to the following potential limitations:

- cost
- expertise
- availability.

The assignment brief scenario

Where relevant, you should make reference to the brief in your answer.

How it will be marked

8-10 marks: Clear and detailed evaluation of the effectiveness of roles. The personnel involved are clearly discussed in terms of potential limitations.

4-7 marks: Some evaluation of the effectiveness of relevant roles. Description of the roles of personnel involved is also evident.

1-3 marks: Limited evaluation of the effectiveness of the relevant roles. Response is largely descriptive and may only be a list of personnel involved.

TOPIC 1.2

Assess the usefulness of investigative techniques in criminal investigations

Getting Started

Working in small groups, imagine that raiders armed with shotguns have robbed a bank. One of the raiders fired their weapon, wounding a customer.

If you were in charge of the investigation, what evidence would you want to collect? You might want to consider the following:

1. Who was in the bank at the time of the robbery? How would you investigate them?
2. What could you find out about the weapon?
3. What other information might be available in a bank?

Investigative techniques

Police and other investigators use a variety of methods and techniques to investigate crime. In this Topic, we assess the usefulness of a range of investigative techniques.

Use of intelligence databases

The term 'intelligence' refers here to information that has been obtained from many sources, often including confidential sources, and has been recorded and evaluated. This information may be stored in a variety of different databases that police officers can access, such as the following.

The Police National Database contains intelligence about suspected criminal activity as well as the data on the PNC. It holds over 3.5 billion searchable records and is itself made up of 220 linked databases.

The Police National Computer (PNC) contains several separate databases.

- It stores details of over 12 million people's arrests, convictions and police cautions, with links to biometric databases for fingerprints and the National DNA Database.
- Vehicle registration data and information on 48 million people who hold a driving licence, and on those who are disqualified.
- The PNC also holds information on missing and wanted persons.

Crimint and the Gangs Matrix Crimint holds information on criminals, suspects and protestors, and the Gangs Matrix holds information on suspected gang members.

International databases UK police can also access databases that share information between police forces in different countries. These include the INTERPOL databases on child sexual exploitation, biometric records (DNA and fingerprints), stolen property (e.g. art works), firearms and organised crime networks.

Limitations The gangs matrix has been criticised as racially discriminatory and in 2021 the Metropolitan Police had to remove over 1,000 young Black men from the database. It has also been subject to leaks. In 2017, the names and addresses of 203 alleged gang members were accidentally leaked and subsequently fell into the hands of rival gangs. Some of those named suffered serious violence.

Forensic techniques

'Forensics' refers to the scientific techniques and tests that are used to assist in investigating crime. As we saw in Topic 1.1, there are a range of forensic experts and specialists, but most often forensic techniques involve investigators recovering evidence from a crime scene and submitting it for analysis in a laboratory.

Forensic evidence can include biological materials (e.g. blood, semen, skin flakes and hair), along with fingerprints, shoeprints, weapons, fibres and threads from clothing, paint flakes and many other items.

It is essential that access to the crime scene is strictly controlled and that investigators wear appropriate protective clothing to avoid contaminating forensic evidence. Once collected, the evidence can be examined by forensic specialists such as those we looked at in the previous Topic and the results shared with police to assist their investigation.

DNA evidence

DNA analysis is the area in which forensics has made greatest progress. DNA is found in almost every cell of the body, and each person's DNA profile is unique (except for identical twins). In recent years, highly sensitive techniques have been developed for the extraction and rapid analysis of minute quantities of DNA samples. This has made DNA profiling the most important development in solving serious crime since fingerprinting was invented.

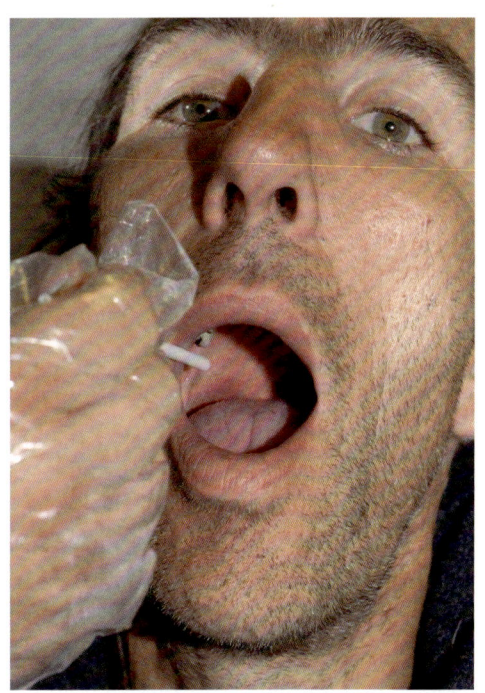

A mouth swab, taking saliva from a suspect to obtain a DNA sample for analysis.

Case study   First ever forensic use of DNA profiling

DNA profiling was developed by the scientist Alec Jeffreys in 1985 and it was first used to investigate the rape and murder of two girls in Leicestershire in 1983 and 1986. Using the new technique, Jeffreys established that semen left in both cases came from the same man. Police then took blood samples from all 4,583 men in the area and eventually found a match with Colin Pitchfork, who was convicted of both murders.

The test also exonerated (cleared) Robert Buckland, a 17-year-old with learning difficulties who had admitted to the 1983 killing. Buckland became the first person ever to be cleared of a crime using DNA analysis.

However, Pitchfork was in fact only caught when a co-worker revealed to workmates that he had taken the blood test masquerading as Pitchfork, because Pitchfork told him he had already given a sample while pretending to be a friend who wanted to avoid being harassed by police because of a previous conviction. A woman overheard the conversation and reported it to the police. The DNA analysis confirmed Pitchfork's guilt but it was witness evidence that enabled police to catch him. The forensic evidence was not the only factor.

Using relatives' DNA profiles

While each individual's DNA profile is unique, blood relatives have similar profiles to one another and samples from family members have been used to aid the identification of perpetrators.

This proved decisive in the case of Colette Aram, who was raped and murdered in 1983 by Paul Hutchinson – before DNA profiling existed. However, by 2008 police were able to develop a profile of her killer due to advances in DNA technology. Hutchinson's son had been arrested for a motoring offence and a routine DNA sample was taken which partially matched DNA taken from the crime scene. His father was arrested and convicted of the murder.

Because blood relatives share similar DNA profiles, the method has also been used to identify deceased victims of homicides, suicides and accidents.

ACTIVITY | Media

DNA evidence   Go to www.criminology.uk.net

Problems with DNA evidence

Despite the advantages of DNA analysis, there are several problems with the use of DNA evidence.

Contamination of DNA evidence

Contamination can lead to miscarriages of justice, as the case of Adam Scott in *Topic 1.1* shows. Scott was wrongly charged with rape in 2011 and spent five months in prison on remand on the basis of a contaminated DNA sample. The danger of contamination is if anything greater now, since the minutest quantities of DNA can now be analysed.

Problems matching samples to suspects In order to obtain a match with DNA from a crime scene, the offender (or a close relative) must already be on the National DNA Database. However, advances in forensic technology mean it may soon be possible to identify the colour of a perpetrator's hair, eyes and skin, and their approximate age, from a DNA profile.

Civil liberties

There have been civil liberties concerns about the police retaining DNA data taken from people who have not been convicted of a crime (e.g. those arrested but released without charge). This led to a change in the law in 2012 requiring most profiles taken from people not convicted to be eventually destroyed.

Cost Until recently, DNA tests were quite expensive. However, the cost of analysing a DNA sample is now around £20.

Surveillance techniques

CCTV

Surveillance means watching over something or someone, for example using CCTV to monitor who comes and goes in and out of a building.

Police often use CCTV footage in criminal investigations since it can give 24-hour coverage of a location, providing a visual record of the crime and helping to identify the perpetrator. In major cases such as murder inquiries or the 2011 riots, CCTV images can be released to the media with appeals for the public to report the identity of anyone they recognise.

However, because a camera is fixed, it cannot follow a target round a corner. CCTV cameras are also fairly easy to spot and criminals may avoid them or disguise themselves. Furthermore, the recorded images are not always of good quality, making identification difficult or impossible.

Covert surveillance

CCTV monitoring is generally not pre-planned; it simply records what occurs. By contrast, covert (hidden) surveillance is planned in advance and carried out in such a way that those who are being monitored are unaware of it. Covert surveillance can take several forms:

- attaching tracking devices to vehicles and using GPS to monitor their movements
- intercepting mail and tapping phones
- static surveillance from a fixed point, e.g. an unmarked, parked police vehicle, perhaps using binoculars or cameras
- highly trained mobile surveillance teams, on foot or in a vehicle.

ACTIVITY / Media

Covert surveillance   Go to www.criminology.uk.net

Covert Human Intelligence Sources (CHIS) can also be used. These are individuals who maintain a relationship with the 'target' in order to covertly gain information. They may be:

- undercover police officers using a false identity to infiltrate a criminal group
- informants who are themselves criminals.

Criticisms of covert surveillance

There are strict rules governing covert police surveillance, since it may involve unwarranted intrusions that breach the target's human rights to a private life, as well as entrapment (encouraging someone to commit a crime so they can be prosecuted for it). Despite this, there have been a number of high profile cases, including those of Colin Stagg and the Justice for Stephen Lawrence campaign.

In the case of Colin Stagg, wrongly accused of the 'Wimbledon Common' murder of Rachel Nickell in 1992, police used an undercover female officer in a covert operation in an effort to trick him into a confession. (See the case study on page 22 for details.)

There have also been cases of undercover police using the identities of dead babies to create a cover story complete with birth records, tricking women they had targeted into sexual relationships, and infiltrating peaceful protestors.

CCTV surveillance captures a crime in progress. Two men rob a phone shop, swinging an axe at the shopkeeper.

ACTIVITY / Media

Criticisms of police covert surveillance   Go to www.criminology.uk.net

Observation

The police distinguish between surveillance, which is pre-planned, and observation, which is not. For example, a police officer out on patrol who unexpectedly comes upon suspicious activity taking place may keep the situation under observation to decide whether a crime is being committed.

Interview techniques

Interviewing witnesses to a crime or interviewing forensic and other experts can be an important part of an investigation and court case.

Eye-witness testimony

Eye-witness testimony (EWT) is the evidence given by a witness to a crime. Juries are often willing to accept EWT as an accurate account of an incident and they frequently give more weight to it than to other kinds of evidence. For example, the Devlin Committee in 1976 found that juries convicted in 74% of cases where line-up identification was the only prosecution evidence.

However, their faith may be misplaced. For example, the Innocence Project in the USA has found that in over 70% of 352 wrongful convictions that were later overturned on the basis of DNA evidence, eye-witness misidentification played a role in convicting an innocent person – including 15 cases where the person spent time on death row.

> **ACTIVITY** | **Media**
> Eye-witness testimony
> Go to www.criminology.uk.net

Memory problems of EWT

Many of the problems with relying on EWT concern witnesses' memories. There are three aspects to memory:

- **acquisition**: witnessing the crime and absorbing what is happening
- **retention**: storing the information in the memory
- **retrieval**: recalling the memory, e.g. when being interviewed by police or identifying someone in a line-up.

Protest against undercover police who infiltrated peaceful protest movements over a 24-year period.

Memory acquisition

Several factors affect how successfully we form a memory of a crime, including:

- **Duration** The longer we are exposed to an event, the better we remember it.
- **Time of day**: Kuehn found that witnesses gave the most detailed statements of events seen either in full daylight, or at night (when they paid greater attention because of poorer visibility). In twilight, they overestimated the viewing conditions and could recall less detail.
- **Time distortion** Witnesses overestimate how long emotional or dramatic events (e.g. an assault) actually last.
- **Violence distraction** Witnesses recall violent events less accurately, probably because witnessing violence produces high anxiety levels that impair memory.
- **Weapon focus**: Loftus et al found that where a weapon is involved, witnesses focus on the weapon and this prevents them forming detailed memories of the offender.

Memory retention

Two main factors affect how well witnesses retain memories of a crime:

- **Time** Memory traces in the brain fade over time and information is lost. However, there is one exception: memory for faces does not seem to fade over time, so a witness who can't remember details of a crime may still be able to identify the offender.
- **Discussion of the event** with other witnesses, friends etc. aids more detailed recall, but it also reduces the accuracy of the memory.

Memory retrieval

Witnesses have to retrieve a memory when a police interviewer asks them to recall a crime. However, misleading information and leading questions can affect a witness's memory and produce inaccuracies, as research by Loftus and Palmer shows.

They showed people a film of a car crash and then asked some of them 'How fast were the cars going when they hit?' Others were asked the same question but with 'bumped' or 'smashed' instead of 'hit'. The 'smashed' group estimated the speed at an average of 40mph, whereas the 'bumped' group put it at 38mph and the 'hit' group at just 34mph.

Later Loftus and Palmer asked them a leading question: 'Did you see any broken glass in the film?' 32% of the 'smashed' group said they had, but only 14% of the 'hit' group. In fact, there was no broken glass in the film.

This research suggests that witnesses' recall of a crime could be distorted by the way questions are worded in a police interview or a cross-examination in court, thus making their evidence unreliable.

The cognitive interview

Given these problems, it is important to ensure that police interview techniques maximise the chances of gaining accurate information from witnesses. Psychologists recommend using cognitive interviews rather than standard police interviews. These use as many 'cues' as possible to encourage recall, using strategies such as:

- **reinstating the context**: the witness is asked to imagine themselves back in the situation
- **reporting everything they saw** – even things that might seem irrelevant.

These techniques help to create more cues to retrieve memories of the crime and cognitive interviews have been shown to produce more recall and a high level of accuracy.

Expert witnesses

As we saw in Topic 1.1, forensic experts can play an important role in criminal investigations. Police can interview experts and specialists for information and advice on different aspects of their investigation. These interviews are often conducted after the expert has submitted a report.

Police can then ask questions for clarification and to develop their lines of inquiry into the crime.

Experts include forensic specialists with knowledge of areas such as the following:

- Experts in blood patterns, fires, explosions and gunshot residues can answer questions about crime scenes.
- Psychologists can offer an analysis of the offender's likely personality, behaviour patterns and psychological characteristics, often as part of an offender profile.
- Pathologists can analyse the likely cause of death in homicide cases, based on post mortem examinations.
- Entomologists (specialists in insects) can calculate time of death based on how developed the blowfly maggots are that are found on a corpse (blowflies lay their eggs on dead bodies.)
- Forensic anthropologists can assist police in identifying deceased victims by analysing human remains.

Entomologists can estimate time of death from the size of blowfly maggots.

ACTIVITY | Media

Forensic entomology Go to www.criminology.uk.net

Experts may also be questioned in court. Unlike eye witnesses, whose evidence must consist solely of an account of the facts that they witnessed, expert witnesses may also be asked to give an opinion based on their expert knowledge. However, experts may sometimes get it wrong and this can lead to miscarriages of justice, as we saw in the case of Sally Clark in Topic 1.1, wrongly jailed for the murder of her two sons.

Profiling techniques

Offender profiling is based on the idea that we can predict the characteristics of an unknown offender by examining the characteristics of their offence and their victim. Just as an offender may leave physical evidence like fingerprints behind at the crime scene, they also leave behavioural evidence. For example, in a murder this could involve how the victim was killed and how their body was left.

Advantages Profiling can have several advantages. It may:

- link crimes committed by the same offender
- help predict future offences, allowing offenders to be caught earlier and avoiding further victims
- help police target their resources and prioritise suspects.

There are four main types of offender profiling. These are typological profiling (also called crime scene analysis), clinical profiling, geographical profiling and investigative psychology.

Typological profiling (crime scene analysis)

A typology is a classification system, and typological profiling aims to classify offenders into different 'types' with different characteristics based on how they behave at the crime scene. (This is why it's also called crime scene analysis.)

By carefully analysing the crime scene, it may be possible to identify the type of offender and their likely characteristics, such as their personality, lifestyle, relationships and motives. The profiler therefore gathers all the available information about the crime scene, the victim and the forensic evidence.

Typological profiling divides crime scenes and offenders into two types: organised and disorganised. The table uses the example of murder cases to show the difference between the two types.

Type of murder	Likely characteristics of the murderer
Organised crime • The crime is planned, e.g. murderer takes weapon and restraints to the crime scene • Attempts to control the victim • Leaves few clues at the crime scene (removes evidence) • The victim is a targeted stranger.	**Organised murderer** • Above average intelligence (but possibly an underachiever) • Manipulative, cunning, outwardly normal, concealing sadistic personality • Socially and sexually competent • Usually living with a partner • Angry/depressed at time of the attack • Follows media coverage of the attack.
Disorganised crime • Spontaneous – little planning or preparation, e.g. weapon improvised at the crime scene • Random, disorganised behaviour • Minimum use of constraint • Little attempt to hide evidence at the crime scene, e.g. leaves murder weapon behind.	**Disorganised murderer** • Lives alone, near to the crime scene • Sexually and socially inadequate • Suffers severe forms of mental illness • Physically or sexually abused in childhood • Frightened and confused at time of the attack.

The profile can then be used by police to identify likely suspects and narrow down their search. It can also be used to predict the likely future behaviour of the offender, such as whether and where they might strike next.

Typological profiling was originally developed in the 1970s in the USA by the FBI. Since then, further typologies have been developed to classify rapists, based on their behaviour when offending. For example, the 'power assertive' type uses rape to assert his masculinity, while the 'power reassurance' type is motivated by fear of sexual inadequacy. Other types include 'anger-retaliatory' and 'anger-excitement' rapists.

Evaluation of typological profiling

The investigative psychologist David Canter makes several criticisms of this approach:

- Information available at the crime scene may be quite limited and not collected under strict conditions.
- Speculations about the offender's likely personality, relationships or motives are not much help to police in finding them.
- The profile is based on the profiler's subjective opinion about which evidence is important, so different profilers might produce completely different profiles of the same case.
- The typology is based on interviews that the FBI conducted with just 36 convicted serial killers and rapists. This is a very small sample, and the offenders may be untypical of those who are not caught, as well as being manipulative and dishonest.

However, typological profiling has helped to solve some high-profile crimes in several countries. It can also help police to predict the likelihood of future crimes.

Clinical profiling

Clinical profilers are usually psychiatrists or clinical psychologists. They use their professional experience to get inside the mind of the offender. The aim is to gain insights about the offender that will allow them to predict their behaviour. Rather than using typologies that try to classify crimes into general 'types', they tend to see each case as unique and individual.

The best-known clinical profiler in the UK is probably Paul Britton. He prefers to immerse himself in the evidence and produce intuitive insights into the offender's thoughts and feelings when committing their crime. Britton is said to be the model on whom the TV series *Cracker* was based.

Evaluation of clinical profiling

Several criticisms of clinical profiling have been made. Firstly, it is based on the profiler's clinical experience of working with convicted offenders, which may be untypical or limited.

Secondly, it can produce unsupported speculations about the offender's characteristics and motivations. This can sidetrack an investigation and result in the arrest or even the conviction of innocent people, while allowing the offender to remain free to commit further crimes, as the case study of Rachel Nickell shows.

Case study Clinical profiling

The profiler, the suspect and the murder of Rachel Nickell

Rachel Nickell was murdered in broad daylight on Wimbledon Common in July 1992. Having become convinced that the murderer was Colin Stagg, but lacking forensic or other evidence, the police turned to the profiler Paul Britton for help.

According to the journalist Matthew Weaver, Britton came up with a plan to tempt Stagg into a confession. This involved a 'honey trap' in which an undercover female police officer calling herself 'Lizzie James' faked a romantic interest in Stagg and a liking for Satanism (an interest of Stagg's). However, despite her efforts, he did not confess.

Nevertheless, in August 1993, Stagg was charged with the murder. However, when the case came to court the following year, the trial collapsed. The judge condemned the honey trap as 'a blatant attempt to incriminate a suspect by positive and deceptive conduct of the grossest kind'. He commented on the abusive and unethical way in which psychology had been used. Stagg eventually received £706,000 in compensation.

Meanwhile, in November 1993, Samantha Bisset and her four-year-old daughter Jazmine had been murdered in their home in south-east London. In October 1995, another man, Robert Napper, was convicted of the murders. In 2008, after a re-investigation of the Wimbledon Common case, Napper was also convicted of the murder of Rachel Nickell.

Britton had been a consultant on the murders of Samantha and Jazmine Bisset as well as that of Rachel NIckell, but according to the journalist Richard Edwards, at the time Britton ruled out any links between Napper and the Nickell case. Had Napper been charged with the earlier murder, he might not have remained free to kill again.

Geographical profiling

There are more crimes in some locations than others. This is because offenders make choices about where to offend. These choices are often based on what they do in their *non-criminal* behaviour in everyday life. For example, they may see a crime opportunity on their way to work and return to it later.

This idea forms the basis of geographical profiling. Geographical profiling aims to work back from the locations where offences take place to identify where the offender lives. It is based on two main principles:

- **the least effort principle** Given two identically attractive targets, the offender will choose the one nearer to home.
- **the buffer zone principle** Although offenders will not travel unnecessarily, they will still avoid offending too close to home for fear of being recognised. This is their buffer zone.

Canter and Gregory apply these principles to identify two different patterns of offending:

- **The marauder** has a home range and travels within the vicinity, moving out from home in a different direction each time to avoid returning to the area of their most recent offence. Therefore, if we draw a circle through the locations of the two offences that are furthest apart, we should expect the offender's home to be somewhere near to the centre of this circle. Canter calls this the 'circle theory'.
- **The commuter** travels away from their home area to offend in another area. Once there, the locations of their offences tend to cluster together. If we find that the offences cluster around a main road or a station, for example, we might expect the offender is using this route to reach their victims and police can use this information to focus their search.

Evaluation of geographical profiling

- The method has had some success in predicting where to find the offender in a range of crimes, including rape, arson and burglary.
- However, profilers need to be sure that all the crimes were definitely committed by the same person. This can be difficult if the offender's mode of offending begins to change as they commit further crimes.
- The marauder/commuter model assumes offenders always follow one pattern or the other, but some switch between the two.
- Profilers need to be sure they haven't missed any crimes that lie outside the circle. Otherwise, the point they have identified as the centre will be in the wrong place.
- Geographical profiling relies on accurate data. If crime locations are not recorded correctly, this will make the map inaccurate.

Investigative psychology

Investigative psychology is most associated with David Canter and incorporates ideas from geographical profiling, such as that offenders are likely to offend in areas they know well. However, it also includes other features.

The offender consistency principle

The central idea of investigative psychology is the offender consistency principle, which is that an offender's behaviour is consistent between their offending and their non-offending behaviour. Therefore the way in which they commit their crimes will reflect their everyday behaviour and personality traits.

For example, a rapist who uses degrading language towards his victim may indicate a man who regards women as objects and who has difficult or failed relationships with women at work or at home.

Criminal narrative themes

Investigative psychology also uses the idea that criminals base their offending on 'criminal narrative themes' or personal life stories that give their crimes meaning. The offender may see himself as 'elated hero', 'depressed victim', 'calm professional' or 'distressed revenger'.

For example, the elated hero sees his crime as a brave and manly thing to do, an enjoyable, exciting adventure. By contrast, the depressed victim believes that events in his life are beyond his control and that he has no other choice but to commit his offence. While doing so he feels confused, depressed and lonely.

Evaluation of investigative psychology

- It uses concepts that can be tested in practice, such as the offender consistency principle.
- It uses both large scale data on patterns of offending and narrative themes to understand offenders' motives.
- It has proved successful in cases covering a range of different crimes.
- However, like geographical profiling, it depends on the quality of the data on offences and offenders. If this is inaccurate, so too will be its predictions.

CONTROLLED ASSESSMENT PREPARATION

What you have to do

Using your notes from Topic 1.2, assess the usefulness of the following investigative techniques in criminal investigations:

- forensic techniques
- use of intelligence databases, e.g. National DNA Database
- profiling techniques
- surveillance techniques
- interview techniques, e.g. eye witness interviews, expert interviews.

You should have an understanding of the range of techniques and assess their effectiveness in the following types of criminal investigations:

- situations: crime scene; laboratory; police station; 'street'
- types of crime: violent crime; e-crime; property crime.

The assignment brief scenario

Where relevant, you should make reference to the brief in your answer.

How it will be marked

16-20 marks: Clear and detailed assessment is made of a wide range of investigative techniques.

11-15 marks: A range of investigative techniques are used to make some assessment of their usefulness in criminal investigations.

6-10 marks: Limited evidence of relevant assessment of the use of investigative techniques. At the lower end, some investigative techniques are described.

1-5 marks: A largely descriptive response with very limited, basic/simple assessment. At the lower end, investigative techniques may be simply listed.

Explain how evidence is processed

TOPIC
1.3

Getting Started
Working in small groups, consider the following cases. In each case, (a) what evidence might you find and (b) how would it be gathered and processed?

1. A woman meets a man on a dating site and goes back to his flat. After having a drink, she decides to leave. The man stops her from leaving and sexually assaults her. While trying to fight him off, she bites his hand.
2. Following a burglary, a man tries to sell games consoles and a laptop matching those that were stolen. He puts an advertisement on social media offering the items for sale and the victim of the burglary sees it. The burglar cut his hand on broken glass when entering the property.
3. An armed man enters a busy shop and orders the shopkeeper to hand over cash from the till and cigarettes from behind the counter. When the shopkeeper refuses, he fires his weapon in the air to scare the shopkeeper, who then hands over the money and cigarettes.

Types of evidence

Evidence is central to the process of investigating and prosecuting crime because it is the basis on which a suspect is charged, tried and found either guilty or not guilty. Therefore, the process of collecting and storing evidence must be done with utmost care.

There are many types of evidence, such as material from the crime scene (e.g. fingerprints, blood stains), exhibits such as clothing, CCTV footage, confessions and witness statements. However, we can group evidence into two types:

Physical evidence: actual physical material, such as DNA extracted from blood stains, weapons, stolen goods recovered from the suspect.

Testimonial evidence: written or oral statements by victims, eye witnesses, expert witnesses and defendants.

Physical evidence

Physical evidence (also known as 'real evidence') is an important part of many criminal investigations and collecting, transferring, storing and analysing it must be done with great care to avoid contamination and to ensure it is admissible in court.

Locard's exchange principle

Edmond Locard (1877-1966) was a pioneer of forensic science and investigators always work on the basis of his exchange principle, which he summed up as 'every contact leaves a trace'. In other words, material from the crime scene (including from the victim) will be present on the offender – and vice versa. Paul Kirk describes the importance of the exchange principle and physical evidence as follows:

"Wherever the offender steps, whatever he touches, whatever he leaves, even unconsciously, will serve as a silent witness against him. Not only his fingerprints or his footprints, but his hair, the fibres from his clothes, the glass he breaks, the tool mark he leaves, the paint he scratches, the blood or semen he deposits or collects. It is factual evidence. Physical evidence cannot be wrong, it cannot be wholly absent. Only human failure to find it, study and understand it can diminish its value."

ACTIVITY | Media

Locard's principle

Go to www.criminology.uk.net

Collecting, transferring and storing physical evidence

Different types of physical evidence need to be collected, transferred (e.g. to a forensics laboratory) and stored in order to preserve them and to prevent contamination. Most contamination occurs by handling items without gloves or by breathing, sneezing or coughing over them.

In the case of serious crimes (e.g. rape, murder or arson), investigators wear protective clothing when collecting materials, to avoid contamination and sometimes to protect themselves from hazardous substances. This includes a mask, a hooded 'scene suit', overshoes and two pairs of gloves. For less serious crimes, only a mask and gloves are required.

Bodily fluids and tissues

Bodily fluids such as blood, semen and saliva, and tissue such as skin flakes and hairs, can provide important identification evidence, because DNA can be extracted from them and

Belfast, 2013. A fully-suited CSI gathers evidence after pipe bombs were thrown at police.

compared with control samples from suspects to see if there is a match which would put the suspect at the crime scene.

Blood should be allowed to air-dry. Fabric bearing wet blood should not be folded, as this will cause the blood to transfer to other parts of the item. Items with dry blood on them should be carefully packaged and sent as soon as possible and in any event within 24 hours to the forensics laboratory for analysis.

Semen may be found on clothing and bedding. If wet, it should be allowed to air-dry on the item. Once dry, the item should be placed in a paper bag, which should then be sealed and placed inside a polythene bag, again sealed and labelled. Each item should be packaged separately. Where someone has been the victim of sexual assault, they should be examined as soon as possible by a police surgeon or other doctor and swabs taken.

Saliva from bites inflicted on a victim can also be swabbed to provide a sample for DNA analysis.

Skin flakes We are constantly shedding small quantities of skin. These may be found at the crime scene and can be analysed for DNA.

Hairs may be found at the crime scene that can be matched with those of a suspect. In assault cases, a victim's hairs may be found on the suspect. If hairs are found on clothing the item should be wrapped in paper or placed in a paper bag, sealed, labelled and sent to the forensics laboratory for analysis. Individual hairs found on furniture etc. should be wrapped or bagged in the same way. DNA can be extracted from cells in the root to identify suspects or victims.

Fingerprints

Fingerprints (and palm, toe and sole prints) are unique to each individual and so they are valuable identification evidence. The 'prints' are skin ridges on the fingers and they can leave impressions or marks in or on surfaces. The marks can be from sweat or from contaminants on the skin.

Fingerprints can be of three kinds:

- **Latent prints** are invisible marks left on a surface that can be made visible by 'dusting' with magnesium powder or shining an ultraviolet light on the surface. After photographing them, prints may be lifted using an adhesive strip and placed on an acetate sheet.
- **Patent (or positive) prints** are visible to the naked eye. They may be left in substances such as blood, ink, oil, powder or dust. They should be photographed for analysis and if possible preserved for use in court.
- **Plastic prints** are three dimensional shapes made by pressing the fingers into soft material such as wet clay or the putty on a window frame. ('Plastic' here means easily shaped or moulded.) They should be photographed and if possible a mould made to capture a copy of the impression.

Once collected from the crime scene, fingerprints can be compared with those stored in the police's IDENT1 database, which houses prints of all arrested persons, to see if there is a match. Police also have Livescan scanners and Lantern portable units linked to the database that can scan suspects' prints and obtain a result within minutes.

ACTIVITY / Media

Fingerprints   Go to www.criminology.uk.net

Impression evidence

Impression evidence is created when a suspect 'presses' something against a surface. This can be a hand, as in the case of fingerprints, but impressions can be created in other ways too, for example by biting someone, or by leaving a shoeprint or a tyre mark.

Bite marks on victims often result from sexual assaults. As they often contain traces of the suspect's saliva, they should be examined promptly by a police surgeon and swabs taken for DNA analysis, and the marks should be photographed. It may be possible to take a cast of the bite mark to compare with one taken of a suspect's teeth, which can be analysed for a possible match by a specialist dentist called a forensic odontologist.

Shoeprints left in oil, paint, blood etc. can be used to seek a match with a suspect's footwear. If prints are left in soil, casts can be made. Outdoor prints should be protected from the weather until they can be properly examined. The police have a database called the National Footwear Reference Collection which can be checked to see if they match a known offender's footwear.

Tyre marks can be left in soft soil, on roads etc. Marks may be made by a rotating or skidding wheel. Tyres develop individual characteristics as they wear and so they can be compared with those belonging to a suspect.

Shoeprint at a crime scene. The photographic scale indicates the size of the print.

Trace evidence

Trace evidence is any material that is transferred from the suspect to the crime scene (including to the victim) or vice versa. It includes things like gunshot residue, glass fragments, paint flakes and fibres, soil and even insects. It also includes toxicology (poisons, drugs and alcohol), for example from roadside breathalyser tests.

Fibres can be natural or synthetic. They can be transferred from clothing, carpets and seats. They can be collected using gloves and tweezers, wrapped in paper and sealed in a bag, labelled and sent for analysis. Fibres from clothing come in a wide variety of fabric mixes and dyes, often specific to particular manufacturers. This can aid in identifying the garment they came from and this information may be used in compiling a description of the suspect.

Paint on window frames, doors, cars and other objects comes in many different colours and types (e.g. rustproof, weatherproof, anti-fungal etc.), which can aid identification and allow for matching with flakes found on a suspect's clothing, tools etc.

Glass fragments found at a break-in can be compared with those found on a suspect's clothing. When window glass is smashed, it undergoes 'backward fragmentation', throwing out fine particles towards the person breaking it. These land on him or her in a particular pattern and can therefore show that they were present when it broke.

Soils can vary greatly even over short distances and so soil samples found on a suspect's footwear can help to place him or her at the crime scene.

Insects such as blowflies, which lay their eggs in or on dead bodies, can give an indication of the time of death by a forensic entomologist examining how developed their larvae (maggots) are.

ACTIVITY | **Media**

Trace evidence

Go to www.criminology.uk.net

> ### Case study | Physical evidence
>
> **Barry George and the murder of Jill Dando**
>
> Jill Dando, the presenter of BBC TV's *Crimewatch*, was shot dead outside her home in April 1999. Barry George was arrested and charged with her murder in May 2000 and convicted in July 2001. Part of the case against him was trace evidence in the form of a single microscopic particle of gunshot residue found in his overcoat pocket a year after the murder. The prosecution argued that this had come from a gun fired by George.
>
> In 2006 George appealed on the grounds that two new witnesses said they had seen armed police at the scene when he was arrested – contrary to the police's claim that no armed officers had been present.
>
> The defence called forensic experts, including those from the original trial, who told the Court of Appeal that it was no more likely that the residue was from a gun fired by George than from some other source. The defence argued that the armed officers involved in his arrest could have been the source of the gunshot residue. The court quashed George's conviction and ordered a re-trial, at which he was acquitted in 2008.

Testimonial evidence

Testimonial evidence is a written or spoken statement given to the court by a witness. It can be given to support either the prosecution or the defence's case.

Disclosure Before the case goes to court, prosecution and defence must disclose any written statements that they have taken. Each side must also provide the other side with a list of the witnesses they intend to call to give evidence at the trial. Physical evidence such as CCTV footage must also be disclosed.

Giving evidence

Any evidence that is agreed and accepted as true by both sides can sometimes be read out in court without the witness being present, but normally they must attend in person to testify (give their evidence).

In court, witnesses testify from the witness box. They may then be cross-examined (cross-questioned) by the opposing side to test their evidence. Defendants cannot be forced to testify.

Vulnerable or intimidated witnesses may be allowed to give evidence via a live video link or by a video recording rather than having to attend court in person. If they do have to attend, they may be allowed to give evidence from behind a screen.

Vulnerable witnesses include those under the age of 18, those with a mental health condition or disability, close relatives of someone who died because of a crime, repeat victims (e.g. of stalkers), victims of serious crimes such as sexual offences, and witnesses of gun crime. (See Topic 1.4 for more about vulnerable and intimidated witnesses.)

Admissibility of testimonial evidence

Rules of evidence lay down what kinds of things can and cannot be given in evidence. Some evidence may not be admissible (allowable) and must not be considered in reaching a verdict. This includes:

- **hearsay evidence**, for example where a witness is simply repeating a rumour they have heard rather than describing what they themselves saw.
- **forced confession**, where violence or threats have been used to extract a confession from the defendant

- **entrapment**, where the police have tried to trick the defendant into committing or confessing to a crime in order to be able to then prosecute them. For example, the 'honey trap' set by police for Colin Stagg led to the judge ruling this evidence to be inadmissible (see Topic 1.2.)

Case study — Testimonial evidence

Expert testimony, disclosure and the cot deaths cases

As we saw in Topic 1.1, Sally Clark was convicted of the murder of her two baby sons in 1999 but acquitted after a second appeal in 2003. Her conviction had been the result of two serious shortcomings by expert witnesses in her original trial.

Firstly, Dr Alan Williams, the Home Office forensic pathologist who conducted the post mortems on both babies, failed to disclose key evidence to the defence. He withheld laboratory evidence that infection was a possible cause of the second baby's death, and he changed his original opinion about the first baby's death from respiratory infection to death by smothering. Williams was severely criticised by the judges at the second appeal. The court invited him to explain why he had withheld the laboratory results but he declined to do so.

Secondly, the testimony given by the paediatrician Professor Sir Roy Meadow was flawed. He claimed that the chance of two siblings both suffering cot death was 1 in 73 million. The Royal Statistical Society later issued a statement to say there was 'no statistical basis' for Meadow's claim and expressed concern at the misuse of statistics in the courts.

Meadow had also testified as an expert witness in other cot death cases and had made the same claim. These included the trials of Donna Anthony in 1998 and Angela Cannings in 2002, in both cases for the murder of their two children. Cannings was freed on appeal in 2003 and Anthony in 2005. Meadow was struck off the medical register for gross professional misconduct in 2005 but was reinstated the following year.

CONTROLLED ASSESSMENT PREPARATION

What you have to do

Using your notes from Topic 1.3, explain how evidence is processed. You should have an understanding of the following types of evidence:

- physical evidence
- testimonial evidence.

You should understand how evidence is processed, including:

- collection
- transfer
- storage
- analysis
- the personnel involved.

You should explore how different types of evidence were processed through a range of case studies, such as Barry George, Sally Clark and Angela Cannings.

The assignment brief scenario

Where relevant, you should make reference to the brief in your answer.

How it will be marked

4-6 marks: Clear and detailed explanation of how evidence is processed using relevant examples.
1-3 marks: Basic response that may only list procedures or mention case studies.

Examine the rights of individuals in criminal investigations

TOPIC 1.4

Getting Started

Working on your own, write down what rights you think an individual has if they:

1. are arrested by the police
2. witness a crime
3. are the victim of a crime.

Share your answers with a partner. Do you agree with each other?

For 1-3 above, consider what you think a person's rights *should or shouldn't* be in each of these situations.

In this Topic we examine the rights of the suspects, victims and witnesses who may be involved in a criminal investigation and court proceedings.

The rights of suspects

The police have certain powers to deal with suspects, including rights to stop and search and to arrest a person.

Stop and account An officer has the right to ask you to account for your actions, your presence in a public place, and your possession of a particular item.

Stop and search Police have 19 different powers of stop and search, e.g. for drugs, firearms and stolen goods, and to prevent acts of terrorism. Police also have certain powers to search vehicles and premises. These powers must be used fairly, responsibly and without discrimination against a person on grounds such as race, gender or sexual orientation.

Police power of arrest

Under section 24 of the Police and Criminal Evidence Act 1984, police may lawfully arrest you as a suspect, without a warrant from a court, if:

- you have been involved, attempted to be involved or are suspected of being involved in committing an offence; *and*
- the officer has reasonable grounds for believing the arrest is necessary.

The officer must then tell you that you are being arrested, what you are being arrested for, and why the arrest is necessary. The officer can use reasonable force to detain you if necessary.

Rights at the police station

If you are arrested, you will be taken to a police station, where you will be handed over to the custody officer (an officer of the rank of sergeant or above), who is responsible for the care of arrestees. You will be searched and then held in a cell. Your possessions will be looked after by the custody officer.

The custody officer must explain your rights to:
- get free legal advice by consulting a solicitor (see below)
- have someone told of your arrest and where you are being held
- see the rules the police must follow and see a written notice telling you about your rights.

If you are under 18 or a vulnerable adult, the police must try to contact your parent, guardian or carer. They must also find an 'appropriate adult' to come to the station to help you and be present during questioning and searching. This could be a parent, carer, relative or friend, a social worker or a volunteer.

Rights when being questioned

The police may question you about the crime you're suspected of and you have a number of rights in this situation.

The right to silence

You don't have to answer the police's questions, but there could be consequences if you don't. The police must explain this to you by reading you the police caution:

> "You do not have to say anything. But it may harm your defence if you do not mention when questioned something which you later rely on in court. Anything you do say may be given in evidence."

If your case goes to trial and in your defence you use something that you had failed to tell the police in your interview, your earlier silence about the matter can be used as part of the case against you. However, remaining silent and refusing to answer the police's questions is not proof of guilt in itself – the prosecution must still produce other evidence against you to convict you.

Recording All interviews must be tape recorded. Many police forces also video interviews.

The right to legal advice

You have the right to free legal advice if you are questioned by the police, including the right to have a solicitor present during your interview to represent and advise you. You must be told about your right to legal advice before you are questioned.

Once you have asked for legal advice, the police cannot normally question you until you have it. However, in serious cases, the police can make you wait for legal advice for up to 36 hours (48 hours for terrorist offences).

Fingerprints, photographs and samples

The police have the right to take photographs of you, as well as fingerprints and a DNA sample (e.g. from a mouth swab), and they can swab the skin surface of your hands and arms. They don't need your permission to do this and they can use reasonable force if necessary.

The police need both your permission and the authority of a senior police officer to take blood or urine samples (except when taking them in connection with drink or drug driving).

Rights to information

Information from fingerprints and samples is stored in a police database. You can ask the police to remove your information from their database but they will only do this if an offence no longer exists or if anything in the police process (e.g. how you were arrested) was unlawful.

How long the police can hold you

Police can hold you in custody for up to 24 hours. After that, they have to either charge you with a crime or release you. For indictable offences (serious crimes) you can be held for 36 hours. After that, police can detain you for a further 96 hours (four days) with the approval of a magistrate. However, if you are arrested under the Terrorism Act, you can be held without charge for up to 14 days.

Police bail

Bail involves the temporary release of a suspect. The police can release you on police bail if you are a suspect but there is not enough evidence to charge you. You will have to return to the station for further questioning when required.

Conditional bail The police may charge you and release you with certain restrictions, e.g. they can impose a curfew on you or require you to stay away from certain people or places. They are likely to do this if they think you may commit another offence, fail to turn up at court, intimidate witnesses or obstruct the course of justice.

ACTIVITY / Media

Rights when arrested — Go to www.criminology.uk.net

Rights of appeal

If you are convicted of an offence, you have certain rights of appeal. These rights vary depending on two factors:

- the type of court – magistrates' court or Crown Court
- whether you are appealing against the conviction (you say you are innocent), or against the sentence (you accept your guilt but you believe the sentence is unfair).

If you were tried in a magistrates' court, you can automatically appeal:

- against your conviction, so long as you had pleaded not guilty at your trial
- against your sentence.

If you were tried in the Crown Court, you have no automatic right of appeal – a judge will decide whether to allow it. (For more about appeals, see Topic 2.2.)

The rights of victims

Victims of crime have rights in relation to criminal investigations and court processes. They are set out in the Code of Practice for Victims of Crime (also called the Victims' Code) which was established by the Domestic Violence, Crime and Victims Act (2004). These rights also apply to close relatives of someone who has died as a result of a crime.

Rights when reporting the crime

If you are a victim of a crime, when you report it the police must give you written confirmation, a crime reference number and contact details for the officer dealing with your case. They must also:

- tell you what will happen next and how often they will update you on their investigation
- assess what support you need and ask a victim support organisation to contact you
- ask if you want to write a Victim Personal Statement about how the crime has affected you. You may be able to read it out in court later.

Victim Support hate crimes teams work in the community to offer support to victims.

Rights during the investigation

The police must give you updates and tell you when a suspect is arrested or charged, set free or released on bail, or given a caution. If the police or CPS decide to drop the charge, they must tell you. You can ask for a review if you disagree with their decision.

The right to privacy If the police give information to the media to help with their investigation, they will normally ask the victim's permission first. In cases of sexual assault or rape, it is against the law for anyone to publish the name, photo or anything that could identify the victim.

Rights relating to trials

In relation to court proceedings, victims have several rights:
- The CPS must tell you where and when the trial will be.
- If you have to give evidence, a Witness Care Officer will support you before and during the trial.
- If the defendant is convicted, you may be able to read your Victim Personal Statement to the court.
- After the trial ends, your Witness Care Officer must tell you the verdict within 24 hours, what sentence the offender gets, if found guilty, and if the offender appeals.
- You can claim compensation from the Criminal Injuries Compensation Authority (CICA) if the crime was violent. The court may also order the defendant to pay you compensation for injuries or damage to property.
- If you so choose, you may also be able to meet the offender through a restorative justice scheme. This aims to repair the harm caused by the offence.

Rights of vulnerable victims

You are entitled to extra support if you are a vulnerable victim. Vulnerable victims include those who:

- are under 18
- have a mental health condition or physical or mental disability
- are a close relative of someone who died because of a crime
- have been repeatedly victimised, for example by harassment or stalking.

You are also entitled to extra support if you are the victim of a serious crime such as wounding, attempted murder, domestic abuse, sexual offences, kidnapping, hate crime, human trafficking or terrorism.

Vulnerable victims are entitled to receive information more quickly, to be given specialist advice and – if they are a close relative of the victim – to be assigned a Family Liaison Officer. They also have the right to special help if they have to give evidence as a witness. (See below for details of support for vulnerable and intimidated witnesses.)

ACTIVITY — Media

Restorative justice

Go to www.criminology.uk.net

The rights of witnesses

Witnesses in criminal cases can be either eye witnesses to a crime or character witnesses who give evidence about a defendant's character. Witnesses can appear for either the prosecution or the defence. Many witnesses are of course also the victims of the crime.

The Witness Charter

Witnesses have a number of rights. The Witness Charter sets out standards of care for witnesses that should be provided by the police, the Crown Prosecution Service, court staff, the Witness Service and defence lawyers. These standards include the following:

- Witnesses will have a main point of contact throughout the process who will keep them informed of the progress of the case.
- Measures to ensure that the court is a safe environment and that prosecution and defence witnesses wait in separate areas.
- Information about the court process in advance of giving evidence so witnesses know what to expect.
- Prosecution witnesses will be informed of any appeal against conviction or sentence.

However, the rights in the Charter are not legally binding; they simply set out the level of service witnesses should expect. Witnesses are also entitled to claim for travel expenses and loss of earnings resulting from attending court.

ACTIVITY — Media

Being a witness

Go to www.criminology.uk.net

Vulnerable and intimidated witnesses

The Witness Charter also includes special measures to support vulnerable and intimidated witnesses.

- **Vulnerable witnesses** include anyone aged under 18 and those with mental or physical disabilities.
- **Intimidated witnesses** include victims of a sexual offence or human trafficking, witnesses to gun or knife crimes, and witnesses whose evidence is likely to be affected by fear or distress about testifying in court.

Special measures for vulnerable and intimidated witnesses include:

- giving evidence from behind a screen or via live video link, or video recording their statement to be played in court later
- judges and lawyers removing their wigs and gowns to create a less intimidating atmosphere
- help from a communications specialist (called a 'registered intermediary') for witnesses who have difficulty understanding questions in police interviews or in court.

CONTROLLED ASSESSMENT PREPARATION

What you have to do

Using your notes from Topic 1.4, examine the rights of the following individuals in criminal investigations:

- suspects
- victims
- witnesses.

You should consider the rights of all individuals from investigation through to appeal.

The assignment brief scenario

Where relevant, you should make reference to the brief in your answer.

How it will be marked

4-6 marks: The rights of individuals in criminal investigations are clearly examined from investigation through to appeal.

1-3 marks: The rights of individuals in criminal investigations are simply listed or may have limited description.

Explain the requirements of the Crown Prosecution Service for the prosecution of suspects

TOPIC 2.1

Getting Started

Working with a partner and using your knowledge from the previous four Topics:

Imagine you are the prosecutor who has to decide whether a case should go to court.

1. What would you want to know about the case?
2. In what ways might the type of crime affect your decision?

Share your ideas with the rest of the class.

The Crown Prosecution Service

The Crown Prosecution Service (CPS) is the main public prosecutor in England and Wales. It was set up in 1986 under the Prosecution of Offences Act 1985. As we saw in Topic 1.1, the CPS took over the prosecuting role from the police because there was a risk of bias in allowing them to both investigate and prosecute cases. The police do continue to prosecute some very minor offences, but the CPS prosecutes all serious or complex cases.

The CPS advises the police in their investigations about lines of inquiry and about what evidence might be required to build a case. It independently assesses the evidence submitted by the police, decides whether to prosecute and if so, what charges should be brought. Under the Criminal Justice Act 2003, the CPS then issues a written charge accompanied by a notice informing the defendant when they are required to appear in court. It then prepares and presents the prosecution case in court.

To make a decision about whether to prosecute, the CPS applies tests that are laid down in the Code for Crown Prosecutors. In this Topic, we focus on the Code and its tests.

However, the tests are not intended to decide whether a person is guilty of an offence – that is the role of the court, not the CPS. They are simply to decide whether there is a case for the court to consider.

The Full Code Test

For the CPS to prosecute a case, it must normally first pass the Full Code Test. This test is applied once the police have completed all reasonable lines of inquiry. The Full Code Test is made up of two separate stages or tests:

1. The evidential test
2. The public interest test.

ACTIVITY / **Media**

The Full Code Test

Go to www.criminology.uk.net

The Evidential Test

Before prosecuting, prosecutors must first be satisfied that there is sufficient evidence for a realistic prospect of conviction of the suspect. That is, they must decide that the evidence would more likely than not be enough for an objective, impartial and reasonable jury, magistrate or judge to find the defendant guilty.

A case that does not pass the evidential stage must not proceed, no matter how serious or sensitive it is. When deciding whether there is enough evidence to prosecute, prosecutors must ask themselves the following questions.

Is the evidence admissible (allowable) in court?

Prosecutors must assess whether the evidence is likely to be rejected as inadmissible by the court. For example, could it be ruled out as hearsay evidence (mere rumour rather than fact)?

Is the evidence reliable?

Prosecutors must decide whether there are any reasons to question the reliability of the evidence, including its accuracy or integrity. For example, are the witnesses truthful and of good character?

Is the evidence credible (believable)?

Credible evidence is evidence where the available facts, when viewed in light of the circumstances of the case, would cause a reasonable person to believe it to be true. The 'reasonable person' would usually mean the jurors, judge or magistrates.

Prosecutors must decide that the evidence is admissible, reliable and credible. If not, the prosecution must not go ahead.

The Crown Prosecution Service is the independent public prosecutor for England and Wales.

The Public Interest Test

Where there is enough evidence for a realistic prospect of convicting the suspect, prosecutors must then decide whether a prosecution is required in the public interest. In doing so, they should consider each of the questions below. Not all questions may be relevant in every case, and the weight attached to each one will also vary according to the facts of the individual case.

1. **How serious is the offence?** The more serious the offence, the more likely the suspect is to be prosecuted.
2. **What is the suspect's level of culpability?** The greater their culpability (blame or responsibility), the more likely they are to be prosecuted.
   - What was their level of involvement? Was the offence planned? Did they benefit?
   - Do they have previous convictions? Are they likely to re-offend?
   - A suspect who has been compelled or exploited will usually have a lower level of culpability.
3. **What harm has the victim suffered?** The more vulnerable the victim, the more likely it is that a prosecution is required – for example where:
   - the suspect holds a position of trust or authority (e.g. a carer or teacher)
   - the suspect targeted or exploited the victim
   - the offence was motivated by prejudice against the victim.

   Prosecutors should also take the victim's views into account about the impact the offence has had on them.
4. **The suspect's age and maturity.** The younger the suspect, the less likely it is that they will be prosecuted.
   - Prosecutors must consider the best interests and welfare of those under 18 – the aim being to keep young people out of the criminal justice system wherever possible.
   - However, prosecution may still be in the public interest, for example if the offence is serious or because of the suspect's past record.
5. **What is the impact of the offending on the community?** The greater the impact, the more likely it is to be prosecuted.
   - The 'community' can mean both a neighbourhood and a group of people who share the same characteristics (such as gender, ethnicity or sexuality).
6. **Is prosecution a proportionate response?** For example, is the cost of prosecuting excessive when weighed against the likely penalty? In cases with many suspects, it may be better to prosecute only the ringleaders to avoid long, complex trials.
7. **Do sources of information require protecting?** Prosecution may not be appropriate where details need to be made public that could harm sources of information or other investigations.

The Threshold Test

In some cases, a suspect may still be charged even if the evidence requirements of the Full Code Test cannot be met. In these cases, the Threshold Test must be applied. The Threshold Test has five conditions, all of which must be met before a suspect can be charged.

1. There must be reasonable grounds to believe the person has committed the offence.
2. There must be reasonable grounds to believe further evidence can be obtained that will provide a realistic prospect of conviction.
3. The crime is serious enough to justify charging the suspect immediately.

4. There must be substantial grounds to object to bail – e.g. a suspect who is likely to interfere with witnesses.
5. It must be in the public interest to charge the suspect.

Any decision to charge under the Threshold Test must be kept under review and the prosecutor should obtain the additional evidence from the police. The Full Code Test must be applied as soon as this evidence is received.

ACTIVITY — Research

Applying the Threshold Test

Go to www.criminology.uk.net

CONTROLLED ASSESSMENT PREPARATION

What you have to do

Using your notes from Topic 2.1, explain the requirements of the Crown Prosecution Service (CPS) for prosecuting suspects, including:

- the charging role
- the Prosecution of Offences Act 1985
- the Full Code Test.

You should have an understanding of the role of the CPS. You should explain the evidential and public interest tests in the decision to prosecute.

The assignment brief scenario

Where relevant, you should make reference to the brief in your answer.

How it will be marked

3-4 marks: Detailed explanation including clear and relevant examples of the requirements (tests) of the CPS in prosecuting suspects.

1-2 marks: A simple/basic explanation of the CPS with little or no reference to the prosecution of suspects.

Describe trial processes

TOPIC 2.2

Getting Started
Working with a partner, write down the meaning of the following terms:
- a magistrate
- bail
- remand in custody
- plea bargaining
- an appeal.

When you get to the end of the Topic, check your answers.

Types of criminal offence

There are three types of criminal offence in terms of their seriousness and where they can be tried:
- **indictable offences** are serious crimes such as murder, treason, rape, robbery and grievous bodily harm (GBH). These must be tried in the Crown Court, although the first hearing will be in a magistrates' court.
- **summary offences** are less serious cases such as many motoring offences and assaults without injury. These are usually tried in a magistrates' court.
- **triable either way offences** (also called 'hybrid' offences). They include theft, fraud, burglary, handling stolen goods, assault occasioning actual bodily harm (ABH) and criminal damage. These can be tried in either a magistrates' court or Crown Court.

Pre-trial matters

Pre-trial matters are all the decisions that the magistrates' court takes before a trial is held. There are several matters to deal with before the trial:

The pre-trial review This usually deals with points of law such as whether certain evidence is admissible.

The plea

Before the trial begins, the defendant will be read out the charge and asked to plead guilty or not guilty.
- **For guilty pleas**, the magistrates hear evidence of aggravating and mitigating factors (ones that make the offence more serious or less serious). They then either pass sentence immediately or adjourn the case for reports (e.g. from a probation officer) before sentencing at a later date. If the offence is too serious for their sentencing powers, they will send it to the Crown Court for sentencing.
- **For not guilty pleas**, the magistrate must make decisions about reports, legal aid and bail before the trial can go ahead.

Plea bargaining

A plea bargain is an agreement between the prosecutor and defendant (and sometimes also the judge), where the defendant agrees to plead guilty in return for some concession from the prosecutor. A plea bargain may therefore have been struck before the case goes to court.

There are three main types of plea bargain:

- **charge bargaining**, where the defendant pleads guilty to a less serious charge, and therefore receives a lighter sentence.
- **count bargaining**, where the defendant pleads guilty to one charge, in return for others being dropped
- **sentence bargaining**, where the defendant pleads guilty to the original charge, in return for a more lenient sentence.

Plea bargaining may offer the defendant an incentive to plead guilty and will avoid a potentially lengthy trial. However, critics argue that unregulated plea bargaining can apply undue pressure to defendants and undermine their right to a fair trial. For example, the prosecution may file additional or more serious charges, with the aim of bluffing or frightening the defendant into agreeing to plead guilty to a lesser offence.

ACTIVITY — Research

Plea bargaining

Go to www.criminology.uk.net

Cuts to legal aid mean many defendants are no longer eligible, despite being on relatively low incomes.

Legal aid

A basic principle of the legal system is equal access to justice, regardless of a person's wealth. Legal aid exists to enable individuals to defend themselves if they cannot afford to pay for a lawyer. The Legal Aid Agency helps with the costs of legal advice and representation.

For summary offences defendants will be able to talk to a duty solicitor to discuss their plea and the evidence against them. For all not guilty pleas defendants will be given legal aid and representation in all court hearings.

Bail

Bail is the temporary release of an accused person while they are awaiting trial. Because all defendants are presumed innocent until proven guilty, section 4 of the Bail Act 1976 makes a general presumption that everyone has the right to bail.

After being arrested at the police station, the accused may be granted police bail and released. The custody officer may refuse bail if the accused's name and address cannot be established. Likewise, the court can also grant bail after the plea has been made.

There are two types of bail:

- **Unconditional bail** is where the court imposes no conditions except to attend court as required.
- **Conditional bail** is where the court imposes conditions that the defendant must agree to before being released, e.g. to report to a police station every day, not contact certain persons, abide by a curfew, surrender their passport or live at a bail hostel.

Remand in custody If the court refuses bail or the defendant breaches the conditions, they may be remanded in custody (sent to prison) until their trial.

ACTIVITY Research

Bail   Go to www.criminology.uk.net

Refusal of bail

The court may refuse bail if the defendant:

- is likely to fail to surrender to bail (i.e. fail to turn up in court)
- has been previously denied bail or failed to meet bail conditions
- is likely to commit an offence while on bail
- could obstruct the course of justice (e.g. by interfering with a witness)
- is charged with a serious offence such as murder
- needs to be in custody for their own protection.

The magistrates will also consider factors such as the defendant's character (including previous convictions), background, associates, drug use etc., and the strength of the evidence against them. If bail is refused, the magistrates must explain why.

Sending for trial

At the end of the pre-trial phase, if the defendant has pleaded not guilty, the magistrate will either arrange a date for the defendant to appear in the magistrates' court for trial (for less serious, summary offences) or if it is a serious (indictable) offence, send the case to be heard in the Crown Court.

The criminal courts system

Overview of the courts

In the legal system of England and Wales, there are two broad types of criminal court, with different roles and powers:

Courts of the first instance, where the original trial of a case is held. These are:
- magistrates' courts
- Crown Court.

Appellate courts These hear appeals against the verdicts and/or sentences imposed by the lower courts (magistrates' and Crown Courts). There are two important appellate courts:
- the Supreme Court – the highest court in the land
- the Court of Appeal (Criminal Division).

Magistrates' court

Virtually all criminal cases are first heard in the magistrates' courts and over 95% of them are decided there. Magistrates' courts are local courts and they deal with the least serious offences. They must pass on serious (indictable) offences to the Crown Court and they can also choose to pass on any triable-either-way offences that they feel are too serious to deal with themselves, for example serious assaults or large thefts.

Magistrates' courts usually sit with three magistrates, who are laypeople – that is, members of the local community without legal qualifications (but sometimes, a legally qualified District Judge will preside over the court instead).

Magistrates are assisted by a clerk of the court, who is legally qualified and who can advise them on points of law where necessary. Defendants are normally represented by a solicitor, often with legal aid. A CPS representative presents the prosecution's case.

Sentencing powers The magistrates decide whether the accused is guilty or not guilty. They can impose fines of up to £5,000 and/or six months' prison (or £10,000 and 12 months if two or more offences are involved). If they feel the case merits a bigger sentence, they can send it to the Crown Court for sentencing (the Crown Court can impose much heavier sentences).

Crown Court

The Crown Court sits in about 90 centres around the country. It deals with:
- all indictable offences, e.g. murder, rape and robbery
- triable-either-way offences where the defendant has elected to be tried in the Crown Court, or where the magistrates have sent it to the Crown Court because it is too serious for them
- appeals from the magistrates' court.

The defence is usually presented by a barrister and the prosecution's case is put by a representative of the CPS.

The jury

If the defendant pleads not guilty, the case is heard by a jury of 12 members of the public. The jury's role is to listen to all the evidence and to the defence and prosecution arguments. They may examine the exhibits of physical evidence and may take notes, and they can ask questions (via the judge). They retire to the jurors' room to consider their verdict in secret. They are normally expected to produce a unanimous verdict, but the judge may accept a majority (10-2) verdict.

The judge

A judge presides over the Crown Court. Their role is to:
- ensure that the trial is fair and to protect the defendant's human rights
- advise the jury on points of law, court procedure and their duties
- act as the referee between the defence and prosecution. The English legal system is based on the *adversarial principle*, where the two sides put their case before the jury to decide
- pass sentence if the accused is found guilty
- where there is a danger of jurors being bribed or intimidated, the Criminal Justice Act 2003 permits a judge to try a case without a jury.

ACTIVITY / Media

The Crown Court — Go to www.criminology.uk.net

Appeals

If you are convicted of an offence, your right to appeal depends on:
- the type of court that convicted you – magistrates' court or Crown Court
- whether your appeal is against your conviction or just against your sentence.

Appeals from a magistrates' court

If you were convicted in a magistrates' court, you have two automatic rights of appeal (you don't need leave to appeal):
- against conviction, so long as you had pleaded not guilty at your trial
- against sentence.

You must appeal within 21 days of being sentenced. Your appeal is heard as a re-trial in the Crown Court by a judge sitting with two magistrates. The court can:
- uphold (confirm) or quash (dismiss) your conviction, or vary it by convicting you of a lesser or greater charge.
- reduce or increase your sentence.

If you win, you may be entitled to compensation and your legal costs. If you lose, you may have to pay costs. If you lose and you wish to make a further appeal, you must get leave (permission) to do so and it must be on a point of law.

The Court of Appeal

Appeals against Crown Court verdicts are handled by the Court of Appeal (Criminal Division).

Defendants have no automatic right of appeal against a Crown Court decision – a judge will decide whether to allow it. You must seek leave to appeal within 28 days. You can seek to appeal against both your conviction and your sentence. The only ground for appeal is that the conviction was unsafe. Appeals are heard in the Court of Appeal (Criminal Division) by three judges. There is no jury.

The prosecution can only appeal where:
- an error in law by a judge resulted in a dismissal
- the prosecution believes an acquittal was as a result of jury tampering (bribery or intimidation)
- the prosecution believes the sentence was unduly lenient

- there is 'new and compelling evidence' of an acquitted defendant's guilt. This only applies to very serious cases and may result in a re-trial, as in the case of the murderers of Stephen Lawrence.

The Court of Appeal's powers

The Court of Appeal cannot re-try a case, but if it finds that the original verdict was unsafe, it can order a re-trial, vary the conviction or decrease the sentence. Any further appeal would be to the Supreme Court.

Appeals to the Supreme Court

This is the highest court in the legal system and its decisions are binding on all other courts. As with the Court of Appeal, leave is required to appeal – there is no automatic right to appeal to the Supreme Court. The Supreme Court normally only hears cases where a point of law of general public importance is at stake.

The Supreme Court was created in 2009. Before then, its role was performed by the House of Lords, via the twelve Law Lords (the country's most senior judges) who sat in the House and who now sit in the Supreme Court.

The Supreme Court: the highest court in the land

CONTROLLED ASSESSMENT PREPARATION

What you have to do

Using your notes from Topic 2.2, describe the following trial processes:

- pre-trial
- plea bargaining
- bail
- roles
- courts
- appeals.

You should have knowledge of each of the stages of the trial process, including the roles of the personnel involved.

The assignment brief scenario

Where relevant, you should make reference to the brief in your answer.

How it will be marked

3-4 marks: Describe in some detail the stages of the trial process, including the personnel involved.

1-2 marks: A simple/basic description of trial processes and/or personnel involved. May only be a list.

Understand rules in relation to the use of evidence in criminal cases

TOPIC 2.3

Getting Started

Working in small groups and using what you have learned from previous Topics, consider evidence that the prosecution is going to use in court.

In what ways might the evidence that the prosecution wishes to use be unsatisfactory? You could consider problems such as:
- the way police investigated the offence
- they way physical evidence was collected
- problems with witnesses and with their testimony.

Relevance and admissibility

In a criminal trial, the prosecution will try to prove that the defendant committed the offence in question and the defence will try to disprove this. To do so, both sides will present evidence to the court for the jury or magistrates to consider.

However, not all evidence can be used. It must be reliable, relevant to the case and admissible (allowable) in court. We shall look at each of these issues in turn.

Reliability of evidence

The reliability of evidence concerns whether the court can count on the evidence as being true. For evidence to be reliable, it must be:

- **Credible** (believable by a reasonable person) For example, does the court believe that the witness was telling the truth when she said she saw the defendant stab the victim, or is she shown to be a liar? But even if she is not lying, her honesty alone is not enough: the prevailing conditions (night time, say) may have made it impossible in fact for her to see clearly.
- **Authentic** (genuine) A document presented in evidence may in fact be a forgery.
- **Accurate** (correct in all details) For example, is the evidence of an expert in fact supported by the rest of the scientific community, or is it unsound? As we saw in Topic 1.3, the evidence of paediatrician Professor Sir Roy Meadow in several cot death cases was later shown to be inaccurate and unreliable.

Relevance of evidence

The law makes a distinction between two types of fact in a trial: facts in issue and relevant facts.

Facts in issue

Facts in issue (sometimes called 'principal facts') are the matters which are in dispute in a case and which the court has to decide about. They are those facts that the prosecution attempts to prove and the defence to disprove.

For example, if David is accused of murdering Jack by beating him with a club, the facts in issue will be whether David did in fact beat Jack with the club; whether the beating did in fact cause Jack's death; whether David did in fact intend to cause Jack's death, and so on.

Relevant facts

Relevant facts, on the other hand, are facts that are needed in order to prove or disprove the facts in issue.

For example, the presence of David's fingerprints and Jack's blood on the club would be relevant facts in connection with whether David did in fact beat Jack with it. (Of course, this in itself doesn't *prove* that David beat Jack with the club – we can imagine other explanations that David's defence might put forward for the jury to consider.)

ACTIVITY | **Research**

The relevance of evidence   Go to www.criminology.uk.net

Admissibility of evidence

Not all evidence may be admissible in court. There are several types of evidence that may not be allowed by the judge or magistrates, including the following.

Illegally or improperly obtained evidence

Illegally or improperly obtained evidence involves the prosecution using dishonest or improper means to gain evidence that supports their case.

- **Illegally obtained evidence** is gained by breaking the law or violating a person's human rights. This would include evidence obtained in an illegal search conducted without a warrant, and using torture or degrading treatment to obtain a confession.
- **Improperly obtained evidence** includes the use of entrapment, where police use deception to persuade a suspect to commit or admit to a crime, as in the case of the 'honey trap' used against Colin Stagg (see Topic 1.2). It may also occur in 'sting' operations mounted by police, where an undercover officer poses as a criminal (e.g. a drug importer) and induces a suspect to commit a crime.

The court in fact can permit illegally or improperly obtained evidence if it helps to discover the truth. However, if it endangers a fair trial, the judge can rule it out as inadmissible. If the *probative value* of the evidence (its value in proving the case) outweighs its *prejudicial effect* (the risk of it producing an unfair trial), the judge will usually allow it to be used.

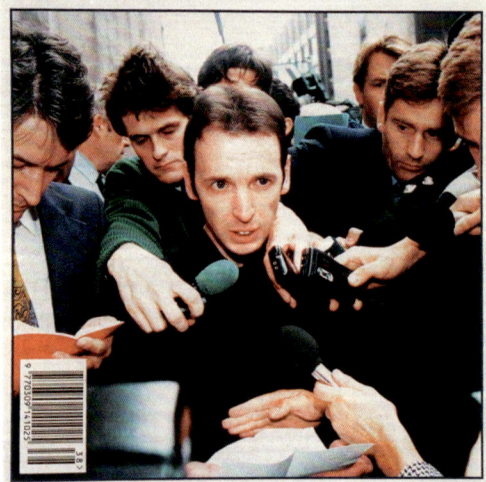

Colin Stagg, after the case was dropped due to police use of a honey trap.

The right to remain silent

It is a basic principle of the law that the accused is presumed innocent until the prosecution can prove him or her guilty of the offence with which they are charged, beyond all reasonable doubt. The accused does not have to prove their innocence and so in theory they do not have to say anything in their defence, either before or during the trial. They have the fundamental human right to remain silent.

However, the Criminal Justice and Public Order Act 1994 allows the jury to draw inferences (conclusions) about a defendant's guilt if they remain silent in the following circumstances:

- **Failure to answer police questions** When questioned under caution, failure to answer can be used as evidence to infer the defendant's guilt. So too can failing to account for a particular object in their possession (e.g. a weapon or stolen goods) or for their presence in a particular place (e.g. a crime scene), when questioned by police.
- **Failure to testify in court** may be used to infer the defendant's guilt, unless they can give a reason for not doing so that the jury finds acceptable.

However, a jury cannot convict solely on inferences about the accused's silence in court. To secure a conviction, the prosecution must provide other evidence.

Evidence of bad character

To assess whether the defendant's evidence is credible (believable), it may be helpful for the court to know whether he or she is of bad character. The Criminal Justice Act 2003 (CJA) defines bad character as 'evidence of or disposition towards misconduct'. Misconduct includes previous convictions and cautions as well as things such as racism, bullying, a bad disciplinary record at work, or having a child taken into care.

However, to prevent this unjustly damaging the defendant's reputation or credibility, character evidence is only admitted under certain circumstances, such as where it shows that the defendant has a tendency to lie, or to commit similar offences to those they are charged with. The CJA also permits the defence to rely on evidence of reputation to prove the defendant's *good* character.

In general, character evidence cannot be used in relation to non-defendants (such as victims, police officers involved in the case, and defence witnesses). However, feminists have criticised the tendency in rape cases for defence lawyers to introduce evidence about victims' sexual history.

Contaminated evidence If the judge decides that the evidence of the defendant's bad character is contaminated, they may direct the jury to acquit the defendant, or order a re-trial.

ACTIVITY / Media

Why rapes are not reported   Go to www.criminology.uk.net

Disclosure of evidence

For a trial to be fair, the defendant must be able to see the materials that are part of the evidence against him or her. For this reason, the law puts a duty on the prosecution to disclose evidence to the defence so that they can prepare to answer the case against them.

The prosecution's duty of disclosure

The prosecution has a duty to:
- notify the accused of all the evidence they intend to rely on
- make available to the defence any unused material relevant to the case that they do not intend to present to the court.

Unused material includes anything that might undermine the prosecution's own case or assist the defence's case, such as any material casting doubt on the credibility of the prosecution's witnesses or the reliability of a confession.

Failure to disclose

The number of cases where charges were dropped due to the prosecution's failure to disclose has increased in recent years. In the case of Liam Allan in 2017, for example, his trial for rape was halted when it emerged that evidence on a computer disc showed that the alleged victim had pestered him for casual sex. The disc had already been examined by police, but they had failed to disclose this to the defence.

This could be an increasing problem as digital evidence becomes increasingly important. For example, if the police have possession of a suspect's phone but fail to read through possibly thousands of text messages, they may miss evidence that clears the suspect of blame and so fail to disclose it to the defence. Police have also sometimes deliberately withheld such evidence when they firmly believed that the accused is guilty. This amounts to perverting the course of justice and is itself a criminal offence.

Limits to disclosure: public interest immunity

The prosecution may not have to disclose certain materials to the defendant. They may seek a public-interest immunity (PII) certificate from the court. This exempts them from having to disclose sensitive materials that pose a real risk to an important public interest, such as endangering national security or revealing the identity of undercover police officers. (For more on PII certificates, see Topic 2.4.)

The defence's duty of disclosure

The main burden of disclosure falls on the prosecution, but the defence must also disclose certain information. This includes the nature of the defence they intend to offer, any matters of fact that they will rely on or will challenge, and any points of law. Unlike the prosecution, they do not have to disclose unused material.

Hearsay evidence

Hearsay evidence is a statement that has been made by someone *out of* court to a witness who is appearing *in* court, and which the witness wishes to rely on as evidence of a fact.

For example, Joan is a witness in a murder trial. She testifies that Colin told her he had seen the defendant shoot the victim. Colin's statement is hearsay, because it is being put forward by someone (Joan) who did not see the incident herself but merely heard about it from Colin, yet she is relying on it to prove that the defendant shot the victim.

In other words, hearsay evidence is basically second-hand evidence. Joan didn't witness the shooting herself and she (and the court) cannot know if Colin is telling the truth, because he is not in court to swear to tell the truth and to have his evidence tested by the defence cross-examining him in front of the jury. For this reason, hearsay evidence is generally not admitted in court.

Exceptions

However, although hearsay is not generally admissible, there are some exceptions to the rule. Hearsay evidence is admissible:
- where all parties (prosecution, defence and judge) agree
- where the judge rules that it is in the interests of justice
- where common law permits it, e.g. in the case of publicly available information, reputation or expert evidence
- where a witness is absent abroad, dead, unfit to testify due to fear or to their bodily or mental condition, or has disappeared.

ACTIVITY — Research

Hearsay evidence

Go to www.criminology.uk.net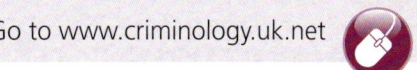

CONTROLLED ASSESSMENT PREPARATION

What you have to do

Using your notes from Topic 2.3, show a detailed understanding of the following rules in relation to the use of evidence in criminal cases:

- relevance and admissibility
- disclosure of evidence
- hearsay rule and exceptions
- legislation and case law.

You should have an understanding of how evidence is used in court.

The assignment brief scenario

Where relevant, you should make reference to the brief in your answer.

How it will be marked

3-4 marks: Detailed understanding of the rules in relation to the use of evidence in criminal cases.

1-2 marks: A simple/basic understanding of the rules in relation to the use of evidence in criminal cases.

TOPIC 2.4

Assess key influences affecting the outcomes of criminal cases

Getting Started

Working in small groups, imagine that a child has been abducted in your town or city. A suspect has been arrested and charged. You receive a summons to serve on the jury for the trial.

List any factors that might influence your view of the case.

Feed your points back to the rest of the class.

As a whole class:

1. Determine which of these influences might affect your verdict when serving on the jury.
2. Consider whether your view of the case might change and if so why.

A range of factors can influence the outcome of criminal cases and in this Topic we shall consider the following key influences on cases:

- the evidence presented to the court
- witnesses, including expert witnesses
- barristers and legal teams involved in cases
- the judiciary (judges and magistrates)
- political factors
- the media.

Evidence

Evidence lies at the heart of the process in criminal cases. In reaching their verdict, the jury or magistrates must take into account all the physical and testimonial evidence of witnesses presented in court, and only this evidence.

Before a case can go to court, the police or other investigators must first provide enough evidence to convince the Crown Prosecution Service that there is a case for the suspect to answer, and the CPS must be confident that there is a realistic prospect of a successful prosecution. That is, they must believe that they are more likely than not to secure a conviction when the case is tried.

Once the case goes to court, the prosecution will present evidence and arguments against the defendant. The defence will challenge the prosecution case, cross-examining the prosecution's witnesses on their evidence and presenting evidence of their own. By the end of the trial, the prosecution must have convinced the jury or magistrates that the accused is guilty 'beyond reasonable doubt' on all aspects of the charge. Otherwise, the defendant must be acquitted.

Witnesses

Both parties – defence and prosecution – are entitled to call witnesses to give evidence (testimony). Normally, witnesses must give their evidence to the court in person, with two exceptions:

- where the witness's evidence is agreed by both parties, it can be given in the form of a written statement
- vulnerable or intimidated witnesses (see Topic 1.4) may be allowed to give their evidence by a live video link or video recording rather than attending court, or from behind a screen in court if they need to protect their identity.

Witnesses can be called by both sides to give evidence in support of their case; this is known as the examination-in-chief. For example, the prosecution will call its own witnesses to give evidence by questioning them in the witness box. The defence may then choose to cross-examine them by questioning them on the evidence they have given.

Jurors or magistrates may give whatever weight they choose to the evidence of witnesses. The quality of a witness's evidence can determine the outcome of a trial. For example, if they are shown to have lied, or if their evidence appears inconsistent, unreliable or not credible, this may sway the verdict one way or the other.

Stereotyping

There is a danger that racial prejudices or gender stereotypes held by jurors may influence how willing they are to believe a witness's testimony. For example, Kaufmann et al found that jurors' judgement of how credible they found a rape victim's testimony depended strongly on the emotions the victim showed when giving their evidence, and not on the actual content of the evidence. Brodsky et al found that jurors' view of the witness's knowledge, likeability, trustworthiness and confidence were key factors in deciding whether to believe their evidence.

It may therefore be that factors such as a witness's gender, ethnicity, class or age, or their appearance, demeanour, accent or personality, affect how much weight juries give to their evidence and therefore affect the outcome of a case.

Eye witnesses

Juries are also often ready to believe eye witnesses, yet their evidence is not always accurate. As we saw in Topic 1.2, studies by psychologists show that eye witnesses' memory can be highly

Pete Williams, jailed based on eye-witness testimony, freed by the Georgia (USA) Innocence Project using DNA evidence after serving 21 years.

inaccurate. Similarly, the Innocence Project found that in over 70% of 352 wrongful convictions that were later overturned on the basis of DNA evidence, eye-witness misidentification helped to convict an innocent person.

Experts

Expert witnesses are people with specialist knowledge that ordinary members of the public do not have. Unlike other witnesses, who may only give evidence of what they know or have observed, expert witnesses can give an opinion to the court based on their special expertise.

In complex cases that rely on highly technical evidence, the testimony given by expert witnesses can be crucial in determining the outcome of a case. As ordinary members of the public, jurors are unlikely to have specialist knowledge of forensic pathology, for example. They must therefore rely heavily on the accuracy of evidence provided by experts.

One danger is that jurors may automatically assume that the expert is right, or misunderstand what the expert is telling them. And some experts may be better than others at communicating their knowledge to laypeople.

Miscarriages of justice Even if the jury understand what the expert is telling them, they are probably unable to check its accuracy. This can lead to miscarriages of justice, as in the cases of Sally Clark, Angela Cannings and Donna Anthony, who were convicted of murdering their children based on inaccurate statistical evidence about cot deaths given by the paediatrician Sir Roy Meadow (see Topic 1.3).

However, in some cases, both defence and prosecution call expert witnesses, who may disagree on how to interpret the facts of the case. While jurors must still try to make sense of their evidence, this at least allows them to consider alternative technical explanations.

ACTIVITY — Media
The misuse of statistics

Go to www.criminology.uk.net

Barristers and legal teams

Barristers and solicitors are both qualified lawyers. Barristers work in higher level courts where they act as advocates, speaking on behalf of their clients. They can act for either the defence or the prosecution. When in court, they wear a wig and gown.

Barristers will often be briefed on the case by a solicitor, who will prepare relevant papers and gather evidence for the barrister to use in court. While barristers work inside the court, solicitors mainly work outside it (though they may also represent clients, mainly in the lower courts).

The quality of the barristers can affect the outcome of a case. This is because trials work on the adversarial system where the two adversaries – prosecution and defence – each try to persuade the jury. In this situation, a more eloquent, persuasive or charismatic barrister might sway a jury's decision where their less able opponent might fail.

Cost

Barristers are highly paid and the best can earn thousands of pounds a day. This means that the rich may be able to afford better representation in court and a greater chance of the verdict going in their favour.

Plea bargaining

Legal teams are often involved in plea bargaining – for example where the defendant agrees to plead guilty to a lesser offence with a lower sentence, instead of pleading not guilty to a more serious one. The prosecution team may agree to this, for example if they feel it will result in a greater chance of winning the case. This will obviously influence its outcome. (For more about plea bargaining, see Topic 2.2.)

Juror infatuation

There have been occasional reports of jurors 'falling for' a barrister and possibly changing their verdict as a result. In 2001, five Hull police officers applied for a review of an inquest verdict. The verdict was that a Black ex-soldier, Christopher Alder, had been unlawfully killed while in their custody. The officers' legal counsel argued that a woman juror had become infatuated with the family's barrister in the inquest and that this had tainted the verdict. However, their application was rejected.

The judiciary

At different stages of a trial, judges can have an important effect on the outcome of a case.

Affecting the verdict

The judge is an expert in the law and in legal procedure. In a trial, the judge has several key powers and responsibilities:

- to clarify the law for the jury and direct them on how it is to be applied in the case they are trying.
- to rule on the admissibility of evidence and on whether the line of questioning taken by the prosecution or defence is permissible
- to sum up the main issues and evidence in the case for the jury before they retire to consider their verdict.

The judge also has the power to dismiss a case, order a re-trial or even direct the jury to bring in a particular verdict. However, juries do not in fact have to follow this direction and they are within their rights to bring in a 'perverse decision' which goes against what the law says but which the jury feel is in the interests of justice – known as 'jury equity' or fairness. (For more about perverse decisions and jury equity, see Topic 2.5.)

Deciding the sentence

The law lays down minimum and maximum sentences for different offences, and there are also Sentencing Guidelines on the level of sentence to be given in different cases. However, within these limits, judges and magistrates have discretion in what sentences they hand down and this will affect the outcome of cases before them.

For example, in the wake of the riots in 2011, the courts handed down more severe sentences. Magistrates sent 37% of those they convicted to jail, compared with only 12% for similar cases in 2010, and the average sentence was almost three times as long. Critics argue that this was the result of a moral panic about the riots and pressure from the media and politicians to crack down on offenders and 'teach them a lesson'.

Juryless trials

Under the Criminal Justice Act 2003, a judge may sit without a jury:

- where there is a risk of jury tampering (where jurors are bribed or intimidated into bringing in a particular verdict)

- in complex fraud cases, where a jury might have difficulty in understanding, or in attending court for months on end.

In these cases, the judge alone decides the outcome of the case. (For more about jury tampering, see Topic 2.5.)

ACTIVITY / Research

Juryless trials

Go to www.criminology.uk.net

Court of Appeal judges have the power to decide the outcome of a case where the verdict of the Crown Court has been appealed. They re-hear the case without a jury and can uphold or reverse the original verdict.

Judicial bias

As we have just seen, the judge can influence the outcome of a case in many ways. One danger is therefore that if the judge is biased, the way they exercise their powers could lead to an unfair result. Bias may arise for several reasons.

Class background

Judges come mainly from the higher social classes. For example, in 2019:

- 65% of senior judges were privately educated (compared with only 7% of the general population)
- 75% had attended Oxford or Cambridge Universities (compared with under 1% of the population).

This may mean they tend to be overly sympathetic to the higher classes. However, clear evidence of class bias is not always easy to identify.

Gender

68% of court judges are male. In recent years there has been an increase in the number of female judges, but progress has been very slow: at the current rate it will take until the year 2062 before there are equal numbers of male and female judges.

Particularly in rape cases, there is a danger that male judges may lack sympathy for female victims – who may feel that they are the ones on trial. For example, Carol Smart quotes one male judge as saying:

> "Women who say no do not always mean no. It is not just a question of how she says it, how she shows it and makes it clear. If she doesn't want it she only has to keep her legs shut."

Politics

Our laws have two main sources: common law, which comes from precedent (where courts follow rulings made by judges in previous cases) and statute law, which is made by Parliament passing Acts or statutes.

Politics plays a central role in making statute law, since it is the politicians sitting in Parliament who pass the Acts of Parliament. The government proposes legislation (laws), which Parliament then debates and sometimes amends. Because the government is formed by the party with a majority of the MPs, it can usually get its legislation passed by Parliament.

Politicians in Parliament can therefore affect the criminal law and the outcome of cases in three ways:

- **Creating new offences** For example, following a media-inspired moral panic, Parliament passed the Dangerous Dogs Act 1991, outlawing certain dog breeds. The Firearms (Amendment) Act 1997 banning handgun ownership was passed after a public outcry over the Dunblane massacre.
- **Abolishing existing offences** Parliament can repeal or amend existing laws that previously made something a crime. For example, the Sexual Offences Act 1967 decriminalised homosexual acts between males aged 21 and over.
- **Changing the penalties** for particular offences. For example, Parliament abolished the death penalty for murder in 1965. In 1997, the Crime (Sentences) Act introduced mandatory minimum sentences for repeat offenders, such as automatic life sentences for a second serious sexual or violent crime.

Public-interest immunity certificates

Another way in which politics may influence the outcome of criminal cases is through public-interest immunity (PII) certificates. These can be issued by a government minister to prevent sensitive evidence such as official secrets being revealed in court. In other words, there is a public interest in not allowing certain evidence to come to light. However, although a minister issues the certificate, it is the judge who decides whether the evidence should be kept out of court.

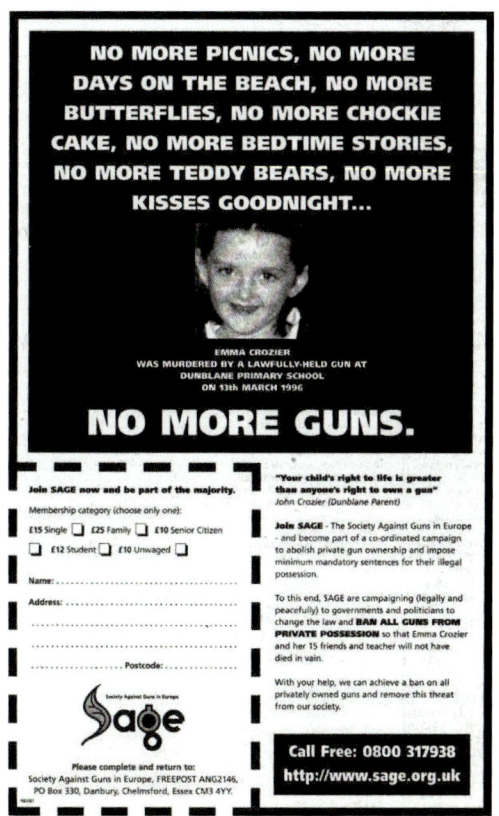

Campaign advert demanding that the law ban guns following the Dunblane massacre.

The 'arms to Iraq' case In 1991, the directors of Matrix Churchill aerospace company were prosecuted for exporting machines used in weapons manufacture to Iraq, apparently without government approval. Approval had in fact been given, but to avoid embarrassment the government issued PII certificates to stop this coming out at the trial by withholding documents which would have cleared the defendants. Eventually, however, the minister responsible admitted he had been 'economical with the truth', the judge ruled out the PII certificates and the case collapsed.

The media

The media can influence the outcome of criminal cases in several ways. For example, moral panics can affect the outcome of cases:

- by demanding tougher sentences for certain offences or offenders, such as those involved in the 2011 riots
- by demanding new laws to deal with some particular 'threat', as in the case of the Dangerous Dogs Act 1991.

Trial by media: the tabloid press

In law, the accused is innocent until proven guilty after a fair trial. In a fair trial, the jury or magistrates must only consider the evidence presented to them in court. It would be unfair if a juror's verdict was prejudiced by media reports they had seen about the case.

Certain high-profile cases attract a great deal of media interest and sensationalised reporting, often with extremely negative coverage of the defendant's character or private life, and this may make a fair trial impossible.

In effect, the media have already found the accused guilty and their blanket coverage of the case before the trial will most likely have been seen by the jurors, potentially prejudicing them against the defendant.

For example, Cheryl Thomas found that a fifth of jurors serving on high-profile cases said they had found it difficult to disregard pre-trial media coverage of the case. They were more likely to recall the defendant being portrayed as guilty than as innocent.

Tabloid libelling of Jefferies could have prevented a fair trial if he had been charged.

Case study Trial by media

The character assassination of Christopher Jefferies

A disturbing example of trial by media is the case of the retired teacher Christopher Jefferies, who was arrested and questioned by police for the murder of his tenant Joanna Yeates in 2010.

The tabloid press ran highly prejudicial articles about Jefferies. For example, the *Sun* claimed he had been 'branded a creepy oddball by ex-pupils, a teaching colleague and neighbours', had invited pupils to his home, was domineering and was believed to be gay. The paper went on to describe him in these words:

> "WEIRD 'Strange talk, strange walk'; POSH 'Loved culture, poetry';
> LEWD 'Made sexual remarks'; CREEPY 'Loner with blue rinse hair'."

Other papers joined in. The *Daily Mirror* claimed Jefferies was a Peeping Tom; the *Daily Star* described him as a foul-tempered angry weirdo. Most of the quotes about him were from unnamed sources. The papers published photos of him shabbily dressed and with unkempt hair (in fact the clothing had been given to him by police after they had taken all his own clothes for forensic analysis).

However, subsequent police investigations revealed that in fact the killer was a neighbour, Vincent Tabak. The *Sun* and the *Mirror* were found guilty of contempt of court for publishing articles that could have prejudiced a fair trial, since it would have been virtually impossible to find a jury who had not been exposed to the tabloids' character assassination. Jefferies received damages for libel from the papers and has since become a campaigner for privacy.

Trial by social media

It is not just the traditional tabloid media that may affect the outcome of criminal cases: trial by *social* media is a growing danger. For example, the trial of two teenage girls accused of the brutal murder of Angela Wrightson in 2014 had to be discontinued because comments on Facebook about the defendants had made a fair trial impossible. They were re-tried and convicted in 2016.

There is also concern about jurors using the internet to research the cases they are trying. For more on jurors and the internet, see Topic 2.5.

ACTIVITY — Research

Do media reports influence juries?   Go to www.criminology.uk.net

CONTROLLED ASSESSMENT PREPARATION

What you have to do

Using your notes from Topic 2.4, assess the following key influences affecting the outcomes of criminal cases:

- evidence
- witnesses
- experts
- barristers and legal teams
- judiciary
- politics
- the media.

You should have an understanding of the many factors that can influence the outcome of a trial and be able to assess their impact.

The assignment brief scenario

Where relevant, you should make reference to the brief in your answer.

How it will be marked

8-10 marks: Assesses key influences affecting the outcomes of criminal cases. There is clear and detailed understanding of their impact.

4-7 marks: Understanding of the key factors affecting the outcomes of criminal cases is shown and some assessment made of their impact.

1-3 marks: Key influences affecting the outcomes of criminal cases are largely described.

TOPIC 2.5

Discuss the use of laypeople in criminal cases

Getting Started

Working with a partner, discuss and answer the following questions:

1. What advantages might there be in having your case decided by members of the general public rather than by a judge?
2. Why might members of the public not be fair when deciding on a case?
3. Can you think of any other disadvantages to members of the public deciding the verdict in criminal cases?

Laypeople in the legal system

Laypeople are ordinary members of the public, who do not have specialised or professional knowledge of the law or legal procedure. In the English legal system, laypeople serve in two key roles: as members of juries, and as magistrates.

Juries

Juries sit in most Crown Court cases and in a number of other situations, such as some inquests into sudden deaths.

The jury's role

In most Crown Court trials, the verdict is normally decided by a jury of 12 laypeople. The jury hear the evidence and arguments put forward by the prosecution and defence. If they wish, they can take notes and, via the judge, ask questions. The judge will advise them on relevant law.

They then retire from the courtroom to decide whether they find the defendant guilty, not guilty, or guilty of a less serious crime, such as manslaughter rather than murder. To bring in a guilty verdict, they must be convinced 'beyond reasonable doubt'.

The jury's decision is taken in secret and the Criminal Justice and Courts Act 2015 makes it an offence for anyone to question jurors about their verdict or how they reached it. Jurors are only allowed to disclose their deliberations in situations such as to report misconduct by other jurors.

Selection Jurors are selected randomly by computer from the names on the electoral register. Those selected will receive a summons to attend court. Jury service is normally for two weeks, though it will be for longer if a trial goes on beyond this period.

Eligibility To be eligible to serve as a juror, the Juries Act 1974 and Criminal Justice Act 2003 state that you must:

- be aged 18 to 75
- be a citizen of the UK, the Irish Republic or a British Commonwealth country
- have resided in the UK, the Channel Islands or the Isle of Man for five years.

Disqualification Certain people are disqualified from jury service, including those on bail and those who have ever received a prison sentence of five years or more. Anyone who has received a shorter sentence is disqualified for 10 years.

Exemption Those selected for jury service are legally required to attend court. However, it is possible to be excused on medical and other grounds, such as a holiday you have already paid for.

ACTIVITY — Media

The role of a juror   Go to www.criminology.uk.net

Strengths of the jury system

Jury equity

Unlike judges, jurors are not bound by what a law says or by precedents (verdicts reached previously in similar cases). As ordinary members of the public, they are free to decide a case based on what they feel is fair or morally right, regardless of the law or how the judge might direct them to apply it to a case. This is called jury equity.

Case study — The trial of Clive Ponting

A good example of jury equity is the acquittal of the senior civil servant Clive Ponting. During the Falklands War with Argentina in 1982, the British navy sank the Argentinian cruiser, the *General Belgrano*, with the loss of 323 lives. Britain had declared an exclusion zone around the Falkland Islands and said that any Argentinian ship inside it would be attacked. The *Belgrano* had been outside the exclusion zone when it was sunk and was only attacked after a top-level government decision to change the British navy's rules of engagement.

Three years later Ponting leaked secret government documents about the sinking to an MP and was subsequently charged with breaching the Official Secrets Act 1911. Ponting did not deny his action (he had admitted it even before he was arrested) but argued in his defence that he had acted in the public interest by revealing the facts.

The judge ruled that Ponting had no defence and directed the jury to convict him as he had clearly contravened the Act by leaking official secrets. The jury nevertheless acquitted him.

1 May 1982: the *General Belgrano* is sunk. Life rafts saved many but 323 died in what some critics described as a war crime.

Kay Gilderdale

In a case in 2010, Kay Gilderdale was charged with attempting to murder her 31-year-old daughter Lynn, who had been seriously ill for 17 years. Evidence showed Kay was a devoted and caring mother. Lynn had sought to commit suicide by injecting herself with morphine. When this apparently failed to work, her mother administered other drugs and she died some hours later. Kay pleaded guilty to assisting Lynn's suicide, but the CPS chose to prosecute her instead for attempted murder. However, the jury acquitted her.

Justice is seen to be done

Juries make the legal system more open and justice can be seen to be done because it is ordinary members of the public who decide the outcome. Also, because the judge has to explain points of law to the jury in open court, both the defendant and the public at large are able to understand the case more clearly.

Impartiality and a fairer trial

Many people believe that jury trials are fairer than being tried by a judge or magistrates. You are being tried by your peers (literally, your equals) rather than by a single individual judge or three magistrates who may be unable to relate to your circumstances or may have particular prejudices. Being tried by a randomly selected cross-section of society makes it more likely that individuals' prejudices will be cancelled out and an impartial jury created.

Also, because a jury usually only sits for two weeks and only hears a few cases, it does not become case hardened. By contrast, judges and magistrates have been accused of being prosecution-minded.

Secrecy

Because by law the jury's deliberations are held in secret, jurors are protected from outside pressures and influences. This allows them to bring in verdicts that may be unpopular with the public. Secrecy also allows them to exercise jury equity and bring in verdicts that ignore the strict letter of the law. Secrecy may also make people more willing to serve on a jury than if they knew their deliberations could be made public.

Public confidence and democracy

The jury is seen as a key element in a democratic society. The right to be judged by one's fellow citizens rather than by the state is essential in keeping the state's power in check and preserving liberty. As the senior judge Lord Devlin argued, the jury is 'the lamp that shows that freedom lives' and is a 'little Parliament' – a democratic institution.

The right to be tried by one's peers is very old and the public have confidence in its fairness and impartiality. For example, government attempts in recent years to restrict the right to trial by jury, both for minor theft cases and for complex frauds, have met with opposition and been defeated.

The jury system is also democratic because it allows ordinary citizens to become involved in the administration of justice, rather than leaving it all in the hands of the state.

Weaknesses of the jury system

Racial bias

There is concern that some jurors are racially biased and that this may result in unjust verdicts. In the case of Sander v United Kingdom (2000), concerning the 1995 trial of an Asian man, Kuldip Sander, a juror wrote to the judge pointing out that two other jurors had been making racist remarks and jokes. Although the judge allowed the trial to continue, the European Court of Human Rights upheld Sander's appeal that he had been denied a fair trial – by which time he had served three years in prison.

However, it is not clear how far racial bias affects juries' verdicts. According to the independent review conducted by the Black MP David Lammy into the treatment of minority ethnic individuals by the justice system, verdicts delivered by juries do *not* appear to be influenced by the ethnicity of either the jurors or the defendant.

Lammy also notes that Black, Asian and minority ethnic defendants are more likely than White defendants to opt for a jury trial at Crown Court where possible. This is because they believe they are more likely to receive a fair hearing there than in the magistrates' court – despite the risk of a tougher sentence if found guilty in Crown Court.

Media influence

Jurors may be influenced by media coverage of a case, especially in high-profile cases that receive a great deal of media attention. One example of this is R v Taylor and Taylor (1993). The jury had found the Taylor sisters guilty of murder, but the Court of Appeal quashed the conviction because the 'extensive, sensational and inaccurate' press coverage of their trial created a risk that the jury had been prejudiced by it.

Fraud trials

Fraud cases can often involve complex technical evidence that jurors, as ordinary members of the public, may struggle to understand. As a result, their verdict may be unsound.

These cases can also be very long and may require jurors to be away from their work for months. Long trials are also more expensive both for the prosecution and the defence.

However, the problem of jurors not understanding may go beyond fraud trials. Cheryl Thomas used simulated trials involving almost 800 jurors to study their understanding. The jurors were all given the same judge's directions on the law. When they were tested afterwards, it was found that more than two thirds of the jurors had not fully understood the directions. Even when given a written summary of the directions, over half still did not fully understand them.

Jury tampering

Jury tampering involves attempts to pervert the course of justice by bribing or intimidating jurors, usually to acquit the defendant. As a result, section 44 of the Criminal Justice Act 2003 allows the prosecution to apply for trial by a judge alone in cases where there has been an attempt to tamper with the jury.

The first judge-only trial was R v Twomey and others in 2009, where it was estimated that it would have cost £6m and 82 police officers to protect a jury for the duration of the trial. The defendants were charged with an armed robbery from a Heathrow warehouse. Three trials had already collapsed, with a serious attempt at jury tampering in the last one. The judge found all the defendants guilty.

High acquittal rates

Juries are sometimes criticised for acquitting too many defendants – about 60% of those pleading not guilty at Crown Court are acquitted. However, most of these are where the judge has dismissed the case without a jury even being sworn in, or where the jury were directed by the judge to acquit – usually for lack of evidence against the defendant. Of the remaining cases, juries in fact convict over 60%.

Perverse decisions

Because the jury are free to ignore what they regard as an unjust law, this may lead to a perverse decision which goes against the facts of the case. For example, in the case of R v Randle and

Pottle in 1991, the two defendants were charged with having aided the Soviet spy George Blake in escaping from prison some 25 years earlier. They were only prosecuted after writing about their role in the escape. The jury found them not guilty, perhaps in protest at the amount of time between offence and prosecution.

The jury also acquitted the defendants in another case where the facts clearly pointed to their guilt. In R v Kronlid and others in 1996, the defendants admitted causing £1.5 million criminal damage to a warplane, but pleaded not guilty on the grounds that they were preventing it from being sent to Indonesia where the government would use it to attack the people of East Timor who were seeking independence from Indonesia.

Secrecy

Secrecy of the jury room means that no reasons can be given for the verdict, so we have no way of telling whether the jury understood the case and reached their verdict for the right reasons. As a result, appeals against a verdict based on information about the jury's deliberations generally fail.

For example, the Law Lords ruled in 2004 that they could not inquire into discussions in a jury room. They considered the following two cases in the appeal.

R v Mirza

The defendant was a Pakistani man who had an interpreter during the trial and the judge had ruled that the jury must not draw any negative conclusions from this. Mirza was convicted on a 10-2 majority. Six days after the verdict, one juror claimed that other jurors had said the use of the interpreter was a 'devious ploy'. It therefore appeared that there was racial bias in their verdict and also that the judge's directions had not been followed.

R v Connor and Rollock

In this case, a juror wrote to the court after the verdict. She stated that jurors disagreed about which of the two defendants had stabbed the victim but decided to convict both, to 'teach them a lesson'. She also said that jurors had wanted a 'quick decision' and refused to spend time deciding which defendant was the guilty party.

In both cases the Law Lords rejected appeals, on the grounds that the law forbids disclosure of what occurs in the jury room.

> **ACTIVITY** — **Media**
>
> The jury system
>
> Go to www.criminology.uk.net

Jurors and the internet

The Criminal Justice and Courts Act 2015 makes it an offence for jurors to search the internet for information relevant to the case, and an offence to disclose such information to another juror. Judges also instruct jurors not to research their cases on the internet. However, Cheryl Thomas found that 12% of jurors admitted they had looked on the internet for information about cases they were trying.

Such information may affect the trial outcome. For example, if jurors read about the defendant's previous record or the victim's reputation, this may prejudice their verdict. Both Dr Theodora Dallas in 2011 and Lionel Tweed in 2017 were jailed for researching the cases they were trying on the internet and reporting their findings to their fellow jurors. In Dallas' case, the jury had to be dismissed and a re-trial held.

> **ACTIVITY** **Research**
>
> Jurors and the internet   Go to www.criminology.uk.net

Magistrates

Like jurors, magistrates are lay members of the public rather than legal professionals. There are around 13,000 magistrates, sitting in about 160 local magistrates' courts up and down the country.

The magistrate's role

Magistrates are unpaid, part-time volunteers who are members of their local community. They are sometimes referred to as Justices of the Peace, or JPs. Magistrates receive training but they are not legally qualified. Instead they are assisted by a legally qualified clerk who advises them on law and procedure. Magistrates must be aged 18-65 when appointed and they can serve up to the age of 70.

As we saw in Topic 2.2, virtually all criminal cases are first heard in the magistrates' courts and over 95% of them are decided there. Cases are usually heard by a panel of three magistrates. They try less serious cases, such as motoring offences, shoplifting, criminal damage and public disorder. Specially trained magistrates also sit in youth courts.

Where a defendant pleads not guilty, a trial will be held before the magistrates. If they find the defendant guilty, they can impose a fine of up to £5,000 or up to 6 months in prison (£10,000 and 12 months for two or more offences).

However, for more serious offences, magistrates pass cases to the Crown Court, either for sentencing if the defendant has been found guilty in the magistrates' court or, if the defendant has pleaded not guilty, they will face a Crown Court trial before a judge and jury.

Strengths of magistrates

Democracy

Using laypeople to try less serious cases brings an element of democracy to the criminal justice system. It allows ordinary local citizens to become involved in the administration of justice, rather than leaving it entirely in the hands of the state's paid judges.

Local knowledge

Magistrates serve in their local court and have knowledge of the local area which they can apply to cases and reflect local needs and priorities when sentencing offenders.

For example, in the case of Paul v DPP (1989), magistrates had to decide whether a kerb crawler was likely to pose a nuisance to others. Because the magistrates knew the area, they knew kerb crawling was a real problem. The former Lord Chief Justice, Lord Woolf, commented that this was precisely the kind of case in which a magistrate's local knowledge was important.

However, many magistrates' courts have been closed in recent years, meaning that magistrates are now dealing with cases from further afield, where they may lack local knowledge.

Representative of the population

Magistrates are quite representative of the population in terms of gender and ethnicity. For example, in 2019:

- 13% of magistrates were from Black, Asian or minority ethnic backgrounds (the figure for the UK as a whole is 14%)
- 56% of magistrates were women (51% for the UK population as a whole).

This compares favourably with judges: in 2019, only 32% were female and only 7% were from Black, Asian or minority ethnic backgrounds.

Because magistrates sit in panels of three, it may be possible to achieve a mix of gender, ethnicity and age to reflect the diversity of the local population.

Limited number of appeals

Magistrates deal with a very large number of cases (around 1.5 million in 2019) but very few of these go to appeal (about 5,000 per year). Most of these are appeals against the sentence, not against the guilty verdict. Less than half of the appeals are successful. This suggests that magistrates are getting it right most of the time in terms of both their verdicts and the sentences they hand down.

Cost

Because magistrates are unpaid (they only receive expenses), they are an economical way of administering justice. One estimate suggests that if paid professional judges had to be used, it would cost about £100m per year.

Weaknesses of magistrates

Unrepresentative of the population

Age While magistrates are broadly representative of the population in terms of gender and ethnicity, in terms of their age profile, they are very unrepresentative. For example, in 2020:
- Only 1% of magistrates were under 30 (for the UK as a whole, the figure is roughly 25%)
- 49% of magistrates were over 60 (compared with only 25% for the UK as a whole).
- At the same time, the great majority of defendants are under 25.

Social class Magistrates are also unrepresentative in terms of social class: the great majority come from middle-class professional and managerial backgrounds. This is partly because people in such jobs often find it easier to take time off work to perform their duties as magistrates. Their higher income also means they are more likely to be able to afford to take on an unpaid role as a magistrate. Their class background may mean they lack understanding of the local community, especially those living in poorer areas.

Inconsistency in sentencing: a postcode lottery

Magistrates are trained to follow official Sentencing Guidelines to ensure that cases are treated consistently and that similar cases heard in different magistrates' courts receive similar sentences. Despite this, however, there is concern that this does not happen and sentences are often inconsistent.

For example, in 2010, Bristol magistrates handed down custodial sentences to 11.1% of offenders and community sentences to 32.2%. By contrast, Coventry, which had a similar number of offenders to Bristol, only imposed custodial sentences on 6.8% of offenders and community sentences on 14.4%.

Critics therefore argue that sentencing in magistrates' courts is a 'postcode lottery' where the sentence an offender receives is as much about where they live as about the offence they have committed.

ACTIVITY — Media

Magistrates Go to www.criminology.uk.net

Bias

Magistrates convict over 90% of all cases, and critics have suggested that this is because they are case hardened and biased in favour of believing the police and prosecution.

For example, in the case of Bingham Justices (1974), which involved a conviction for speeding in which the evidence of the motorist and that of a police officer contradicted one another, the chairman of the magistrates said, 'My principle in such cases has always been to believe the police officer'. The conviction was quashed on appeal because of the magistrate's obvious bias.

Such bias may be partly due to the fact that magistrates' courts are local courts and so magistrates are likely to see the same police officers and CPS prosecutors time and again, with the danger of a cosy relationship developing and a loss of impartiality.

However, magistrates have also been accused of racial bias. As we saw earlier, Lammy found that Black, Asian and minority ethnic defendants were more likely than White defendants to opt for a Crown Court trial in front of a jury of their peers, because they feared racial bias from magistrates.

Over-reliance on legal advisers

Critics argue that magistrates rely too much on the legal adviser to the court. Although in theory the legal adviser is not allowed to help decide a sentence, magistrates – who are laypeople, not lawyers – may defer to the view of the legal adviser, who is a professional expert.

Over-use of short prison sentences

Magistrates have been criticised for over-using relatively short custodial sentences (they can sentence offenders to up to 12 months in prison in certain cases). Such sentences are expensive, contribute massively to prison overcrowding and costs, and do little to prevent further offending.

CONTROLLED ASSESSMENT PREPARATION

What you have to do

Using your notes from Topic 2.5, discuss the use of the following laypeople in criminal cases:
- juries
- magistrates.

You should be able to discuss the strengths and weaknesses of both juries and lay magistrates.

The assignment brief scenario

Where relevant, you should make reference to the brief in your answer.

How it will be marked

4-6 marks: The uses of lay people (juries and magistrates) are discussed fully in relation to their strengths and weaknesses in criminal cases.
1-3 marks: A basic/simple description of juries and magistrates.

TOPIC 3.1

Examine information for validity

Getting Started
Working in small groups and using knowledge you have gained from this Unit so far, discuss this question:

How far can we rely on the following sources of information about crimes and suspects?

- **a.** the testimony of experts
- **b.** forensic evidence
- **c.** the tabloid press
- **d.** social media
- **e.** eye witnesses
- **f.** the police
- **g.** the judiciary's judgements.

You might want to refer to any relevant cases you know about.

Think about these sources in terms of issues such as:

- Is the information accurate or inaccurate?
- Is it factual or just opinion?
- Is it biased or impartial?

Sources of information

In this Topic, we examine the following sources of information in relation to criminal justice: evidence, trial transcripts, the media, court judgements, and law reports.

In each case, we look at how valid the information source is. That is, how far does it provide us with true and correct information – can we rely on it? Does it have legal force and authority?

For example, the tabloid press are often accused of giving a biased, stereotyped view of suspects as monsters or weirdos. This coverage could prejudice jurors against the defendant and lead to an invalid verdict – one not based on the true and full facts of the case presented to the court. Likewise, not all witness testimony is valid and some kinds (such as hearsay) may be ruled inadmissible in court.

Evidence

The prosecution and defence will present evidence in a criminal trial and it is up to the jury or magistrates to decide how valid that evidence is in reaching their verdict.

As we saw in Topic 2.1, before proceeding with a prosecution, the CPS requires evidence to be:

- **admissible** For example, hearsay evidence or confessions obtained by threats will not be valid in the eyes of the court.
- **reliable** Is the evidence accurate; is a witness dishonest or of bad character? Is a document authentic or a forgery?
- **credible** Is the evidence believable, given the circumstances? Even if the witness is honest, could they really have seen clearly what they claimed to have seen?

The fact that the prosecution's evidence in court has to first convince the CPS gives some indication that it may be valid, but this is not guaranteed. For example, the defence may be able to demonstrate shortcomings or inconsistencies in a witness's testimony during cross-examination.

Eye-witness testimony

As we saw in Topic 1.2, although juries tend to give a lot of weight to eye-witness testimony, it is not always valid. Many convictions based on evidence from eye-witnesses have been overturned when more accurate and reliable evidence has come to light, such as DNA.

Research by psychologists such as Loftus et al shows that witnesses' memory and the evidence they give can be affected by many factors, such as:

- the time when the event took place
- whether they discussed what they saw with other people
- how long ago they witnessed it
- the way questions about the event are put to them in court.

All this suggests that eye-witness evidence may lack validity. For example, if the event took place a long time before the trial, the information lacks currency and recall becomes less accurate over time. Likewise, the circumstance in which the memory was formed can undermine validity. For example, Loftus et al found that where a weapon was involved, 'weapon focus' by witnesses meant they did not form a detailed memory of other aspects, such as a good description of the offender.

Evidence from experts

In complex technical cases, the verdict often hinges on the evidence of an expert such as a medical specialist or forensic scientist. By definition, the expert is supposed to know more about a particular subject than either the legal professionals or laypeople such as jurors.

As a result, the evidence of expert witnesses has a special status: unlike other witnesses, they are entitled to give their *opinion* as experts on the matter in hand. And jurors may find the expert's opinion especially credible and give it great weight when reaching a verdict.

Miscarriages of justice

Relying on experts carries the risk of a miscarriage of justice if their evidence is inaccurate, or if they pass off what is merely an opinion as a scientific fact. We have seen several examples of this elsewhere in this Unit.

For instance, as we saw in Topic 1.3, Sally Clark, Donna Anthony and Angela Cannings were all convicted of killing their children on the strength of expert evidence from Sir Roy Meadow. He inaccurately told the court in each case that there was only a one in 73 million chance of two cot deaths (sudden infant death syndrome) occurring in the same family by chance.

Evidence from experts who are biased or incompetent can also undermine validity of the information. For example, the forensic scientist Dr Frank Skuse was involved in a number of miscarriages of justice involving defendants charged with IRA terrorism offences, including the Birmingham Six who were wrongly convicted of bombing two Birmingham pubs in 1974.

Sir Roy Meadow arrives at a hearing of the General Medical Council, charged with serious professional misconduct.

Forensic evidence

Expert testimony often involves interpreting forensic evidence such as DNA. While each individual's DNA is unique to them and can therefore provide highly valid information about a suspect or victim, it can be contaminated and lead to someone being accused of a crime they did not commit, as in the case of Adam Scott (see Topic 1.1).

Trial transcripts

A trial transcript is a complete and exact written record of every word spoken in court by the judge, lawyers, witnesses and defendant.

Originally, transcripts were made by court stenographers using a type of shorthand and later using special stenotype machines. Nowadays courts record proceedings digitally instead, using Darts (the Digital Audio Recording Transcription and Storage system).

Anyone can apply for a transcript of a court hearing if the hearing was recorded, but the court can refuse to provide one (for example, if the hearing was confidential). Crown Court hearings are always recorded, whereas magistrates' hearings are never recorded. There is usually a fee for the transcript.

Uses of transcripts

Trial transcripts are important in ensuring justice for two reasons:

- They are evidence that a defendant can use in an appeal, for example to show irregularities in the proceedings or biased summing up by the judge.
- They are used by the Parole Board when considering a prisoner's application to be released on parole. The Board can read the sentencing remarks made by the judge at the original trial. For example, the judge may have commented on the risk that the offender poses to the public, and this will affect the Board's decision.

How valid are transcripts?

Trial transcripts are recognised as valid sources of information because they are seen as highly accurate and unbiased accounts of the words spoken in court. They are also current records of the words at the moment when they were spoken, and not a reconstruction at a later time of what had been said in court. It is for these reasons that transcripts are accepted as true records in appeals and by the Parole Board.

However, although the Darts recording system is highly reliable, there is always a small risk of malfunctioning with any technology. It is also possible that some spoken words may not be recorded clearly. Where stenographers were used, there was a small risk of human error in mishearing or mistyping the spoken word. The circumstances of the courtroom (for example, noise levels) can also affect the recording or transcription.

Media

Political bias

Different media outlets show different political biases. Newspapers tend to support one party or another. For example, the *Mirror* tends to be more left-wing and support Labour, while the *Sun* tends to be more right-wing and support the Conservatives. By contrast, radio and TV have a duty to provide balanced coverage of political issues. For example, the BBC is required to treat controversial subjects with 'due impartiality' rather than taking sides.

These differences mean that coverage of crime and justice issues varies from one media source to another. For example, right-wing papers tend to favour tougher laws and more prison sentences to tackle crime. This can affect the validity of their coverage, with a one-sided approach that selects information supporting this view. Newspapers are also free to put their opinions forward and this is likely to colour the information they present.

We must therefore treat media sources with caution and take full account of the political biases of the particular media outlet when assessing how valid or truthful the information is.

Moral panics

The media need to attract an audience in order to make a profit or improve their ratings. This may lead to sensationalised coverage, for example of the riots of 2011, dangerous dogs in 1991, or the mods and rockers in the 1960s. Distorted and exaggerated reporting of events produces information that doesn't give an accurate or valid picture of the amount or severity of criminality that is actually occurring.

How objective and reliable are media accounts as a source of information on crime and disorder?

Stereotyping

As we saw with the case of Christopher Jefferies in Topic 2.4, the tabloid press often portray suspects in police investigations in a very negative light. Frequently, the portrayal is based on stereotypical views of what an offender looks and acts like: sexually deviant, a creepy loner with weird behaviour patterns and so on. Odd or unflattering photos are often used to reinforce the image, along with quotes from unnamed neighbours, colleagues etc.

Such coverage amounts to trial by media and, as the Jefferies case shows, the information produced by these sources is often riddled with inaccuracy and bias, and has little or no validity.

A further problem with some media coverage of crime is racial stereotyping. For example, Hall et al describe how the media in the 1970s portrayed 'mugging' as committed only by Black youth.

Judgements

The judgements made by courts are not always valid. This can be due to several reasons, such as unintentional bias and unconscious stereotyping, political bias, and incorrect rulings by judges and coroners.

Unintentional bias in judgements

Unbiased judgement is essential if defendants are to receive a fair trial, but research shows that unconscious biases can influence the judgement of jurors. For example, simulations show that jurors who believe the justice system is too lenient are more likely to judge a defendant guilty.

Race

Unconscious racial stereotypes can influence judgements and decisions. For example, Plant and Peruche found that in a video-game simulation, US police officers were more likely to shoot unarmed Black suspects than unarmed White ones, an effect known as 'weapon bias'. Other US studies have found trial judges and death penalty lawyers to have biases against Black people.

Gender

Ellison and Munro found that in simulations of rape trials, jurors used victims' lack of signs of physical injury or emotional response, and their delays in reporting the attack, as reasons for bringing in not guilty verdicts. These reasons are based on unconscious assumptions and stereotypes about rape victims.

Political bias in judgements

Judges have their own personal political views and so there is a risk that these will influence their judgements. One case where this may have occurred was that of former Chilean dictator General Pinochet.

In 1973 Pinochet had seized power in a bloody military coup that overthrew the democratically elected government of President Salvador Allende. In 1998, Pinochet was visiting Britain when he was arrested on an extradition request from the Spanish government, who wanted to try him for crimes against humanity.

Pinochet claimed that as an ex-head of state, he had immunity from arrest, but the House of Lords ruled that he had no such immunity. However, it subsequently reversed its decision on the ground of bias. Lord Hoffman, one of the judges in the case, had failed to disclose his links with the human rights organisation Amnesty International (he was chair of its fund-raising body), which had backed Pinochet's extradition.

The Lords did not suggest that Hoffman was actually biased. Instead they argued that 'justice must not only be done, but must be seen to be done' and Hoffman's close ties with Amnesty could give rise to a *suspicion* of bias in his verdict. Ultimately there is no way of knowing for certain whether Hoffman's verdict was biased, or whether it was based purely on an objective view of the facts.

Chile, 2016. Demonstrators carry pictures of people missing believed murdered by the military in the 1973 coup. Allende, also killed in the coup, is pictured in the centre.

Inquests

When a sudden death occurs due to the actions of public organisations such as the police, they receive state-funded legal representation at the inquest. By contrast, the bereaved families have no automatic entitlement to legal aid. The pressure group INQUEST argues that this is a form of institutional bias and undermines the right to fair treatment. It can be particularly difficult for families to challenge a verdict that they believe to be invalid, as the Hillsborough disaster shows.

The Hillsborough disaster

On 15 April 1989, 96 Liverpool fans died and 766 were injured in a crush on the terraces at Sheffield Wednesday FC's Hillsborough Stadium at the start of an FA Cup semi-final. The crush occurred after the police match commander, Chief Superintendent David Duckenfield, ordered an exit gate to be opened, which led to a surge of supporters into the already overcrowded fenced-in pens behind the goals. The match was abandoned at 3.05 pm, five minutes after kick-off.

Rescue efforts were chaotic and some police at first tried to stop fans escaping the pens, believing it to be a pitch invasion. In the weeks that followed, police fed false stories to the media blaming hooliganism and drunkenness by Liverpool fans.

The first inquest

A report by Lord Justice Taylor blamed the police, but in 1990 the Director of Public Prosecutions (DPP) announced that no officers would face charges. In 1991, inquest verdicts declared the deaths were accidental. The coroner ruled that all 96 had died prior to 3.15 pm, which meant that the emergency services' response after that time could not be examined.

In 2000 the families of the 96 took out a private prosecution against Duckenfield and another officer. Despite Duckenfield admitting he had lied, the jury failed to reach a verdict.

In 2009 the government set up the Hillsborough Independent Panel. It published its report in September 2012 – the first thorough investigation of the disaster. It found that:

- fans were not responsible; the main cause was lack of police control
- up to 41 of the dead might have survived had the emergency services' response been better
- there had been a police cover-up, including altering 116 statements to remove negative comments about their role
- the police had blamed fans and sought to smear the reputations of the dead (e.g. conducting alcohol tests on their bodies).

The second inquest

In December 2012 the High Court quashed the accidental death verdicts. In 2016, a new inquest found that:

- all 96 were unlawfully killed
- Duckenfield's actions amounted to 'gross negligence'
- the police and ambulance service contributed to the deaths
- stadium design faults contributed to the deaths (it had no valid safety certificate).

Following the inquest verdicts, Duckenfield was charged with manslaughter by gross negligence and the football club's ex-secretary Graham Mackrell with breaching sports ground safety laws.

From the almost 20-year story of the disaster, it is clear there were serious errors of judgement by many in authority, including:

- the police and ambulance service on the day
- the DPP in 1990 deciding not to prosecute anyone
- the coroner's court accidental deaths verdict in 1991
- the court trying Duckenfield in 2000.

Equally, the police's lies, cover-ups, victim-blaming and falsifications of evidence mean that their account of the events and their role in them lacks any validity.

ACTIVITY | Media

Hillsborough   Go to www.criminology.uk.net

Hillsborough, 15 April 1989. Some fans are rescued from the crush but 96 others died.

The inquest on Mark Duggan

The judgements in inquests into suspicious deaths have often been challenged. For example, the family of Mark Duggan, whose shooting by police sparked the 2011 riots, sought to overturn the inquest verdict of lawful killing.

Duggan was killed by a police firearms officer who believed, incorrectly, that Duggan was armed with a handgun. At the inquest, the coroner directed the jury that if they accepted that the officer honestly believed he was in danger and was acting in self-defence, they should return a verdict of lawful killing. This was in fact their verdict.

On appeal, Duggan's family argued that the coroner had misdirected the jury. He should have told them that they must also consider whether the officer's belief was based on reasonable grounds and if not, that they should return a verdict of unlawful killing.

However, the Court of Appeal rejected the family's appeal on the grounds that it was a matter of common sense that the jury would consider this, and that the coroner giving them detailed directions could confuse them.

The validity of the initial judgement and that of the Court of Appeal can be debated and there remains disagreement about whether the jury understood that it was possible to bring in a verdict of unlawful killing.

ACTIVITY | Media

The Mark Duggan case   Go to www.criminology.uk.net

Vigil outside Tottenham police station after the inquest found Mark Duggan was lawfully killed.

Law reports

Law reports are reports of decisions made by courts. They are published on a regular basis – many of them weekly. Their purpose is to inform lawyers and judges about important judgements in the courts and to prevent two courts reaching differing decisions on identical facts.

A report contains the following sections:
- the case header: the names of the parties involved, the date, the court and the judge
- the key words relating to the case (e.g. hearsay evidence) and the key issues involved
- the headnote: a summary of the facts, the court's decision and any case law considered
- the judgement: a transcript of the exact words used by the judge to explain his or her reasoning.

The principle of precedent

Only about 2% of all cases are reported in law reports. These are the cases that set a precedent – that is, they lay down a new principle of law.

In England and Wales, the principle of precedent governs how courts reach many of their decisions. Precedent involves following the decisions that have been made in previous similar cases. Where the point of law in the present case and a previous one is the same, the court should follow the decision of the previous case.

Following precedent promotes consistency and fairness between similar cases, and it also provides certainty – people can know what to expect in a case, given the decision that was reached in a similar previous case.

Why are law reports important?

The courts can only follow precedent if they actually know what the previous decision was and the reason for it. It is therefore vital to have details of the earlier case, and this is the role of law reports.

A report provides a full and accurate record of all the relevant information. This means the court can rely on it as an authoritative statement of the legal principle on which the case was decided. This enables the court to see whether the earlier case sets a precedent for the one they are currently dealing with.

How valid are law reports?

Official law reports can be seen as valid, authoritative sources of information on the law.

- **Accuracy** They are accurate accounts of cases, with an exact transcript of the judgement, and with key details of important cases written up in a standard format.
- **Currency** They are current (up to date) – many reports are published on a weekly basis.
- **Bias** They are objective, unbiased reports of the facts of cases.
- **Opinion** They contain the opinions of the court, since this is essential for other courts to understand the reasons for the judgement. They do not contain the opinions of the person who writes the report.

CONTROLLED ASSESSMENT PREPARATION

What you have to do

Using your notes from Topic 3.1, examine the following information for validity:

- evidence
- trial transcripts
- media reports
- judgements
- law reports.

You should examine the validity of the above information in terms of:

- bias
- opinion
- circumstances
- currency
- accuracy.

You should show the ability to review the information sources and make judgements on the suitability of the content they provide against a number of criteria.

The assignment brief scenario

Where relevant, you should make reference to the brief in your answer. To reach the top mark band, you must include reference to the brief.

How it will be marked

11-15 marks: Detailed examination of a relevant range of information sources (including reference to the brief). There is a clear review of their suitability in terms of validity.

6-10 marks: A range of information sources are examined and reviewed in terms of their validity. At the bottom end, the range of information sources and/or the review will be limited.

1-5 marks: Limited information sources are described (listed at the lower end). At the top end, some information sources are discussed in relation to validity.

Draw conclusions from information

TOPIC 3.2

Getting Started
Working with a partner, consider what you have studied so far in this Unit and answer the following questions:
1. What factors might lead to a trial being unfair?
2. Why might there be more not guilty verdicts in cases decided by juries rather than ones decided by judges or magistrates?

Safe verdicts

A safe verdict is one that is reached on the basis of all the relevant facts of the matter after a fair trial. To achieve a safe verdict, two things are needed:
- **the evidence** must be admissible, reliable and credible, as well as sufficient to justify the verdict
- **court procedures** must have been followed correctly during the trial.

Unsafe verdicts and miscarriages of justice

Unsafe verdicts and miscarriages of justice generally occur when there are either problems with the evidence or problems with the trial process itself. In such cases, the defendant may seek to appeal against the 'guilty' verdict.

Miscarriages of justice

Miscarriages of justice are cases where the innocence of the appellant (the person making the appeal) is proven. They are almost always based on fresh evidence. For example, this might be as a result of new forensic techniques such as advances in DNA analysis that were not available at the time of the original trial.

If the Court of Appeal decides that a conviction is a miscarriage of justice, then there will not normally be a need for a re-trial. The case against the appellant will be dismissed, because the new evidence proves their innocence.

ACTIVITY Research

The Innocence Project   Go to www.criminology.uk.net

Unsafe or wrongful convictions

Unsafe verdicts are usually called unsafe or wrongful convictions. Miscarriages of justice are one type of wrongful conviction (they are wrong because the accused was actually innocent). However, wrongful convictions can also occur where it is not clear whether the accused was innocent or guilty.

In these cases, the conviction is usually overturned because there was something wrong with the trial process. This led to the accused not receiving a fair trial and so we cannot be sure beyond reasonable doubt that he or she was guilty.

Defects in the trial procedure such as the following may cause wrongful convictions:
- the judge misdirecting the jury
- the judge making mistakes in their legal rulings, such as wrongly excluding or including evidence, e.g. admitting hearsay evidence
- failure to call relevant witnesses or present relevant evidence
- jury irregularities, e.g. tampering, jurors researching the case on the internet etc.

These defects may not show that the appellant was innocent, but they cast doubt on his or her guilt. In these cases, the Court of Appeal will quash the original conviction but may order a re-trial.

The Birmingham Six

There have been a number of high-profile miscarriages of justice in the last 50 years or so. One of the best known is that of the Birmingham Six.

Arrest and trial

On 21 November 1974, two Birmingham pubs were bombed, it is believed by the Provisional IRA, with the loss of 21 lives. Soon after, six Northern Irish-born Catholic men who lived in Birmingham were arrested. While in police custody, they were deprived of food and sleep, interrogated for up to 12 hours without a break, threatened and beaten, and subjected to a mock execution. Four of the men signed confessions.

On 12 May 1975 the six were charged with murder and conspiracy to cause explosions. The judge deemed the confessions admissible as evidence. Giving evidence for the prosecution, the forensic scientist Dr Frank Skuse claimed he was 99% certain that two of the men had explosives traces on their hands. This was opposed by the defence's expert Dr Hugh Black, the former Chief Inspector of Explosives for the Home Office. The six were found guilty on 15 August 1975 and each given 21 life sentences.

Appeals

In March 1976 the men's application for leave to appeal was dismissed and they remained in jail. In 1985, the first of several *World in Action* TV programmes casting doubt on their convictions was broadcast. In 1986, a book by Chris Mullin MP set out the case for their innocence, including Mullin's claim to have met some of those who were actually responsible for the bombings.

In 1988, after the longest criminal appeal ever, the Court of Appeal ruled that the convictions were safe and dismissed their appeals. Over the next three years, journalists and campaigners produced new evidence throwing doubt on the safety of the convictions.

Freedom

In a new appeal in 1990, fresh evidence of police fabrication, wrongful exclusion of evidence by the trial judge, and challenges to the confessions and the forensic evidence, led the prosecution not to offer a case.

The Court of Appeal said that 'in the light of the fresh scientific evidence, which at least throws grave doubt on Dr. Skuse's evidence, if it does not destroy it altogether, these convictions are both unsafe and unsatisfactory'. The six were freed on 14 March 1991.

ACTIVITY	Media
The Birmingham Six	Go to www.criminology.uk.net

The West Midlands Serious Crime Squad operated from 1974 to 1989, when it was disbanded after an investigation into allegations of serious misconduct, some of which resulted in wrongful convictions, including the Birmingham Six. Over 100 other cases either failed or were quashed on appeal. Malpractice by officers included physical abuse of prisoners (such as putting plastic bags over their heads), fabrication of confessions and planting of incriminating evidence.

ACTIVITY — Research

Miscarriages of justice

Go to www.criminology.uk.net

Some of the Birmingham Six with Chris Mullin (wearing glasses), after their release by the Court of Appeal.

Just verdicts

A just verdict is one that is deserved, lawful and proper. It is a verdict that does justice to the facts of the case, finding the guilty, guilty, and the innocent not guilty. The criminal justice system has not always produced verdicts that are just, as with the double jeopardy rule.

Double jeopardy

Until the double jeopardy rule was changed in 2003, someone who had been acquitted of an offence could not be prosecuted again for that offence. In most cases this is just and fair, because it prevents the abuse of state power. It stops prosecutors from repeatedly prosecuting someone for the same crime until they finally secure a conviction, which would be regarded as oppression.

However, in certain cases, it becomes clear that a 'not guilty' verdict in the original trial was unjust. This can happen when the defendant, after being acquitted of a crime, then admits to having committed it. The justice of a verdict can also be questioned when new evidence comes to light after the acquittal.

In *Criminology Book One*, we examined the case of Billy Dunlop. Dunlop had been tried and acquitted of the murder of Julie Hogg, but subsequently admitted to the crime. Julie's mother Ann Ming successfully campaigned for a change in the double jeopardy rule to allow Dunlop's re-trial and conviction.

Stephen Lawrence

The racist murder of Stephen Lawrence in 1993 also gave impetus to the campaign to change the double jeopardy rule. The police investigation had been incompetent and racist, and did not result in prosecutions of any of the five suspects (two were initially charged but the charges were later dropped).

Stephen's parents brought a private prosecution against three of the suspects. However, they were acquitted after the judge ruled that identification evidence given by Duwayne Brooks was inadmissible. Duwayne had been with Stephen when he was murdered.

The Macpherson Report

In 1999 the Macpherson Report into the case called for the removal of the double jeopardy rule. In 2003 the Criminal Justice Act amended the law so that a second prosecution could be allowed for very serious crimes if 'new and compelling' evidence is uncovered. Even then, the Director of Public Prosecutions (the head of the CPS) must personally agree that re-opening the case is in the public interest. Only one re-trial is permitted.

'New and compelling evidence': Dobson's jacket was found to have tiny flakes of Stephen Lawrence's blood on it.

Just verdicts In the Lawrence case, the change led to the re-trial and conviction of one of the five suspects, Gary Dobson, in 2012. Another of the original suspects, David Norris, who had not been tried previously, was also convicted. It could therefore be said that a just verdict had finally been reached, but only after 19 years and only in the case of two of the suspects.

ACTIVITY | Media

The Stephen Lawrence case

Go to www.criminology.uk.net

Jury equity or jury nullification

Sometimes the law may seem unjust. In these situations, to bring about a just verdict, a jury may deliberately reject the evidence and decide to acquit a defendant who has broken the law – even when the judge has directed them to bring in a guilty verdict. This is known as jury equity (see Topic 2.5) or jury nullification, because the jury nullifies the law. That is, they ignore the letter of the law to reach what they believe is a just or equitable verdict.

Juries sometimes do this when they believe the existing law or the punishment for breaking it is unfair, inhumane or immoral. They can do this because a jury's verdict to acquit is unassailable (cannot be challenged). If juries consistently refuse to convict defendants charged under a particular law, this may send a signal to lawmakers that the law needs changing.

There are some famous cases of juries nullifying a law and acquitting defendants in the interests of justice.

Capital punishment

In early 19th century England, the theft of items worth more than forty shillings (two pounds) carried the death sentence, but juries were often unwilling to condemn petty thieves to death and they either brought in not guilty verdicts or even – in one case involving the theft of £20 – found the defendant guilty of stealing only 39 shillings (£1.95) instead, which saved him from the gallows.

Runaway slaves

In the United States in the 1850s, juries in the Northern states, where slavery was outlawed, practised nullification to protest against the Fugitive Slave Act. The Act required runaway slaves captured in the Northern states to be returned to their owners in the South, where slavery was legal. Across the North, juries regularly acquitted defendants accused of harbouring fugitive slaves.

Anti-war protest

In 2000 two anti-war protesters, Rosie James and Rachel Wenham, were twice acquitted of criminal damage involving spray painting 'Death Machine' and 'Illegal' on the side of the nuclear submarine *HMS Vengeance*. In addition, in both a first and a second trial, the jury failed to agree on a further charge of damaging the submarine's equipment.

James and Wenham admitted these actions but pleaded not guilty, arguing that they were acting to prevent a war crime and that their actions were justified under international law. A spokeswoman for the protestors said: 'Our case clearly caused a serious dilemma for the jury and it shows that instinctive morality is alive and well'.

The case of James and Wenham has similarities with that of the civil servant Clive Ponting, who was acquitted by a jury of leaking official secrets over the sinking of the *General Belgrano*, despite openly admitting he had done so (see Topic 2.5).

Cannabis laws

In 1998 Alan Blythe was charged with cultivating cannabis with intent to supply, an offence usually punished by a prison sentence. He pleaded 'duress of circumstance' (being forced by circumstances to commit a crime), explaining that he had grown cannabis and supplied it to his wife, a terminally ill multiple sclerosis sufferer. This was the only thing that eased her pain and he feared that without it, she would commit suicide.

The judge said that duress was not a legitimate defence and instructed the jury to find Blythe guilty. However, the jury returned not guilty verdicts on all charges other than simple cannabis possession, resulting in a £100 fine instead of prison. Blythe's case has some similarities with that of Kay Gilderdale (see Topic 2.5).

Nullification as a cause of injustice

While we might agree that some or all the above were just verdicts, jury nullification can also produce the opposite result. For example, in the United States in the past there have been cases of all-White juries refusing to convict members of the Ku Klux Klan (a violent racist, White supremacist group) of lynching Black men, despite overwhelming evidence of the defendants' guilt.

Just sentencing

An important part of a fair justice system is fair or just sentencing – that those who are found guilty of a crime receive an appropriate and legal sentence. When judges and magistrates sentence an offender, they are guided by two factors:
- **the law** laying down the possible sentences that can be given for a particular offence
- **the Sentencing Guidelines** published by the Sentencing Council.

For example, for the offence of theft, the law (the Theft Act 1968) allows a range of possible sentences from a discharge to seven years imprisonment. The Sentencing Guidelines help the court to decide where to fix the sentence within this range. The Guidelines require the court to consider factors such as culpability (e.g. was the crime pre-planned?), harm to the victim, previous convictions, age or maturity, whether the offender pleaded guilty etc.

On this basis, a first offender with learning difficulties who stole a chocolate bar on the spur of the moment and admitted their guilt at the first opportunity would expect a lower tariff (sentence) – perhaps a conditional discharge. By contrast, a 30-year-old with a long list of previous convictions who stole to order from a vulnerable adult would attract a much higher tariff – probably a custodial sentence.

Judicial discretion

As the examples above show, judges or magistrates have to weigh up the relative importance of numerous factors in deciding on the sentence and they have some room for discretion (choice) in how they do this. As a result, two very similar cases may still result in somewhat different sentences.

Partly because of this discretion, cases arise where the sentence appears too lenient or too harsh, given the particular circumstances of the offence or the offender. We shall look at each of these in turn.

Unduly lenient sentences

In certain cases, where victims, prosecutors or members of the public feel a sentence is unduly lenient, they can apply to the Attorney General or Solicitor General (government law ministers) for it to be reviewed under the Unduly Lenient Sentences (ULS) scheme. If they agree that the judge made a gross error in sentencing, they will ask the Court of Appeal to review and if necessary increase the sentence. The court will only increase the sentence if it is significantly below the sentence that the judge should have passed – the sentence must be not just lenient, but *unduly* (excessively) so.

The ULS scheme only applies to serious offences. These include murder, manslaughter, rape, robbery, people trafficking, child sex crimes, certain fraud and drug offences, some terror-related offences, and racially or religiously aggravated offences. In 2018, 140 cases were referred to the Court of Appeal and of these, 99 had their sentences increased.

Sentences increased for being unduly lenient include the following cases:

- **Joshua Gardner**, the Croydon 'zombie knife' attacker, originally received a suspended sentence for trying to smash his way into a car to attack the driver. In 2019, his sentence was increased to three and a half years in a young offender institution.
- **John Dennis** had his jail sentence doubled in 2015 from 10 to 20 years for raping four women. The Court of Appeal described him as highly predatory and his offending as 'a chronicle of cold, callous sexual degradation', with the youngest victim a vulnerable 15-year-old.
- **Mohammed Ghani** had his jail sentence increased from two years to five in 2018 for sexually assaulting a girl over a seven year period during 'professional visits' (he was an imam) to her home. The girl had been under 14 at the time.
- **Robert Brown** had his jail sentence increased from nine years to ten and a half years in 2018 for the hit-and-run killing of two brothers aged two and six. He had taken a cocktail of drugs and was driving at 60mph in a 30mph zone.

Unduly harsh sentences

Some sentences may be seen as too harsh. For example, the courts in 2011 took a particularly dim view of anyone involved in criminality during the riots that had taken place that year and the sentences they handed down were much harsher than would usually be the case. For example:

- A mother of two who was at home asleep during the riots in Manchester was jailed for six months for accepting a pair of looted shorts from a friend.
- A Brixton man was jailed for six months for taking a case of water worth £3.50 from a smashed-up Lidl store.
- Two men in Cheshire were jailed for four years each for using Facebook to incite a riot that never took place.

None of the above had previous convictions.

Moral panic

One possible reason for the stiffer sentences is the moral panic that surrounded the riots, with widespread calls from the media and politicians for a crackdown on those involved. For example, in the wake of the riots, Her Majesty's Courts and Tribunals Service, which oversees the courts, advised magistrates to consider custodial sentences for riot-related offences that would normally be punished less severely.

A similar pattern of harsh sentencing has accompanied other moral panics, such as the mods and rockers in the 1960s. Stanley Cohen notes that magistrates routinely refused bail, so that young people with no previous convictions and charged with only minor offences were remanded to prison, in some cases for several weeks. Magistrates also sentenced more people to detention centres for first offences.

Penal populism

Critics argue that sentencing has become increasingly politicised: politicians have advocated tougher sentencing as a way of gaining popularity with the voters. This is known as 'penal populism' and it has resulted in longer sentences.

For example, the Crime (Sentences) Act 1997 introduced mandatory minimum sentences for certain crimes. One effect of tougher sentences has been a sharp increase in the prison population over the last 30 years, at a time when crime rates have generally been falling. (For more on penal populism and prison, see *Criminology Book One*, Unit 2, Topic 4.1.)

CONTROLLED ASSESSMENT PREPARATION

What you have to do

Using your notes from Topic 3.2, draw objective conclusions from information on criminal cases in relation to the following:

- safe verdict
- miscarriage of justice
- just verdict
- just sentencing.

You should show the skills needed to analyse the information in order to draw conclusions based on reasoned evidence.

The assignment brief scenario

Where relevant, you should make reference to the brief in your answer. To reach the top mark band, you must include reference to the brief.

How it will be marked

11-15 marks: Draws objective conclusions on criminal cases (including reference to the brief), using evidence and clear reasoning/argument in support of conclusions.

6-10 marks: Draws some objective conclusions on criminal cases, using some evidence and reasoning in support of conclusions.

1-5 marks: Draws conclusions on criminal cases. Conclusions may be mainly subjective, with limited evidence used in support.

Preparing for the Unit 3 controlled assessment

When you have completed Unit 3, you will sit the controlled assessment. This section gives you some guidance on how to prepare for it.

What does it involve?

The controlled assessment involves a set of tasks covering the eleven Unit 3 Assessment Criteria (ACs) and you must address them all in your answers. They are dealt with in the eleven Topics covered in this book.

Using the brief You will be given a brief, which is a scenario describing a criminal case. Think of it as a prompt to remind you about some of the ACs that you need to deal with in your answers. You should make reference to the brief in your answers, but only where it is particularly relevant to do so. However, for AC 3.1 and AC 3.2, you *must* make reference to the brief in order to score in the top mark band.

Prepare your file in advance

Before you sit the assessment, it is essential that you have thoroughly prepared your notes for all eleven ACs, because you will need to take them with you into the assessment.

On the next page is a checklist of what you need to do for each AC. Use this to make sure you have written your notes on all of them so that you have everything covered *before* you sit the assessment. For help making notes on each AC, refer back to the Topic with the same number.

On the day of the assessment

On the day of the controlled assessment, make sure you bring all your Unit 3 materials and have your file in good order.

You are allowed to have access to your class notes and to information sources, but you are not allowed to access the internet. You can't take in any electronic documents or devices. Everything you need must be on paper, so if you have any electronic notes you must print them off if you want to take them into the assessment.

Use your headings!

When completing your controlled assessment task, it's a very good idea to use the eleven ACs as headings and write about each one in turn, so that you make sure you have covered everything and maximised your marks.

AC	What you need to do	Max. mark
	In all ACs, link your answer to the brief where it is relevant.	
1.1	Evaluate the effectiveness of the roles of personnel involved in criminal investigations. A clear and detailed evaluation of a range of personnel is needed. Include strengths and limitations and give examples of relevant cases. You should consider cost, expertise and availability when evaluating each role's effectiveness.	10
1.2	Assess the usefulness of investigative techniques in criminal investigations. Include a range of techniques and give a clear and detailed assessment of each one. Give examples of cases where possible and focus on how effectively or ineffectively the techniques were used in those cases.	20
1.3	Explain how evidence is processed. Include both physical and testimonial evidence. Give a clear, detailed explanation of how evidence is processed. Include the collection, transfer, storage and analysis of evidence, and the personnel involved, e.g. CSIs collect and transfer evidence from the crime scene; forensic scientists analyse it. Include examples of physical evidence from the brief and other cases.	6
1.4	Examine the rights of individuals in criminal investigations. Include the rights of suspects, victims and witnesses. Give a clear explanation of each one.	6
2.1	Explain the requirements of the Crown Prosecution Service for prosecuting suspects. Give a detailed explanation of the CPS's role in prosecuting suspects in criminal trials. Explain the tests that must be passed for a prosecution to take place. Use examples to support your points.	4
2.2	Describe trial processes. Describe all the stages of the trial process in detail, including the roles of the different personnel involved.	4
2.3	Understand rules in relation to the use of evidence in criminal cases. Explain the rules concerning evidence used in court. Refer to examples and cases.	4
2.4	Assess key influences affecting the outcomes of criminal cases. Assess the following influences: evidence, witnesses, legal teams, the judiciary, political factors and the media. Give examples of cases.	10
2.5	Discuss the use of laypeople in criminal cases. Give a detailed discussion of the strengths and limitations of using juries and magistrates to try criminal cases. Give examples of cases.	6
3.1	Examine information for validity. Examine the following information sources in detail: evidence, trial transcripts, media reports, judgements and Law Reports. Consider the validity of these sources in terms of bias, opinion, circumstances, accuracy and currency (whether it is up-to-date). Make a judgement about the validity of each source. Support your points with examples of valid and invalid verdicts in criminal cases. Make reference to the brief in your answer.	15
3.2	Draw conclusions from information. Draw objective conclusions on criminal cases, supported by evidence and clear reasoning/argument. Consider safe verdict, miscarriage of justice, just verdict and just sentencing. Make reference to the brief in your answer.	15
TOTAL		**100**

UNIT 4

CRIME AND PUNISHMENT

Overview

This Unit is about social control – that is, about how society seeks to control our behaviour and ensure that we obey the law. It focuses on the criminal justice system and its efforts to achieve social control.

We begin by looking at how the law is made by Parliament and by the decisions of judges. We then go on to examine how the criminal justice system is organised to uphold the law and punish those who break it. This involves looking at how agencies such as the police, Crown Prosecution Service, the courts, prisons and probation service fit together.

We also look at the different values on which a criminal justice system can be based. For example, it can emphasise the need to protect the rights of the accused against the power of the state, such as the principle that you are innocent until proven guilty. Or it can focus on protecting the public by suppressing crime, even at the cost of some innocent people being wrongly convicted.

Next we look at punishment and what it is for. For example, should the aim of imprisonment just be to protect the public by taking offenders off the streets? Or should it be about rehabilitating criminals so that they 'go straight' and lead a crime-free life? As we shall see, the justice system uses punishment to try to achieve several different aims.

But do the prisons, police and other agencies of the criminal justice system actually succeed in achieving their aims? For example, does prison succeed in preventing people re-offending? When you have completed this Unit, you will be in a position to evaluate how effective the different agencies are in achieving social control and ensuring that society's members obey the law.

Describe processes used for law making

TOPIC 1.1

Getting started

Working with a partner, complete the following:

1. From what you have studied so far in your course or from your own knowledge, note down what you know about how laws are made. For example, who is involved in making the law?
2. Consider the law to make stalking a criminal offence (see *Criminology Book One*, page 160). Who campaigned for the new law and why did the campaign succeed?

Share your answers with the rest of the class.

This Topic deals with who makes the law. In England and Wales, there are two main sources of the law:

- **the government**, through Parliament
- **the judiciary.**

We shall look at each of these two sources and how they make the law.

Government (parliamentary) processes of law making

Parliament

The United Kingdom is a parliamentary democracy. This means that most of the country's laws are made by passing Acts of Parliament. Laws made by Parliament are also often referred to as 'statutes' or 'legislation'.

Parliament is made up of three parts:

- **the monarch** (the queen or king)
- **the House of Lords**
- **the House of Commons**.

The monarch has only a formal role in law-making. The king or queen simply gives the Royal Assent – their agreement to the new law.

The Lords

Members of the House of Lords are called peers. There are about 800 peers. In the past, all peers were noblemen (such as dukes and barons) and they were hereditary positions that passed from father to eldest son. However, today there are only 92 hereditary peers; there are also 26 Church of England bishops and archbishops. The rest of the members are life peers who cannot pass their position on to their children. The main job of the Lords is to act as a 'double check' on new laws.

The Commons

The House of Commons is the most important part of Parliament because it is made up of the elected representatives of the people: the 650 Members of Parliament (MPs). Each MP is elected at a general election to represent a constituency (a geographical area of the country).

ACTIVITY | Media

Parliamentary democracy   Go to www.criminology.uk.net

The government

While Parliament's job is to represent the people, the government's job is to run the country. The government is formed by the political party that has a majority of the 650 MPs. The prime minister is the leader of the majority party. Most proposals for new laws come from the government. A proposal for a new law is called a Bill.

Bills must be agreed by both Houses of Parliament and receive the Royal Assent before they can become Acts of Parliament (laws).

Green Paper Before putting a Bill before Parliament, the government usually publishes a Green Paper. This is an initial report to provoke public discussion of the subject. It often includes questions for interested individuals and organisations to respond to.

White Paper After the consultation, the government publishes a White Paper, which is a document setting out their detailed plans for legislation. It often includes a draft version of the Bill they intend to put before Parliament.

The monarch opening Parliament, the UK's supreme law-making body.

The parliamentary stages of a Bill

For a Bill to become law, it must go through a series of stages in Parliament.

First reading

The government first introduces the Bill into the Commons (or occasionally the Lords), where it receives a first reading. This is just a formal announcement of the Bill and it is followed by a vote to allow it to move to its next stage.

Second reading

At the second reading of the Bill, its main principles are considered and debated by the whole House of Commons and a vote is taken. As the government has the support of a majority of MPs, they will usually win this vote. If so, the Bill then moves on to the committee stage.

The committee stage

The Bill is now examined in detail, line by line, by a small committee made up of MPs from different parties. The committee will report back to the whole House and will often propose amendments (changes) to the Bill.

The report stage

The report stage gives MPs an opportunity to consider the committee's report and to debate and vote on any amendments they might wish to make to the Bill. For major Bills, the debates may be spread over several days.

Third reading

The report stage is normally followed immediately by a third reading of the Bill. This is the final chance for the Commons to debate the Bill's contents. No amendments are allowed at this stage – the House votes either to pass the Bill or to reject it.

The Lords

After the third reading, the Bill goes to the House of Lords, where it goes through the same stages as in the Commons. If the Lords have amended the Bill, it must return to the Commons so MPs can decide whether to accept or reject the Lords' amendments. The House of Commons has the final say because it is made up of the people's elected representatives.

Royal Assent

Once the Bill has been passed by both Houses of Parliament, it goes to the monarch for signing, known as the Royal Assent. This is the monarch's agreement to make the Bill into an Act of Parliament or law and is a formality.

The new law will now come into force immediately, unless the Act specifies that it will only apply from some later date (known as a commencement order).

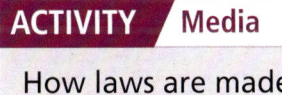

How laws are made

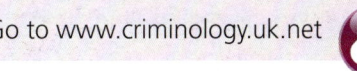

Go to www.criminology.uk.net

> **Box Some examples of criminal statutes**
>
> The following are some of the criminal laws introduced by government and passed by Parliament that you have already looked at in your course.
>
> **The Criminal Justice Act (2003)** introduced a change in the double jeopardy rule, following Ann Ming's successful campaign and the recommendations of the Macpherson Report on the murder of Stephen Lawrence. The change enabled the killer of Ann Ming's daughter and one of the suspects in the killing of Stephen Lawrence to be tried for a second time. Both were convicted.
>
> **The Crime (Sentences) Act (1997)** introduced mandatory minimum sentences for a range of repeat offences, such as an automatic life sentence for a second serious sexual or violent offence.
>
> **The Dangerous Dogs Act (1991)** Most legislation involves detailed scrutiny and usually takes months to become law, but this Act was rushed through Parliament in just a few weeks as a knee-jerk over-reaction to a media-led moral panic. As a result, it wasn't given due consideration and many flaws became apparent, such as that it 'blames the breed, not the deed': most dog attacks are not in fact committed by the four breeds banned by the Act.

Judicial processes of law making

As well as government and Parliament, judges too can make law. This is done through two processes: judicial precedent and statutory interpretation. We shall look at each of these.

Judicial precedent

Judicial precedent is a source of law-making where the past decisions of judges create law for future judges to follow.

Judicial precedent is based on the principle of standing by or following what judges have decided in previous cases. (This idea of 'standing by a decision' is also known by its Latin name, *stare decisis*.)

As we saw in Unit 3, Topic 3.1, this means that where the point of law in a case today is the same as in the previous case, the judge should follow the decision made in the previous one. Treating similar cases in the same way creates certainty, consistency and fairness in the legal system.

Much of the law of the land has developed from following the decisions made in earlier cases. This helped to create a single set of laws common to the whole country, and so the system has come to be known as common law.

The court hierarchy

The legal system has a hierarchy of courts, with the Supreme Court at the top and the magistrates' courts at the bottom. A decision taken in a case by a higher court automatically creates an *original* or *binding precedent* for all lower courts – one that they have to follow when dealing with similar cases.

Exceptions to precedent

There are two main situations where a court does not have to follow precedent. These are distinguishing, and overruling:

- **Distinguishing** A precedent from an earlier case is only binding on a present case if the legal principle involved is the same *and* if the facts are similar in both cases. 'Distinguishing' means

that the judge finds the facts in the present case are different enough from the earlier one to allow him or her to reach a different decision and not have to follow the precedent of the earlier case.
- **Overruling** is where a court higher up the hierarchy states that a legal decision in an earlier case is wrong and overturns it. For example, the Supreme Court can overrule a lower court's decision when it hears an appeal.

The law on marital rape is an example of overruling a precedent. In the case of R v R (1992), a husband had been convicted of attempting to rape his wife. He appealed on the grounds that there was a centuries-old precedent that a husband could not be guilty of raping his wife because the marriage contract gave a wife's 'irrevocable (i.e. irreversible) consent' to sex. But the appeal court overruled this on the grounds that the idea of irrevocable consent was unacceptable today because a couple are now seen as equal partners in a marriage.

Statutory interpretation

As well as making the law by creating precedents for others to follow, judges can make law by the way they interpret the statutes or Acts of Parliament. A statute is a written law and so judges need to interpret the meaning of its words and apply them to the case they are judging.

Judges have three main interpretation rules to help them do this: the literal rule, the golden rule and the mischief rule.

The literal rule

Under this rule, judges should use the everyday, ordinary meaning of the words in a statute. However, one problem with this method is that a word can have several different literal, dictionary meanings. For example, in R v Maginnis (1987), a case involving illegal drugs, different judges found different meanings of the word 'supply'.

The golden rule

Sometimes, the literal rule can lead to an absurd result and the golden rule allows the court to modify the literal meaning to avoid this.

For example, under the Official Secrets Act (1920), it was an offence to obstruct Her Majesty's Forces 'in the vicinity of' (i.e. near to) a prohibited place, such as a naval base. In the case of Adler v George (1964), Adler argued that he had not broken the law because he was not literally *in the vicinity* of a prohibited place, but was actually *in* it. The court chose to apply the golden rule to avoid an absurd result and Adler was convicted.

The mischief rule

The mischief rule allows the court to enforce what the statute was *intended* to achieve, rather than what the words actually say.

For example, the Licensing Act (1872) makes it an offence to be drunk in charge of a 'carriage' on the highway. In Corkery v Carpenter (1951), Corkery was found guilty even though he had been in charge of a bicycle, not a carriage. The court used the mischief rule to convict him, arguing that the Act's purpose was to prevent people from using *any* form of transport on the public highway when drunk – not just carriages.

 **Media**

Statutory interpretation   Go to www.criminology.uk.net

NOW TEST YOURSELF

Practice Question

How does the government make laws in the United Kingdom?

Answer by Sophie

The government makes laws through Parliament. These are called Acts of Parliament or statutes. This involves several stages. First it publishes a Green Paper to stimulate discussion about the issues that the law will deal with, e.g. knife crime. This is followed by a White Paper with its detailed proposals for the new law, e.g. to prevent sales of knives to under-16s.

Next there are a series of stages in the House of Commons. The first reading of the bill (the proposed law) is a formal announcement. The second reading is where MPs debate the bill's main principles. If they vote for the bill, it goes to the committee stage, where a small committee of MPs examines it line by line and may propose amendments to the bill. The committee reports back to the whole House and MPs debate and vote on any amendments, e.g. they might raise the minimum age for buying knives to 18. The third reading usually follows immediately, where MPs debate the bill as a whole and vote to pass or reject it.

It's important to note that the government can usually get a majority of MPs to support its bills. This is because normally a majority of the MPs belong to the same party as the government. But if it is a minority government, like Mrs May's Conservative government after 2017, it may find that the Commons rejects some of its bills, e.g. Mrs May's bill to withdraw from the EU.

Once the Commons has passed a bill, it goes through a similar process in the House of Lords. Finally, it goes to the monarch for signing – known as the Royal Assent. At this point it becomes an Act of Parliament – the government has made it the law of the land.

Questions

Using Sophie's answer and the material in this Topic, answer the following questions.

1. What is a bill? How many stages (readings) must a bill go through in the Commons?
2. At which stage does the Commons debate a bill's main principles?
3. Why can a government usually get its bills passed in the Commons?
4. On what principle is judicial precedent based?
5. What are the two exceptions to precedent?
6. What is the literal rule and why might it cause problems?
7. What does the mischief rule allow the courts to do?

Describe the organisation of the criminal justice system in England and Wales

TOPIC 1.2

Getting started
Working with a partner, complete the following:
1. Using Unit 3 Topic 1.1, write a brief summary of the role of the police in the criminal justice system.
2. Using Unit 3 Topic 2.2, write a brief summary of the stages of the trial process, including the roles of the personnel involved.

You will find that what you learned in Unit 3 about the different stages of the trial process and the agencies involved, such as the police, CPS and courts, is relevant to this Topic.

Overview of the criminal justice system

The criminal justice system in England and Wales is made up of a number of interconnected organisations and agencies. As a starting point, we can divide the system into the following main parts:

- **law creation and administration**: the passing of the criminal laws by Parliament and the running of the justice system by government departments
- **law enforcement** by the police
- **the courts** (including prosecution and defence) decide the outcome of criminal cases
- **punishment of convicted offenders** by the prisons and probation service.

From this overview of the system, we can now look in a little more detail at its parts and how they work. We shall do this by taking a journey through the system, from the creation of criminal laws through to the punishment of offenders.

The main agencies of the criminal justice system

Law creation

As we saw in Topic 1.1, Parliament and judges make the laws dealing with crime.
- **Parliament** passes Acts (legislation or statute law).
- **Judges** create law by setting judicial precedents that other courts then must follow, and by interpreting the meaning of statutes (statutory interpretation).

Administration of the system Two government departments oversee most of the justice system and are responsible for its smooth running: the Ministry of Justice and the Home Office.

The police
The police are responsible for enforcing the criminal law. They investigate crimes, collect evidence, and arrest, detain and question suspects. In minor cases, they may issue a caution

or fixed penalty notice, but in virtually all other cases, they will send the files to the Crown Prosecution Service to decide whether to prosecute. There are 43 regional police forces in England and Wales.

The Crown Prosecution Service

The CPS is an independent prosecution service for England and Wales dealing with about half a million cases a year.

- The CPS advises the police in their investigations about lines of inquiry and what evidence is required to build a case.
- It assesses the evidence the police submit to it and decides whether to prosecute and what the charge will be.
- Its decisions are based on applying the Full Code Test to the case (see Unit 3, Topic 2.1).
- It prepares and presents the prosecution case in court.

HM Courts and Tribunals Service

HM Courts and Tribunals Service is responsible for the administration of the courts and tribunals in England and Wales.

The courts

Once a suspect is charged, they are brought before the magistrates' court. The defendant will plead guilty or not guilty, and pre-trial issues such as bail and legal aid will be decided. Guilty pleas will lead to a sentencing hearing. Not guilty pleas will lead to a trial being arranged.

- **Magistrates' courts** deal with less serious offences (about 95% of all cases).
- **The Crown Court** deals with serious offences, which are triable by a judge and jury.

The prosecution (the CPS) and defence lawyers will present arguments and evidence for and against the defendant. Evidence will be testimonial (witness statements), physical (e.g. weapons, stolen goods) or both.

The jury (in Crown Court) or magistrates will decide the verdict. If guilty, the judge or magistrates will decide the punishment. This could be a custodial (prison) or community sentence, a fine or a discharge. It will be based on the relevant statute and the Sentencing Guidelines produced by the Sentencing Council. Offenders may appeal against their conviction and/or sentence. (For more detail on the role of the courts, see Unit 3, Topic 2.2.)

HM Prison and Probation Service

Her Majesty's Prison and Probation Service carries out the sentences given to offenders by the courts.

- **HM Prison Service** supervises offenders in custody.
- **The National Probation Service** supervises offenders who are serving their sentences in the community, including prisoners who have been released on licence to serve part of their sentence outside prison.

As well as supervising the management and punishment of offenders, the prison and probation services seek to rehabilitate offenders so that they can lead a crime-free life.

ACTIVITY Media

The probation service   Go to www.criminology.uk.net

Relationships between the justice agencies

The different parts of the justice system are inter-related. In this section, we examine how they relate to one another.

The police

The police have relationships with:

- **the courts**: giving evidence as prosecution witnesses; providing protection for vulnerable witnesses; holding defendants in police cells and transporting them to and from court.
- **the CPS**: providing evidence for the prosecution of offenders; charging offenders in line with CPS instructions.
- **HM Prison and Probation Services**: police will arrest prisoners who have been recalled to prison for breaching the terms of their licence. As a result of Sarah's Law, the police also cooperate with the prison and probation services in managing the list of child sex offenders living in their area.
- **voluntary organisations**, e.g. referring victims and witnesses of crime to Victim Support, women's refuges, the Witness Service etc.

The Crown Prosecution Service

The CPS has relationships with:

- **the police**: advising on possible lines of enquiry and evidence collection to build a case; instructing them on charging suspects.
- **the courts**: preparing and presenting the prosecution case against offenders; preparing appeals against unduly lenient sentences.

Government departments

Government departments have relationships with:

- **the courts, prison service and probation service** through HM Courts and Tribunals Service and HM Prison and Probation Service. The Ministry of Justice is the department responsible.
- **the police**, where the Home Office is the department responsible, e.g. for setting national policing priorities.

Government departments provide funding for these parts of the justice system. The funds come out of general taxation.

HM Courts and Tribunals Service

The Service has relationships with:

- **courts and judges:** supervising the efficient running of the courts system; funding the individual courts.
- **HM Prison Service**: holding prisoners attending court, pending their transfer/return to prison; arranging video recordings and live links for prisoners giving evidence from prison.

The National Probation Service

The NPS has relationships with:

- **HM Prison Service and the Parole Board**: supervising prisoners who are released on licence.
- **the courts**: preparing pre-sentencing reports on offenders; supervising offenders who have been given a community sentence by the court; supervising drug testing under the court's orders.

> **ACTIVITY** — Media
>
> Relationships between agencies   Go to www.criminology.uk.net

HM Prison Service

The Prison Service has relationships with:

- **the courts**: carrying out the custodial sentences that the court has imposed on offenders; supervising defendants who have been remanded into custody (refused bail) by the court; facilitating visits from defence lawyers to their clients in prison.
- **the police**: facilitating interviews with prisoners involved in ongoing police investigations.
- **the National Probation Service**: liaising when a prisoner is to be released from prison on licence.

Other parts of the justice system include:

Voluntary organisations: e.g. Victim Support is a charity that liaises with the police, courts and CPS to support victims throughout the stages of an investigation and trial. Other voluntary organisations include Nacro, Women in Prison and Women's Aid.

Campaigns to change the justice system, e.g. the Howard League for Penal Reform, the Prison Reform Trust and INQUEST have relationships with the courts, prisons, police, the Ministry of Justice and the Home Office.

> **ACTIVITY** — Research
>
> The work of INQUEST   Go to www.criminology.uk.net

NOW TEST YOURSELF

Practice Question

Describe the relationship of the prison service with other agencies in the criminal justice system.   (6 marks)
   Source: WJEC Criminology Unit 4 examination 2017

Advice

You need to describe the relationship between the prison service and agencies such as:

- The courts: prisons hold prisoners attending court, pending transfer/return to prison. They arrange video links for prisoners giving evidence from prison.
- The police hold prisoners after arrest and transport them to prison if the court remands them in custody. They arrest and return prisoners recalled to prison. Prisons facilitate police interviews with prisoners. Police work with prisons to manage child sex offenders.
- Judges decide the sentence, including the term of imprisonment and whether it is concurrent (one term follows on from another) or consecutive (two terms are served simultaneously).
- The probation service works with prisons to prepare prisoners for release to ensure a smooth transition into the outside world, and supervises them after release. It liaises with prison if the offender has to be recalled due to breaching their order.
- Charities work with prisons to provide support services for inmates and following release.
- Defence solicitors may visit prisons to consult with their clients.
- The Ministry of Justice funds the prisons, via HM Prison and Probation Service.

Describe models of criminal justice

TOPIC 1.3

Getting started

Working in a small group, consider the following two views:

A. To protect society, criminals should be caught and locked up as quickly as possible. It's worth risking a few innocent people going to prison if this helps us to catch most of the guilty ones.

B. To protect the individual, it shouldn't be easy to convict a person of a crime. It's better to risk some guilty people going free than to send an innocent person to prison.

Discuss which view you agree with more. From your discussion, note down any problems you find with each view. Do you agree as a group?

Two models of criminal justice

In 1968 Herbert Packer, an American professor of law and criminology, described two contrasting sets of values which shape the way criminal justice systems work. He sums these up in two opposed models of criminal justice:

- **the crime control model of justice**
- **the due process model of justice.**

The crime control model

- Crime is a threat to people's freedom and so the goal of the crime control model is the *suppression of crime*. It prioritises catching and punishing offenders, deterring and preventing them from committing further crime.
- The model starts from a *presumption of guilt*. It trusts the police to be able to identify those who are probably guilty through their investigations and interrogations.
- Police should be free from unnecessary legal technicalities that prevent them investigating crime.
- Once the 'probably guilty' are identified, it favours a *conveyor belt* or assembly line justice system that speedily prosecutes, convicts and punishes them.
- It argues that if a few innocent people are occasionally convicted by mistake, this is a price worth paying for convicting a large number of guilty people.
- It emphasises the *rights of society and victims* to be protected from crime, rather than the rights of suspects.

Question
What sort of 'legal technicalities' might supporters of the crime control model want to remove so that police can investigate more effectively?

The due process model

- The power of the state is the greatest threat to the individual's freedom and so the goal of the due process model is to *protect the accused from oppression* by the state and its agents. These include the police, prosecutors and judges.
- The model starts from a *presumption of innocence*. The accused is innocent until proven guilty after a fair trial.
- It has less faith in the police's ability to conduct satisfactory investigations. Incompetence, dishonesty etc. mean that suspects' and defendants' rights need to be safeguarded by a set of *due process rules* that investigations and trials must follow. These include rules about arrest, questioning, legal representation, admissibility and disclosure of evidence, cross-examination of witnesses, no secret trials etc.
- Rather than a conveyor belt carrying the accused swiftly to punishment, the rules and procedures protecting their rights form a necessary *obstacle course* that prosecutors have to overcome before they can secure a conviction.
- This means that the guilty sometimes go free on a 'technicality' (e.g. where the prosecution have relied on illegally obtained evidence). However, the model argues that this is a lesser evil than convicting the innocent.
- The model emphasises the *rights of the accused individual* rather than those of the victim or society.

> **Question**
> What kinds of evidence are courts likely to rule out as inadmissible and why?

Links to theories

The two models of justice have links to different theories of crime.

The crime control model and theory

Right realism The crime control model is a right-wing, conservative approach to justice and it has much in common with right realist theories of crime. For example, like zero tolerance policing strategies, it favours giving the police greater powers to investigate and suppress crime.

Functionalism The crime control model also has links with Durkheim's functionalist theory that punishment reinforces society's moral boundaries. As the main function of justice is to punish the guilty, this enables society to express its moral outrage and strengthen social cohesion.

The due process model and theory

Labelling theory The due process model is a liberal approach. It aims to stop state agencies like the police from oppressing people. As such it has links to labelling theory. The police may be tempted to act illegally, harassing groups that they label negatively as 'typical criminals'. The due process model offers some protection against this because it requires the police to follow lawful procedures and not exceed their powers.

Left realism argues that oppressive 'militaristic policing' of poor areas triggers confrontations and makes residents unwilling to assist the police. In the left realist view, police must follow due process by acting in a lawful and non-discriminatory way if they want to fight crime effectively, since this depends on the cooperation of the community.

Crime control and due process   Go to www.criminology.uk.net

The two models and the UK justice system

How far do the two models describe the system of justice in England and Wales? We can see examples of each model by looking at two areas:

- **the rules governing the working of the justice system** Do the rules protect the rights of the accused, or do they favour the prosecution?
- **the way the system works in practice**. Do the police, prosecutors and judges actually follow the rules and procedures as they should?

Rules governing the working of the justice system

There are many due process rules in place to protect the individual's rights during an investigation and trial. For example, in Unit 3, Topic 2.3 we saw that illegally obtained evidence may be ruled inadmissible in court. This includes things such as a confession obtained by using torture or degrading treatment. This could be said to support the due process model, since it protects the defendant's rights.

However, the judge has the power to admit illegally obtained evidence (for example, evidence found during a search conducted without a warrant) if he or she believes it will help to establish the truth. This could be said to support the crime control model, since it may lead to a conviction.

In the table below, we can see how some rules within the English legal system support the due process model and individuals' rights, while others may support the crime control model by helping to secure convictions.

Some rules governing the working of the justice system	
Rules favouring due process	**Rules favouring crime control**
The suspect's right to know why they are being arrested.	Police rights to stop, question, search and arrest. The right to stop and search without giving a reason in some circumstances.
The right to remain silent when questioned by police and in court – based on the principle that it is the prosecution's job to prove guilt, not the accused's job to prove their innocence.	The court may draw negative inferences (conclusions) if the defendant remains silent when questioned by police or fails to testify in court without good reason.
The right not to be detained indefinitely without charge.	Extended police detention is allowed for questioning on suspicion of indictable offences (36 + 96 hours) and terrorist offences (14 days).
The right to legal representation when questioned by police and in court.	Extended period before access to a lawyer is allowed (for serious offences). Restrictions on the availability of legal aid.
The right to trial by a jury of one's peers.	Jury trials are only for serious cases. Magistrates are more likely than juries to convict. Juryless trials are allowed if jury tampering is suspected.
The right to appeal against conviction or sentence.	Appeal rights are not always automatic. Some are only allowed on a point of law, not of evidence.
The right not to be re-tried for the same offence once acquitted.	Change to the double jeopardy rule allows a second prosecution if 'new and compelling' evidence emerges (for serious offences only).
Rules governing the admissibility of evidence in court; e.g. hearsay, entrapment and forced confessions are not admitted.	Evidence of bad character/previous convictions is permitted in certain circumstances.
The prosecution has a duty to disclose evidence against the defendant in advance of the trial.	Public-interest immunity certificates may allow the prosecution to avoid disclosing evidence.

Due process and crime control in practice

We can see from the table how different rules of the justice system might support each of the two models. But we also need to look at how the system works in practice. For example, are the rules that protect suspects' and defendants' rights followed in reality, in the police station and the courtroom?

It may be that in most cases, police, prosecutors and judges respect the due process rights of the accused and follow correct procedure. For example, only a small proportion of defendants who are convicted of an offence seek to appeal against either their conviction or their sentence, which could indicate that most are reasonably satisfied with the way their case was processed by the justice system.

Miscarriages of justice

However, there have also been miscarriages of justice as a result of the police, prosecution or judges failing to follow correct procedures and in some cases even breaking the law themselves. These cases point to the fact that in practice the justice system does not always operate according to the principles of the due process model. Relevant cases include the following:

Colin Stagg was the victim of attempted entrapment following the murder of Rachel Nickell. Despite lacking any evidence against him, the police became convinced that he was the killer and tried to use a 'honey trap' to trick him into confessing to the crime.

Sally Clark was wrongly jailed for the murder of her two baby sons partly as a result of the Home Office pathologist and prosecution witness Alan Williams failing to disclose relevant information to her defence lawyers.

The Birmingham Six were wrongly convicted of 21 murders after police fabricated evidence against them, deprived them of sleep and food, and used violence and threats to extract confessions. The judge wrongly deemed the confessions admissible as evidence while excluding defence evidence, and the prosecution presented dubious and unreliable forensic evidence against the six.

The police have the power to stop, search and arrest. Do they use it fairly?

The West Midlands Serious Crime Squad was responsible for over 100 criminal cases (including the Birmingham Six) involving malpractice by its officers, including perjury (lying under oath), assaulting prisoners, fabricating confessions and planting incriminating evidence on suspects.

The case of Bingham Justices (1974) involved bias by a magistrate. When a defendant's evidence contradicted that of a police officer in a speeding case, the chairman of the magistrates said, 'My principle in such cases has always been to believe the police officer'.

In all the above examples, the cases either collapsed in court or guilty verdicts were quashed on appeal. However, for some it took a second appeal, resulting in longer in jail – 16 years for the Birmingham Six and three years for Sally Clark.

ACTIVITY / Media

Miscarriage of justice   Go to www.criminology.uk.net

NOW TEST YOURSELF

Practice Question

1. Identify **three** features of the crime control model of justice. (3 marks)
2. Identify **three** features of the due process model of justice. (3 marks)
   Source: WJEC Criminology Unit 4 examination 2020

Advice

You should identify three features of the crime control model for Question 1 and three features of the due process model for Question 2.

Deal with each model separately. For each model look at three issues, such as:
- what it sees as the greatest threat to freedom
- whether it presumes the accused is innocent or not
- whether it has faith in the police and prosecutors
- whose rights it gives priority to: the accused or society.

Use specialist vocabulary where possible.
- For the crime control model, this could include terms such as suppression of crime, presumption of guilt, conveyor belt, and rights of society and victims.
- For the due process model, it could include terms such as protecting the accused from oppression/ rights of the accused, presumption of innocence, obstacle course and due process rules (such as rights on arrest or admissibility of evidence).

TOPIC 2.1

Explain forms of social control

Getting started
Working in a small group, complete the following:
1. What are norms, values and moral codes? (If you're not sure, look back at *Criminology Book One*, Unit 2, Topic 1.1.)
2. What sanctions exist for controlling our behaviour in line with society's norms? For example, how is our behaviour controlled in school by peers and teachers?
3. Why do you think people follow the norms and values of society?

Share your answers with the rest of the class. As a whole class, make a list of the ways our behaviour is controlled in society.

What is social control?

For society to function smoothly, people need to behave more or less as others expect them to. Imagine the chaos, for example, if the bus driver decided today to take their bus to the seaside, passengers and all, instead of following the normal route so that people could get to work, school or the shops – or if the postman decided to post all the mail to just one address in each street.

Social control involves persuading or compelling people to conform to society's norms, laws and expectations. Society has various means of achieving control over its members' behaviour, which we can group into two main forms:

- Internal forms of social control
- External forms of social control.

Internal forms of social control

These are controls over our behaviour that come from within ourselves – from our personalities or our values. As such, they are therefore also forms of *self*-control. They lead us to conform to the rules of society and the groups that we belong to because we feel inwardly that it is the right thing to do.

Moral conscience or superego

According to Freud's psychoanalytic theory, we conform to society's expectations and obey its rules because our superego tells us to do so. Along with the id and the ego, the superego forms part of our personality. Our superego tells us what is right and wrong and inflicts guilt feelings on us if we fail to do as it urges.

Our superego develops through early socialisation within the family, as a sort of internalised 'nagging parent' telling us how we ought to behave. Its function is to restrain the selfish, 'animal' urges of the id. If we acted on these urges, they would often lead us into anti-social and criminal behaviour. The superego allows us to exercise self-control and behave in socially acceptable ways.

Tradition and culture

The culture to which we belong also becomes part of us through socialisation. We come to accept its values, norms and traditions as part of our identity. For example, believers follow the religious traditions that they have been raised in, such as the Muslim tradition of fasting during Ramadan or the Jewish tradition of sharing the Shabbat (Sabbath) evening meal. Conforming to such traditions is an important way of affirming one's identity and being accepted as a member of a particular community.

Internalisation of social rules and morality

Both our superego and the traditions we follow become part of our inner self or personality. Yet both of them start as things outside of us – either as our parents' rules and values in the case of the superego, or as those of our culture or social group in the case of tradition.

Socialisation In both cases, we internalise these rules through the process of socialisation – whether from our parents or from wider social groups and institutions such as religion, school and peer groups. In this way, *society's* rules and moral code become our own *personal* rules and moral code. As a result, we come to conform willingly to social norms.

'Rational ideology' is a term that has been used to describe the fact that we internalise social rules and use them to tell us what is right and wrong. This enables us to keep within the law.

ACTIVITY — Media

Socialisation   Go to www.criminology.uk.net

External forms of social control

As well as internal forms of control such as our conscience, society has external forms of control that aim to ensure we conform to its expectations and keep to its rules. Society does this through agencies of social control.

Agencies of social control

These are organisations or institutions that impose rules on us in an effort to make us behave in certain ways. They include the family, peer group and education system. For example, parents may send a naughty child to bed, friends may shun someone who tells tales, and teachers may give a disruptive student a detention.

All these are negative sanctions (punishments), but agencies of social control can give positive sanctions (rewards) to those who conform. For example, a hardworking student may earn praise, gold stars etc. from the teacher. Both positive and negative sanctions help to impose social control. This echoes Skinner's operant learning theory of behaviour reinforcement – punishments deter undesired behaviour and rewards encourage acceptable behaviour.

The criminal justice system

The criminal justice system contains several agencies of social control, each with the power to use formal legal sanctions against individuals in an attempt to make them conform to society's laws. These agencies and their powers include the following.

- **The police** have powers to stop, search, arrest, detain and question suspects.
- **The CPS** can charge a suspect and prosecute them in court.

- **Judges and magistrates** have powers to bail the accused or remand them in custody, and to sentence the guilty to a variety of punishments.
- **The prison service** can detain prisoners against their will for the duration of their sentence, and punish prisoners' misbehaviour (e.g. by putting them in solitary confinement).

All these are negative sanctions, but the justice system also has positive sanctions (rewards) that it can use to control behaviour. For example, assisting the prosecution is likely to earn an offender a lower sentence, while good behaviour by prisoners may earn them more privileges and earlier parole.

Coercion

Coercion involves the use or threat of force in order to make someone do (or stop doing) something. Force may involve physical or psychological violence, or other forms of pressure. The negative sanctions of the criminal justice system above are examples of coercion: sending someone to prison for stealing is a form of coercion aimed at preventing further offending (if only for the period that the thief is in jail).

Fear of punishment

Fear of punishment is one way of trying to achieve social control and make people conform to the laws. In effect, fear of punishment is a form of coercion, because it involves the threat that force will be used against you if you do not obey the law. For example, if you commit an offence you may be arrested, charged, convicted and jailed – all against your will.

Deterrence Some theorists, such as right realists, argue that fear of being caught and punished is what ensures that many would-be criminals continue to obey the law. In other words, fear acts as a deterrent. We shall look at punishment and deterrence in more detail in Topic 2.2.

Control theory

Most criminological theories ask why people commit crimes, but control theorists start from the opposite question: why do people obey the law? The answer given by control theorists such as Travis Hirschi is that people conform because they are controlled by their bonds to society, which keep them from deviating. Hirschi argues that 'delinquent acts occur when an individual's bond to society is weak or broken'.

According to Hirschi, the individual's bond to society has four elements:

1. **Attachment** The more attached we are to others, the more we care about their opinion of us, the more we will respect their norms and the less likely we will be to break them. This is especially true of attachments to parents and teachers.
2. **Commitment** How committed are we to conventional goals such as succeeding in education and getting a good job? The more we are committed to a conventional lifestyle, the more we risk losing by getting involved in crime, so the more likely we are to conform.
3. **Involvement** The more involved we are in conventional, law-abiding activities, like studying or participating in sports, the less time and energy we will have for getting involved in criminal ones. This is part of the justification for youth clubs: they keep young people off the streets and busy with legal activities.
4. **Beliefs** If we have been socialised to believe it is right to obey the law, we are less likely to break it.

ACTIVITY — Media

Social bonds

Go to www.criminology.uk.net

Parenting Many control theorists emphasise the role of parenting in creating bonds that prevent young people from offending. For example, Gottfredson and Hirschi argued that low self-control is a major cause of delinquency, and that this results from poor socialisation and inconsistent or absent parental discipline.

Other control theorists put forward similar ideas. Riley and Shaw found that lack of parental supervision was an important factor in delinquency. They argue that parents should:

- involve themselves in their teenagers' lives and spend time with them
- take an interest in what they do at school and how they spend time with their friends
- show strong disapproval of criminal behaviour and explain the consequences of offending.

Walter Reckless also points to the importance of parenting and socialisation. We have psychological tendencies that can lead to criminality, but effective socialisation can provide 'internal containment' by building the self-control to resist the temptation to offend. He also argues that external controls such as parental discipline can provide 'external containment'.

Feminists have also used control theory to explain women's low rate of offending. Frances Heidensohn argues that patriarchal (male-dominated) society controls females more closely, making it harder for them to offend. For example, women spend more time on domestic duties, leaving them less opportunity to engage in criminality outside the home. Pat Carlen found that females who do offend had often failed to form an attachment to parents because they had suffered abuse in the family or been brought up in care.

ACTIVITY / Media

Forms of social control

Go to www.criminology.uk.net

Hobbies and sporting activities may help to keep young people out of crime.

NOW TEST YOURSELF

Practice Question

Discuss reasons why individuals abide by the law. (9 marks)

Source: WJEC Criminology Unit 4 examination 2018

Answer by Anthony

People abide by (i.e. obey) the law because of the effects of social control. There are two types of control: internal and external. Internal control is where we choose to obey the law without being compelled to do so, e.g. our conscience tells us what is right. According to Freud, our conscience or superego is an internal 'nagging parent' making us feel guilty if we even think of breaking norms.

Good start – defines internal control. Useful link to theory.

We acquire our conscience through socialisation, where we learn society's moral code from institutions like the family and religion. For example, the Ten Commandments teach believers that it is a sin to steal. Socialisation also teaches us our cultural traditions and the behaviour expected, e.g. Muslims must fast during Ramadan. We internalise rules and traditions as part of our personality and conscience. We can then work out for ourselves what is right and wrong and what society deems acceptable, and act accordingly.

Relevant examples and concepts applied.

People also abide by the law because of external social control, where agencies like those in the criminal justice system use coercion (force or threat of it) to make us obey the law, e.g. police can arrest and detain us, magistrates can fine us, prisons can lock us up. Likewise, parents, peers and teachers use negative sanctions (punishments) to make us conform to their rules. External control works through fear of punishment (deterrence): we obey the law for fear of prison etc. Deterrence can be individual (where experiencing punishment deters the offender from re-offending) or general. General deterrence reflects Bandura's social learning theory: seeing others punished for deviance deters us.

External control clearly explained, plus more concepts, examples and theory.

Control theorists like Reckless see both internal and external control as necessary to ensure people obey the law. He argues that socialisation produces 'internal containment' by teaching us self-control to resist temptations to offend, while controls like parental discipline produce 'external containment'. Feminists like Heidensohn argue that women's low rate of offending is due to external control over them by patriarchal society.

Uses theory to round off the answer.

Overall comments

This is a Band Three (top band) response. Anthony deals with a range of reasons why people abide by the law, which he organises into internal and external forms of social control. He uses relevant specialist vocabulary, including socialisation, superego, moral code, norms, cultural traditions, internalisation, coercion, sanctions, deterrence, and internal and external containment. He links some of these ideas to theories (Freud, Bandura, Heidensohn and Reckless) and he applies examples to illustrate his points.

Discuss the aims of punishment

TOPIC 2.2

Getting started
Working with a partner, discuss the following:
1. Why does society punish criminals? Suggest as many reasons as you can.
2. From your knowledge of criminological theories in Unit 2, what types of punishment do you think the following would favour?
   a) biochemical theories
   b) cognitive theories
   c) right realism.

What are the aims of punishment?
Many people believe that punishment is an effective way to prevent or reduce crime. Others argue that offenders deserve to be punished anyway, regardless of whether or not this reduces crime.

In this Topic, we shall discuss the different aims or purposes that punishment can have. These are:
- **retribution** – expressing society's outrage at crime
- **rehabilitation** – making offenders change their behaviour
- **deterrence** – discouraging future offending
- **public protection** from offenders
- **reparation** – making good the harm caused by crime

Theories We shall also look at how these aims of punishment link to some of the criminological theories that you studied in Unit 2.

Retribution

Retribution literally means paying back. It involves inflicting punishment on an offender as vengeance for a wrong or criminal act.

'Just deserts'
Retribution is based on the idea that criminals should get their 'just deserts': offenders deserve to be punished and society is morally entitled to take its revenge. The offender should be made to suffer for having breached society's moral code.

Proportionality
Punishment should fit the crime – it should be equal or proportionate to the harm done, as in the idea of 'an eye for an eye, a tooth for a tooth, a life for a life'. This is why some people argue that murderers should suffer the death penalty.

The idea of proportionality leads to a 'tariff' system or fixed scale of mandatory (compulsory) penalties for different offences: so many years' jail for armed robbery, such-and-such a fine for speeding and so on.

Expressing moral outrage Although retribution might have good effects (such as deterring potential offenders), this is not its purpose. Instead, it is simply a way for society to express its moral condemnation or outrage at the offender. Punishment is morally good in itself, regardless of whether it changes the offender's future behaviour. Retribution is a justification for punishing crimes already committed, not a way of preventing future ones.

An example Hate crimes such as racially aggravated offences carry an 'uplift' or higher tariff sentence. For example, the maximum penalty for grievous bodily harm is five years' imprisonment, but this can be increased to seven years if it is proven to be racially motivated. The uplift reflects society's greater outrage at the offence.

Convicts serving imprisonment with hard labour. Should society take retribution in this way?

Theory

Retribution is linked to right realist theories of criminality such as rational choice theory. Like these theories, retribution assumes that offenders are rational actors who consciously choose to commit their crimes and are fully responsible for their actions. They must therefore suffer the outrage of society for what they have chosen to do.

For functionalist sociologists such as Durkheim, the moral outrage that retribution expresses performs the function of boundary maintenance. Punishing the offender reminds everyone else of the difference between right and wrong.

Criticisms

- It can be argued that offenders deserve forgiveness, mercy or a chance to make amends, not just punishment.
- If there is a fixed tariff of penalties, punishment has to be inflicted even where no good is going to come of it, for example on a remorseful offender who will commit no further crimes.
- How do we decide what is a proportionate penalty or 'just desert' for each crime? People disagree about which crimes are more serious than others.

ACTIVITY / Media

Problems of retributive justice Go to www.criminology.uk.net

Rehabilitation

Rehabilitation is the idea that punishment can be used to reform or change offenders so they no longer offend and can go on to live a crime-free life. Rather than focusing on punishing past offences, as retribution does, rehabilitation uses various treatment programmes to change the offender's *future* behaviour by addressing the issues which led to their offending.

Rehabilitation policies include:

- **education and training programmes** for prisoners so they can avoid unemployment and 'earn an honest living' on release
- **anger management courses** for violent offenders, such as Aggression Replacement Training (ART) and other cognitive behavioural therapy programmes
- **Drug Treatment and Testing Orders**, and programmes to treat alcohol dependence.

Community sentences often include requirements for offenders to engage in such programmes as part of their sentence. (For more about community sentences, see Topic 2.3.)

Support Rehabilitation policies generally require offenders to actively want to change their lives, but they often also require considerable input of resources and professional support from therapists, probation officers or others to help them achieve change. This is particularly so where their offending has led to their exclusion from mainstream society and where they need to be reintegrated into the community, such as upon their release from prison.

Theory

Individualistic theories of criminality see rehabilitation as a significant aim of punishment. They advocate various ways of changing offenders' behaviour:

- **Cognitive theories** favour cognitive behavioural therapies (CBT) to teach offenders to correct the thinking errors and biases that lead to aggressive or criminal behaviour.
- **Eysenck's personality theory** favours the use of aversion therapy to deter offending behaviour.
- **Skinner's operant learning theory** supports the use of token economies to encourage prisoners to produce more acceptable behaviour.

Sociological theories such as left realism also favour rehabilitation in that they regard social factors such as unemployment, poverty and poor educational opportunities as causes of crime. Therefore addressing these needs among offenders will help to reduce offending.

Criticisms

- **Right realists** argue that rehabilitation has only limited success, in that many offenders go on to re-offend even after undergoing programmes aimed at changing their behaviour.
- **Marxists** criticise rehabilitation programmes for shifting the responsibility for offending onto the individual offender's failings, rather than focusing on how capitalism leads some people to commit crime.

Deterrence

To deter someone from doing something is to put them off doing it. The fear of being caught and punished may deter people from committing crime. Deterrence can be either individual or general.

Individual deterrence

Individual (or specific) deterrence uses punishment to deter the individual offender from re-offending. Punishment may convince the offender that it is not worth repeating the experience.

For example, the argument that 'prison works' is based partly on the idea that if sentences are tough enough, offenders will not want to go back to jail again. In the UK in the 1980s, Margaret Thatcher's government introduced a tough new system in juvenile detention centres described as a 'short, sharp shock' to deter young offenders. The United States introduced similar military-style 'boot camps' around the same time and with the same aim.

General deterrence

General deterrence aims at deterring society in general from breaking the law. If the public see an individual offender being punished, they will see what they themselves will have to suffer if they commit a similar crime. Making an example of the individual will have a general effect and teach everyone else a lesson.

In the past, this was often done through public punishments such as executions, floggings or putting offenders in the stocks, so that everyone could see for themselves the consequences of offending. Today, the public are more likely to learn about the costs of offending from media reports instead.

Severity versus certainty

It is important to distinguish between the severity of punishment and the certainty of punishment. For example, however severe the punishment might be for a particular offence, if there is very little chance of being caught and convicted, then it will be unlikely to deter many would-be offenders.

For example, although there is a mandatory minimum sentence of three years' imprisonment for committing a third domestic burglary, only about 5% of reported burglaries result in a successful conviction, so the likelihood of facing the punishment is very low and may not be a deterrent.

On the other hand, if an offender is very likely to be caught, then even a relatively mild punishment may be an effective deterrent.

Theory

Right realism favours deterrence as a means of crime prevention:
- **Rational choice theory** sees individuals as rational actors who weigh up the costs and benefits before deciding whether to offend. Therefore, severe punishments and a high chance of getting caught will deter offending.
- **Situational crime prevention strategies** such as target hardening make it harder to commit an offence successfully and therefore act as a deterrent.

Social learning theory is relevant to understanding general deterrence. If would-be offenders see a model (one of their peers, for example) being punished for offending, they will be less likely to imitate that behaviour.

Criticisms

- There is very little evidence that short, sharp shocks or boot camps reduced youth offending in either the UK or the USA.
- The fact that about half of all prisoners re-offend within a year of release suggests that prison is not an effective deterrent.
- How do we decide how severe a punishment needs to be for it to deter enough would-be offenders?
- Deterrence assumes would-be offenders know what the punishments are, but they may be ignorant of the penalties.
- Deterrence assumes offenders act rationally, carefully weighing up the risks. But some act irrationally, driven by their emotions without thought for the likely punishment.

- People who break laws they see as unjust are unlikely to be deterred by punishment. (See Topic 3.3 on crime committed by those with moral imperatives.)

ACTIVITY / Research

Boot camps   Go to www.criminology.uk.net

Public protection

Incapacitation Punishment may be used to protect the public from further offending by incapacitating offenders. Incapacitation is the use of punishment to remove the offender's physical capacity (ability) to offend again.

Policies There have been many types of incapacitation policy at different times and places, such as the following:

- **execution** of offenders, preventing them from committing any further crimes whatsoever
- **cutting off the hands** of thieves
- **chemical castration** of sex offenders
- **banishment** e.g. in the early 19th century, convicts were often transported to Australia
- **foreign travel bans** to prevent football hooligans attending matches abroad
- **curfews and electronic tagging** to prevent further offending by restricting offenders' movements.

Imprisonment

Imprisonment is the main means of incapacitation in today's societies. It is an important part of the claim that 'prison works': by taking offenders out of circulation, it prevents them committing further crimes against the public.

Incapacitation for public protection has influenced sentencing laws. For example, the Crime (Sentences) Act 1997 introduced mandatory minimum jail sentences for repeat offenders:

1930s electric chair used in New Jersey prison. The death penalty is legal in 27 US states.

- automatic life sentences for a second serious sexual or violent offence
- seven years minimum for a third Class A drug trafficking offence
- three years minimum for a third domestic burglary conviction.

Similarly, the Criminal Justice Act 2003 introduced the idea of 'imprisonment for public protection' (IPP). This allowed courts to give an indeterminate sentence (one with no fixed release date) to a 'dangerous' offender who is convicted of certain serious violent or sexual offences. (However, in 2012, indeterminate sentences were abolished for new cases.)

In the United States, 'three strikes and you're out' laws were introduced in the 1990s. These give offenders long prison sentences (including life) for a third offence, however minor, if either of their two earlier offences was a serious crime. For example, in 1995 Jerry Williams was given 25 years to life without parole, for stealing a slice of pizza (reduced to six years on appeal).

Theory

Biological theories Lombroso argued that criminals are biologically different from the rest of the population and it is not possible to change or rehabilitate them. He favoured sending habitual criminals into exile, for example detaining them on islands away from the public. Other biological theories of criminality have favoured chemical or surgical castration to incapacitate sex offenders.

Right realists see incapacitation as a way of protecting the public from crime. A small number of persistent offenders are responsible for the majority of crimes, so incapacitating them with long prison sentences would significantly reduce the crime rate.

Criticisms

- Incapacitation leads to longer sentences and long-term 'warehousing' of offenders with little hope of release. This leads to an ever-rising prison population and associated costs.
- Incapacitation is a strategy of containment or risk management. It does nothing to deal with the causes of crime or to change offenders into law-abiding citizens.
- The 'three strikes' principle re-punishes individuals for their previous crimes.
- It is unjust because it imprisons them for crimes that the law assumes they may commit in the future.

Reparation

Reparation involves the offender making amends for a wrong they have done, whether to an individual victim, society as a whole, or both. The harm done can be both material and social.

Making amends for material damage can include:

- **Financial compensation** to the victim, e.g. paying for the cost of repairing damage done to someone's property. Courts have the power to impose compensation orders on offenders.
- **Unpaid work** to make reparation to society through Community Payback, for example removing graffiti from public buildings. This is imposed by the court as part of a Community Order.

Restorative justice

Making amends for the social damage done involves the offender recognising the wrongfulness of their actions. This can be done through restorative justice schemes, which bring offender and victim together, often with the help of a mediator.

This allows the victim to explain the impact the crime has had. The offender can come to appreciate the harm they have caused, express their remorse and seek forgiveness. Restorative justice can help bring closure to the victim and reintegrate the offender into society.

ACTIVITY | Media

Restorative justice

Go to www.criminology.uk.net

Theory

Labelling theory favours restorative justice as a way of reintegrating offenders into mainstream society. By enabling them to show genuine remorse, it permits their reintegration and prevents them being pushed into secondary deviance.

Functionalists such as Durkheim argue that 'restitutive justice' – reparation to put things back to how they were before the crime was committed – is essential for the smooth functioning of complex modern societies.

Criticisms

- Reparation may not work for all types of offence. Compensation for damage to property or minor offences may be fairly straightforward, but can reparation be made for sexual or violent crimes? A rape victim may not want to face or forgive the rapist. And by definition, reparation to homicide victims is impossible.
- Some regard reparation as too soft a form of punishment that lets offenders off lightly.

NOW TEST YOURSELF

Practice Question

Discuss retribution and rehabilitation as aims of sentencing. (9 marks)

Source: WJEC Criminology Unit 4 examination 2018

Advice

Deal with each of the two aims separately. Divide your time roughly equally between them.

First define retribution, using key terms such as proportionality, letting the punishment fit the crime, 'just deserts', 'an eye for an eye' or revenge. Note that unlike rehabilitation, retribution doesn't aim to change the offender's future behaviour, but just to punish in proportion to the severity of the offence. Give examples of sentences that aim to achieve retribution. These could be the death penalty for murder, the idea of an 'uplift' (a longer sentence) if a crime is racially motivated, and the idea of a fixed tariff of specific penalties for specific crimes. Link retribution to a theory such as functionalism (Durkheim). Note criticisms of retribution as an aim, e.g. imprisoning large numbers of offenders is costly; recidivism rates are high.

Then define rehabilitation, using key terms such as reform (or reformation), changing the offender's way of thinking/mind set, or removing the causes of the offender's offending (e.g. unemployment, addiction). Note that unlike retribution, which punishes *past* misbehaviour, rehabilitation is forward-looking, aiming to improve *future* behaviour. Give examples of sentences that aim to achieve rehabilitation, e.g. prisons and community sentences may offer anger management courses; education and training so offenders can find work; Drug Treatment and Testing Orders to treat addiction. Rehabilitation may be more effective on young or first offenders. Link rehabilitation to a theory such as left realism or cognitive theories. Note criticisms of rehabilitation, e.g. programmes are often costly and may be seen as a 'soft option'.

TOPIC 2.3

Assess how forms of punishment meet the aims of punishment

Getting started

1. In a small group, using what you already know about imprisonment, discuss how far you feel that it meets each of the five aims of punishment described in the previous Topic. (These were retribution, rehabilitation, deterrence, public protection (incapacitation) and reparation.)
2. Make brief notes of your conclusions and feed back to the rest of the class.
3. As a whole class, discuss the usefulness of imprisonment as a form of punishment. You might like to think about this in relation to different types of offence or offender.

The aims of sentencing

As we saw in the previous Topic, punishment can have several different aims. In this Topic, we look at how far the sentences handed down by the courts meet these different aims of punishment.

The Criminal Justice Act 2003 sets out five aims of sentencing:

- the punishment of offenders (retribution)
- crime reduction, including through deterrence
- rehabilitation of offenders
- protection of the public (incapacitation)
- reparation to victims.

Any or all of these aims may be relevant in a given case and it is for the judge or magistrate to decide how they apply.

The sentencing framework

There are four basic types of sentence that the courts can use to punish offenders. These are: imprisonment, community sentences, fines and discharges. We shall look at each of these in turn.

ACTIVITY Research

Type of sentence Go to www.criminology.uk.net

Imprisonment

Prison sentences are handed down by courts for the most serious offences, or when the court believes that the public must be protected by removing the offender from society. For example, almost half of all prisoners in the UK were convicted of sex or violence offences.

There are three kinds of prison sentence: indeterminate and life sentences, determinate sentences, and suspended sentences.

Life sentences

A life sentence is the most serious punishment a UK court can hand down. The judge sets the minimum time that the offender must spend in prison before they can be considered for release by the Parole Board. The Board then assesses whether their release is safe and suitable. If so, they are released on licence and have to follow specific rules or conditions and be supervised by the probation service. The offender remains on licence for the rest of their life. If at any time they break the terms of their licence, they will be called back to prison.

Mandatory (compulsory) life sentences must be given to offenders who are found guilty of murder. Discretionary life sentences can also be given for other serious offences such as rape. In some very serious cases, a judge may sentence an offender to a whole life term. This means they will never be released.

Indeterminate sentences

These set a minimum time the offender must serve in prison. Offenders have no automatic right to be released after the minimum term has been served. Instead, the Parole Board will decide if the offender is suitable to be released on licence.

In 2018 there were around 10,000 prisoners serving indeterminate sentences. Indeterminate sentences account for around 14% of the prison population — by far the highest in Europe.

Some of these are IPP or 'imprisonment for public protection' prisoners. The Criminal Justice Act 2003 allowed offenders to continue to be detained indefinitely after they had served their minimum sentence, if they were regarded as potentially too dangerous to be released. However, IPP sentences were ruled unlawful in 2012 and the sentence was abolished for new cases. In 2019 there were still about 2,200 IPP prisoners.

ACTIVITY | **Media**

Indeterminate sentences   Go to www.criminology.uk.net

Determinate sentences

A determinate sentence is one with a fixed length. Most prisoners in the UK serve determinate sentences (about 65-70,000 in 2021). In most cases, not all the sentence is served in prison:

- If the sentence is under 12 months, the offender is normally released halfway through.
- If the sentence is 12 months or more, the offender spends the first half in prison and the second half in the community on licence. The licence is supervised by the probation service and includes the conditions they must meet (e.g. undergo drug treatment and testing). If they break any of their licence conditions, the offender could be recalled to prison for all or part of their sentence.
- Offenders sentenced to less than two years are released on post-sentence supervision for 12 months, with regular meetings with a probation officer and specified requirements.

Suspended sentences

In a suspended sentence, the offender is given a prison sentence but does not go directly to prison. They may receive a suspended sentence if they would otherwise be given a prison sentence of less than 12 months. Sentences can be suspended for up to two years. The court may also impose requirements such as probation or drug addiction treatment.

The offender must meet these requirements and must not commit any further offence during the suspension period. If they do, the court can send them to prison to serve their original sentence. In 2019, 15% of those convicted of a serious (indictable) offence received a suspended prison sentence.

Does imprisonment meet its punishment aims?

Does punishing offenders with imprisonment work in terms of the five aims of punishment set out in the Criminal Justice Act 2003?

Retribution

This is the idea that offending deserves to be punished and that the punishment should fit the crime.

Prison punishes people for their crimes by taking away their freedom (and often also imposes unpleasant living conditions on them).

However, it is difficult to say whether imprisonment gives offenders their 'just deserts'. For example, how do we decide exactly what length of sentence 'fits' different crimes? Society disagrees about whether sentences are too long or too short, and about which offences or offenders deserve prison.

Deterrence

It is argued that the risk of being sent to prison deters would-be offenders from committing crimes, and actual offenders from committing further crimes. However, high re-offending rates by ex-prisoners suggest that prison is not an effective deterrent for many. For example, nearly half of adult prisoners are re-convicted within a year of being released from jail.

Deterrence only works if would-be offenders are capable of thinking and acting rationally. But many offences are committed under the influence of drugs or alcohol, and many offenders are poorly educated or have mental health problems. In these circumstances, they may not carefully consider the risk of being sent to prison when they commit an offence.

Public protection (incapacitation)

One argument for imprisonment is that it protects the public by taking offenders out of circulation: if they are in jail, they cannot harm the public (though of course, they can harm themselves, other inmates or staff). In other words, prison 'works' because it incapacitates criminals – it puts them out of action for the duration of their sentence.

Imprisonment may provide public protection in several ways:

- 'Whole life' sentences keep offenders permanently off the streets.

Learning a skill while in prison can reduce re-offending.

- Prisoners serving indeterminate sentences can be kept in jail for as long as they are deemed a danger to the public.
- There has been a trend towards longer sentences, so the public remain protected from offenders for longer. This includes mandatory minimum sentences, e.g. for a third drug trafficking or burglary offence.
- Most prisoners are released on licence and under supervision. If they become a danger to the public during their licence period, they can be recalled to prison.

However, prison can be a 'school for crime', where prisoners acquire skills, attitudes and contacts that lead them to offend after their release and potentially to commit more serious offences. Most prisoners are eventually released, so while prison buys the public temporary protection, it may result in greater harm later.

Also, keeping people in prison is very costly. Critics argue that these funds could be used to pay for other ways of protecting the public.

Reparation

One aim of punishment is for the offender to repair the damage caused by the offence, both to the victim and to wider society. Under the Prisoners' Earnings Act 2011, prisoners who are permitted to work outside of prison to prepare for their eventual release can be made to pay a proportion of their earnings towards the cost of victim support services, forcing prisoners to take responsibility for the harm they have caused.

However, in practice few prisoners have the opportunity to earn money in this way. In general, imprisonment does little to meet the aim of reparation.

Rehabilitation

Rehabilitation involves changing an offender so that they no longer offend and instead lead a crime-free life. Although rehabilitation is a goal of imprisonment, prisons have a poor record of reducing re-offending, as these figures suggest:

- 48% of prisoners re-offend within a year of their release.
- For those who served a sentence of less than 12 months, the figure rises to 64%.
- 6,789 prisoners were recalled to prison for breaching their licence conditions in 2019.

Short sentences are one reason for this failure: nearly a half of all sentences are for six months or less. This means there is not enough time to get to grips with long-term problems that cause offending, such as mental health issues or addiction. As former Justice Secretary Kenneth Clarke put it, it is 'virtually impossible to do anything productive with offenders on short sentences.' Short prison sentences have been found to be less effective than community sentences at reducing re-offending.

Education and training Even for prisoners with longer sentences, opportunities to deal with the causes of their offending and prepare them for a crime-free life are often limited. For example, only a quarter of prisoners have a job to go to on release. This is partly because many lack the education or skills needed: over half of prisoners have the literacy skills of the average 11-year-old.

Yet opportunities for education, vocational training or meaningful work are limited. For example, release on temporary licence (ROTL) can allow prisoners out of prison on day release to attend work or training and improve their future job prospects, but fewer than 400 a month (0.5%) get this opportunity.

Addressing offending behaviour There is a shortage of places on courses that address offending behaviour, such as anger management programmes. Many prisoners on indeterminate 'public protection' sentences remain in prison due to a lack of programmes that could address their violent behaviour.

Community sentences

Community sentences are imposed for offences which are too serious for a discharge or a fine but not so serious that a prison sentence is necessary. A Community Order given by the court will have one or more requirements, such as:

- supervision by a probation officer
- between 40 and 300 hours unpaid work (Community Payback)
- a curfew or exclusion order
- a residency requirement, e.g. to live at a supervised, probation-approved hostel
- a group programme, e.g. anger management, drink-drivers etc.
- treatment for drug or alcohol addiction (including testing), or for mental health problems.

Do community sentences meet their punishment aims?

Community sentences have several aims: punishment (retribution) by society for wrongdoing, reparation to individual victims and/or the community, and rehabilitation to prevent recidivism (re-offending).

Retribution

All community sentences must include an element of punishment or retribution. For example, curfews and exclusion orders restrict offenders' movements to certain times and places. This is a form of retribution, making the offender suffer limits on their freedom.

Likewise, those doing unpaid work have to wear high visibility vests with 'Community Payback' on the back. The public 'naming and shaming' that this involves is also a form of retribution.

Unpaid work in the community: a way of making reparation?

Reparation

Reparation can include doing unpaid work to repair the damage they have caused to a victim's property. Equally, reparation may be to the whole community through unpaid work on Community Payback, e.g. removing graffiti, clearing wasteland or decorating a public building such as a community centre.

Public protection

All sentences must include public protection as one of their aims. Because community sentences do not lock offenders up, they do not achieve the aim of incapacitating offenders. However, breaches of a community sentence can lead to the offender being sent to prison.

Rehabilitation

Offenders often have multiple, complex needs such as homelessness, drug misuse, mental health problems, unemployment and educational needs. These needs are often underlying causes of their offending.

Community sentences may aim to rehabilitate offenders by addressing these needs. For example, they can require offenders to undergo treatment for their addiction problems, or undertake an activity such as training to improve their job prospects.

Studies have repeatedly shown that community sentences are more effective at rehabilitating offenders and preventing recidivism than short prison sentences (the main alternative to community sentences). For example:

- In one Ministry of Justice study, 34% re-offended within 12 months of starting their community sentence. This compared with 64% for those serving prison sentences of less than 12 months.
- The Prison Reform Trust found that community sentences are particularly effective for people with many previous offences. For those with over 50 previous convictions, re-offending is over one-third higher for those given a short prison sentence rather than a community sentence.

Despite this, however, the use of community sentences has declined. Between 2007 and 2020, the proportion of offenders receiving Community Orders fell from 14% to 7%.

ACTIVITY / Research

Alternatives to prison Go to www.criminology.uk.net

Fines

Fines are financial penalties for offending. They are normally given for less serious offences and therefore are very often used by magistrates' courts, but even with more serious (indictable) offences, about 15% of those found guilty receive a fine.

The size of a fine depends on the following factors:

- **the offence itself** The law lays down a maximum fine for a given offence
- **the circumstances of the crime** The Sentencing Guidelines give a range of options depending on whether it was a first offence, how much harm was done etc.
- **the offender's ability to pay** A poorer defendant will probably receive a smaller fine, and/or be allowed to pay in instalments

- **which court is hearing the case** For example, magistrates can only impose fines up to £5,000 (or £10,000 for two or more offences).

Do fines meet their punishment aims?

Fines have two main aims:

Retribution Hitting someone in the pocket can be a good way to make them suffer for the harm they have done.

Deterrence A fine may make an offender reluctant to re-offend for fear of further punishment. As the use of fines is a common way of disposing of first offenders, fines may be used as a signal that worse will follow if they re-offend.

Failure to pay

Offenders who fail to pay their fines without good reason may face prison. Courts can deduct fines from an offender's benefits or send in bailiffs to seize their property in the event of non-payment. However, many fines do not get paid. For example, by 2019 the backlog of unpaid fines and court surcharges had reached £623m. Many of these are written off as uncollectable. This suggests that fines may not always meet their aims of punishment.

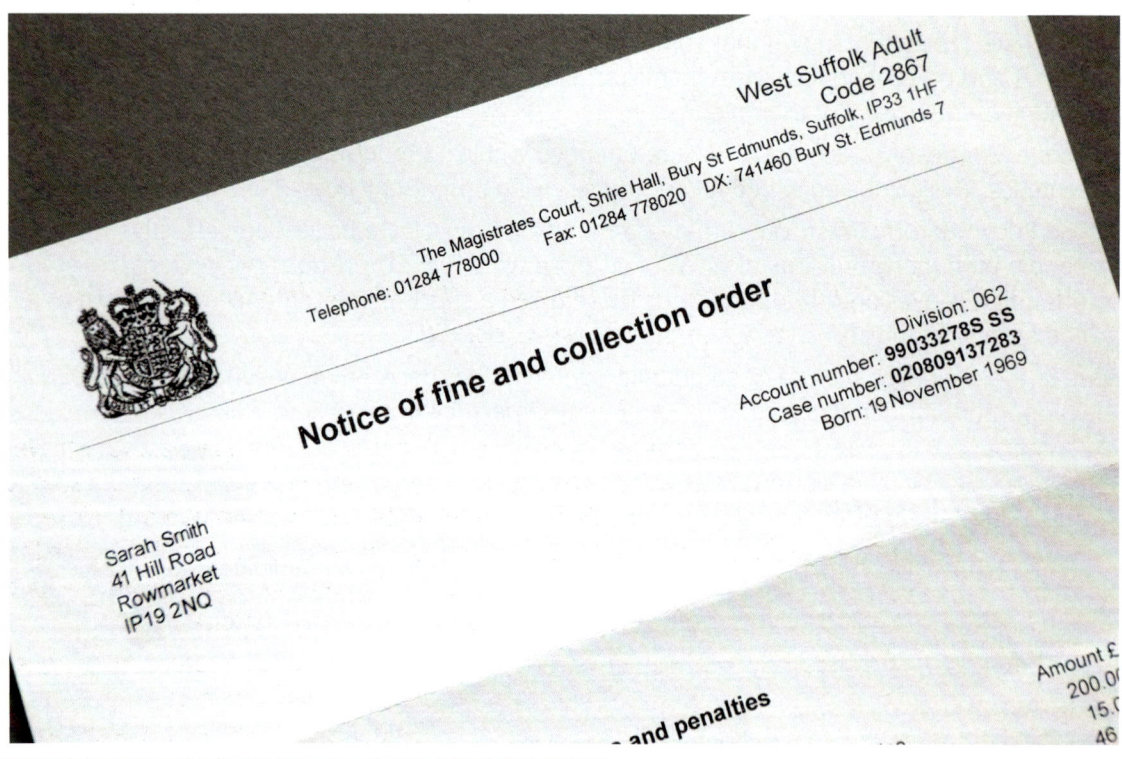

How effective are fines in meeting their punishment aims?

Discharges

When the court finds someone guilty of a minor (usually first-time) offence but decides not to hand down a criminal conviction, they will be given a discharge.

There are two types of discharge:

- **a conditional discharge** means that the offender will not be punished unless they commit another offence within a set period of time determined by the court (up to three years). If they do so, the court can sentence them for both the original offence and the new one. This will result in a criminal record.

- **an absolute (or unconditional) discharge** means that no penalty is imposed. The court may grant an absolute discharge where the defendant is technically guilty but where punishment would be inappropriate, usually because the defendant is morally blameless. It is not classed as a conviction.

Absolute discharges are normally only used for minor offences but in the Thirsk rail crash of 1892 in which ten people died, a signalman was found guilty of manslaughter but given an absolute discharge because of the very unusual circumstances of the case.

ACTIVITY — Research and discussion

The Thirsk rail crash — Go to www.criminology.uk.net

Do discharges meet their punishment aims?

The basic aim of discharges is deterrence. They are the lowest level of punishment and are in effect a warning as to the individual's future conduct. In general, there is a low rate of re-offending following a discharge, especially if it was for a first offence – probably because for many first offenders, the experience of simply going to court is enough for them to mend their ways. In this respect, discharges appear to largely meet their punishment aim.

NOW TEST YOURSELF

Practice Question

Explain how a judge might achieve public protection by passing sentences. (6 marks)

Source: WJEC Criminology Unit 4 examination 2018

Advice

You need to consider a range of different kinds of sentence that a judge may pass to achieve public protection. The most obvious one is a *custodial sentence* (imprisonment), since locking someone up *incapacitates* the offender – they are unable to harm the public for the duration of their sentence. You can mention different custodial sentences, e.g. the judge's power to recommend a 'whole life' sentence, or that a minimum period be served before parole. Until 2012 judges could also impose indeterminate 'imprisonment for public protection' (IPP) sentences under some circumstances.

You also need to explain how *non-custodial sentences* may achieve pubic protection. Various community sentences can be imposed, e.g. orders restricting offender's movements such as curfews that limit the times they can be in contact with the public, or orders banning them from certain areas or addresses (e.g. those of their victims). Electronic tagging may be used to monitor offenders' compliance with these orders. Disqualification from driving can also protect the public from dangerous drivers.

TOPIC 3.1

Explain the role of agencies in social control

Getting started

1. Working with a partner, make a list of the different criminal justice agencies that you know about. For each one, list the ways in which they are involved in controlling people's behaviour. (For example, the police have the power to arrest suspects.)
2. Share your answers with the class.
3. As a class, compile a full list of criminal justice agencies and the different ways in which they control people's behaviour.

Agencies involved in social control

As we saw in Topic 2.1, social control involves getting people to conform to society's norms and laws. There are a range of agencies involved in maintaining social control. Some are sponsored and controlled by the government. These include the police, the Crown Prosecution Service (CPS), the judiciary, the prisons and the probation service.

Others lie outside government control, including voluntary organisations such as charities and pressure groups (organisations and campaigns that aim to change government policies). There are also a number of privately run prisons.

In this Topic we shall look at the role of these different agencies in social control. We have examined aspects of some of these agencies in Unit 3, such as the police, the CPS and the judiciary, and what you learned there will be relevant here.

The police

Philosophy

The philosophy of the police was summed up by Sir Robert Peel, who in 1829 founded the Metropolitan Police, the first modern professional police force in Britain. According to Peel:

- The basic mission of the police is to prevent crime and disorder.
- The police's ability to perform their duties depends on the public's cooperation and approval.
- The use of physical force is a last resort.
- The police's duty is to impartially serve the law.
- The police are the public and the public are the police. The police are just citizens in uniform, paid to do full-time what all citizens must do, that is, uphold the law.

In Peel's philosophy, the police are the servants of the public and the law. Policing relies on the consent of the public and this is to be achieved by upholding the law with the minimal use of force. Peel's principles are embedded in the Police Code of Ethics, which stresses that the police are public servants who need to maintain the respect and support of the public in order to perform their duty.

> **ACTIVITY** / Media
>
> The Police Code of Ethics   Go to www.criminology.uk.net

Aims and objectives

According to the Association of Chief Police Officers, the aims of the police are to:
- keep the peace and maintain order
- protect life and property
- prevent, detect and investigate crime
- bring offenders to justice.

The police seek to achieve these aims using the powers that we saw in Unit 3, Topic 1.4. They have specific legal powers to stop, question, search, arrest, detain in a police station and interview a member of the public in relation to a crime. Most of these powers are given under the Police and Criminal Evidence Act 1984.

Funding

In 2020/21, the total police budget was £15.2 billion. This comes from three sources:
- about two-thirds comes from central government
- most of the rest comes from local council tax
- a small amount comes from charging for services such as policing football matches.

The police's funding fell by 19% between 2010 and 2018. This led to a fall of 20,000 in police numbers during the same period. By 2020, there were 123,000 police officers in England and Wales.

Policing by consent requires good relations with the public.

Working practices

National and local reach

In the UK today there are:
- 39 regional police forces in England and four in Wales, e.g. the Metropolitan Police, South Wales Police.
- One police force for Scotland and one for Northern Ireland.

There are also specialist police organisations with UK-wide reach, such as the National Crime Agency, the British Transport Police and the Border Force.

Types of criminality and offender

The police deal with virtually all types of offence and offender, although some specialist law enforcement agencies do deal with certain kinds of crime and criminal. For example, HM Revenue and Customs deals with tax evasion and tax fraud.

Police duties

Most police have general duties, including patrolling a particular area or 'beat', working with the local community, responding to the public's calls for assistance (both routine and emergency), securing crime scenes, gathering evidence from witnesses and apprehending offenders.

Specialist policing

There are also departments with specialist duties, including the work of detectives in the CID (criminal investigations department), fraud and drugs squads, and Special Branch. These are found in most police forces. Some police forces also have other specialist units, such as covert operations and surveillance teams, traffic and mounted police, air support, river police, underwater search teams and dog handler units.

Some other policing specialists operate nationally as part of the National Crime Agency, such as child exploitation and online protection (CEOP), or as part of the Metropolitan Police, such as SO15, the counter terrorism command ('SO' stands for Special Operations).

Unarmed policing With the exception of certain specialist units, the police in Britain are largely unarmed. This reflects Peel's philosophy that use of force is a last resort in upholding the law. This is unlike the position of the police in most other countries, who are generally armed.

Special Constables are unpaid, part-time volunteers who undergo the same training and have the same legal powers as paid officers.

Police Community Support Officers (PCSOs) have more limited powers, often dealing with anti-social behaviour on the streets, e.g. issuing fixed-penalty notices for littering or confiscating alcohol from under-age drinkers. They can also ask a police officer to arrest a person.

Police and Crime Commissioners (PCCs) are elected representatives of the people of the area covered by a police force (e.g. Bedfordshire, West Yorkshire). They give the local population a voice in policing by being directly accountable to the electorate. Their aim is to cut crime and ensure efficient and effective policing. They set the local force's policing priorities and their budget, and they hold the Chief Constable to account for the force's performance (including dismissing him or her where necessary).

The Crown Prosecution Service

We examined the work of the Crown Prosecution Service in Unit 3, Topic 2.1, so you may want to re-visit that Topic to refresh your memory.

Aims and objectives

The Crown Prosecution Service (CPS) is the main public prosecutor in England and Wales. It was set up in 1986 under the Prosecution of Offences Act 1985. It took over the prosecuting role from the police because there was a risk of bias in allowing the police to both investigate and prosecute cases. The police still prosecute some very minor offences, but the CPS prosecutes all serious or complex cases.

The CPS's role involves the following:

- It advises the police in their investigations about lines of inquiry and the evidence needed to build a case.
- It independently assesses the evidence submitted to it by the police and keeps cases under continuous review.
- It decides whether to prosecute and if so, what charges should be brought.
- It prepares the prosecution case and presents it in court, using its own lawyers and self-employed specialists.
- It assists, informs and supports victims and prosecution witnesses.

Philosophy and values

The CPS says that the values that underpin its work are:

- **independence and fairness** – prosecuting without bias and always seeking to deliver justice
- **honesty and openness**
- **treating everyone with respect**
- **behaving professionally and striving for excellence**
- **equality and inclusion** – to inspire greater confidence in the CPS from victims and witnesses.

Funding

Most of the CPS's income comes from the government, with a budget of around half a billion pounds per year. In addition, the CPS recovers some of its costs when the courts award costs against defendants, and it also recovers assets confiscated from criminals.

However, the CPS has suffered significant funding cuts. In 2018, the then head of the CPS, Alison Saunders, reported that its budget had fallen by 25% and that it had lost a third of its staff. This has led to concerns that it is unable to perform its role effectively.

Working practices

Types of criminality and offender Except for some very minor offences, the CPS deals with the full range of offences and criminals. It takes responsibility for all serious cases.

National and local reach The CPS is a national body throughout England and Wales, with 14 regional area teams prosecuting cases locally. Each one is headed by a Chief Crown Prosecutor and works closely with local police forces and other criminal justice partners. CPS Direct is a 'virtual' 15th area, providing charging decisions to police nationwide, 24/7, 365 days a year.

The head of the CPS is the Director of Public Prosecutions (DPP). Max Hill was appointed as DPP in 2018.

Decisions to prosecute

At the heart of the CPS's working practices is the Code for Crown Prosecutors. The Code sets out two tests that prosecutors must apply in deciding whether to prosecute a case:

1. the evidential test
2. the public interest test.

The evidential test

Prosecutors must first be satisfied that there is enough evidence for a realistic prospect of convicting the suspect. In particular, they must decide that the evidence is admissible (allowable in court, e.g. not hearsay), reliable and credible (believable). If not, it fails the evidential test and the prosecution must not go ahead.

The public interest test

Prosecutors must next decide whether the prosecution is in the public interest. To do so, they must consider the following seven questions. Not every question may be relevant in a particular case.

1. How serious is the offence?
2. What is the suspect's level of culpability (blame)?
3. What harm has the victim suffered?
4. The suspect's age and maturity.
5. What is the impact of the offence on the community?
6. Is prosecution a proportionate response to the offence?
7. Do information sources require protecting, e.g. in relation to other investigations?

The Threshold Test

Even if there is not enough evidence currently available for an immediate prosecution, a suspect may still be charged under certain circumstances. In these cases, the CPS must apply the Threshold Test:

- There must be reasonable grounds to believe that the suspect is guilty and that enough further evidence can be obtained later to secure a conviction.
- The offence is serious enough to justify immediate charging and it would be too risky to allow bail. Any decision to charge must be kept under review.

The judiciary

The judiciary consists of all the judges in the country's courts. There are over 3,000 court judges.

Philosophy

The philosophy of the judiciary is summed up in six principles in the Guide to Judicial Conduct (2016). These lay down the standards for judges' ethical conduct. The six principles are:

1. **judicial independence**: judges should be independent and free from government interference in their decisions. This enables them to uphold the rule of law and safeguard the rights of citizens against the power of the government.
2. **impartiality**: not showing favour to one side or the other
3. **integrity**: being honest and with strong moral principles
4. **propriety**: upholding society's accepted standards of behaviour and morals
5. **ensuring equal treatment** to everyone who comes before the courts
6. **competence**: the knowledge and ability to do the job.

On appointment, judges swear two oaths:

- **the oath of allegiance** (loyalty) to the Queen, her heirs and successors
- **the judicial oath** to 'do right to all manner of people after the laws and usages of this realm, without fear or favour, affection or ill will' – in other words, to treat people equally, with impartiality and according to the law.

Aims and objectives

The basic role of the judiciary is to interpret and apply the law to the cases that come before it in the courts.

- **In Crown Court** the judge must manage the trial, ensuring fairness to all parties, explaining the legal issues and procedures to members of the jury, summing up the evidence, and passing sentence if the defendant is found guilty.
- **In the appeal courts** (the Court of Appeal and the Supreme Court), judges make rulings on the appeals that come before them from lower courts in the hierarchy. This may involve creating precedents through the principle of judicial precedent (see Topic 1.1), which then bind the future decisions of the lower courts.

Funding

The pay of the judiciary is based on the advice of an independent body, the Senior Salaries Review Body, which makes recommendations to the Prime Minister and the Lord Chancellor on how much judges should be paid (along with the pay of others such as MPs and senior civil servants). For example, in 2020 the most senior judge, the Lord Chief Justice, received £262,000, while district judges (the lowest rank of the judiciary) earned £112,000.

However, although judges are well paid by most people's standards, some senior lawyers can earn far more than judges. For example, some experienced barristers working in commercial law earn in excess of £1m (although lawyers working in the criminal courts generally earn much less than this). This may be a disincentive for some people to become judges.

Working practices

The position of judges reflects the importance of maintaining their independence so that they can uphold the rule of law and defend the rights of citizens. For this reason:

- **they have security of tenure**: they cannot be removed from office except by a petition to the Queen passed by both Houses of Parliament (this has only ever happened once, in 1830, to remove a corrupt judge).
- **their salary is guaranteed**.

The judiciary is organised in a clear hierarchy. They can be divided into *superior judges*, who sit in the Supreme Court, Court of Appeal and High Court, and *inferior judges*, who sit in Crown Court (and sometimes also in magistrates' courts).

Types of criminality and offender Judges deal with all types of offence and offender, except for the least serious cases, which are usually dealt with by magistrates, or by cautions and fixed-penalty notices issued by the police.

National and local reach At the most senior level, the Supreme Court has nationwide jurisdiction and settles points of law of national importance. Judges working in the lower (inferior) courts such as the 90 or so Crown Court venues around the country handle local cases.

Senior judges in procession from Westminster Abbey to the Houses of Parliament.

Prisons

Philosophy

HM Prison and Probation Service (HMPPS) is the government agency responsible for the UK's prisons. It describes its purpose as 'preventing victims by changing the lives of offenders'.

Aims and objectives

The prison service has three main aims:
- to protect the public from harm
- to help people who have been convicted of offences to rehabilitate so they can contribute positively to society
- to hold prisoners securely and implement the sentences and orders of the courts.

Funding

Prisons are paid for by the government out of general taxation. In 2018, the total budget for prisons was approximately £3 billion – 16% lower than in 2010. This resulted in cuts to staffing levels, with a 15% fall in the number of prison officers between 2010 and 2018. As a result, many more experienced officers left the service: by 2020, almost a third of staff had less than three years' experience. The average cost of keeping a prisoner in public sector prisons in 2019 was £41,136 per year, or £42,591 in private prisons.

Working practices

In 2019 there were a total of 121 prisons, holding around 80,000 prisoners at any one time. Of these, 106 were public sector prisons, run by the government, and 15 were private prisons, run by three private companies –Sodexo, G4S and Serco. In 2019 G4S was stripped of its contract for HMP Birmingham, which was returned permanently to the public sector following failings by G4S, including Britain's worst prison riot in 25 years, in 2016.

Types of criminality and offender

The prison service deals with higher risk offenders who are deemed unsuitable to serve their sentence in the community. However, the range of seriousness of offence varies greatly, from murder down to theft.

National and local reach

The prison service is nationally organised, with prisons situated throughout the UK. When sentenced to prison, an offender is first placed in a local prison and given a security classification based on a risk assessment. They may then be moved to a more appropriate prison elsewhere. (See table.)

Prison type	Category	Risk assessment of prisoners	Examples of prisons
Closed	A (high security)	Those whose escape would be highly dangerous to the public, e.g. those convicted of murder, attempted murder, rape, terrorism or explosives offences.	Belmarsh, Wakefield, Manchester
Closed	B	Do not require maximum security, but for whom escape still needs to be made very difficult.	Pentonville, Wandsworth
Closed	C	Cannot be trusted in open conditions but unlikely to try to escape.	Birmingham, Dartmoor
Open	D	Can be reasonably trusted not to try to escape.	Ford, Kirkham, Askham Grange

Attempted escapes Prisoners who have made escape attempts are placed on an 'escape list' and must be handcuffed and wear bright yellow clothing when being moved (nicknamed 'banana suits'), must change cells frequently and have their clothes and some of their personal property removed from their cell before being locked in for the night.

Prison activities and routines

Although the prison service aims to rehabilitate prisoners, prisons have been criticised for their lack of opportunities for education, training and work experience. For example, in 2020 the chief inspector of prisons said that half the prisons inspected had too few programmes of useful activity. Under two-fifths were assessed as delivering 'good' or 'reasonably good' activities, compared with more than two-thirds in 2009-10. One reason for this is the cuts in the number of prison officers, which mean there are fewer available to supervise prisoners undertaking activities.

HMP Wandsworth. Over 40% of inmates are locked in their cells during the working day.

Incentives and earned privileges

Incentives and earned privileges (IEPs) are rewards that prisoners can earn by keeping to the rules.

There are three IEP levels: basic, standard and enhanced. On entering prison, the prisoner is put on standard level, which might mean they are allowed to spend more of the money they earn, for example.

Misbehaviour will lead to the prisoner being reduced to basic level, where they can only have the minimum that the law says they must have, such as a limited number of letters or visits. Good behaviour will lead to being moved to the enhanced level, with additional privileges, such as a TV in their cell. Different prisons have different rules about what privileges can be earned.

The National Probation Service

Philosophy

The National Probation Service (NPS) describes its core values and ethical principles as:
- the belief that offenders can change for the better and become responsible members of society
- belief in the worth and dignity of the individual
- a commitment to social justice, social inclusion, equality and diversity.

Aims and objectives

The NPS describes itself as 'a statutory criminal justice service that supervises high-risk offenders released into the community and provides statutory support to victims of serious sexual or violent crime.'

Its priority is to protect the public by rehabilitating offenders, by tackling the causes of their offending and enabling them to turn their lives around.

As we saw in Topic 2.3, the probation service supervises two types of client:

1. **Offenders serving a sentence in the community** rather than in prison, as the result of a Community Order by the court. This may involve requirements such as:
   - up to 300 hours unpaid work (Community Payback)
   - an exclusion order or curfew, or a residency requirement
   - a group programme, e.g. for anger management.

2. **Offenders who have been released on licence from prison** before the end of their sentence. For example, prisoners serving 12 months or more are normally released on licence halfway through their sentence. The licence has requirements attached (e.g. undergoing drug treatment) and is supervised by the probation service.

Partnerships The NPS works in partnership to manage offenders with a range of organisations: courts, police, local councils, and partners in the private and voluntary sectors. Until 2020, this included 21 private sector community rehabilitation companies (CRCs), such as Sodexo Justice Services.

CRCs provided probation services for low and medium risk offenders.

ACTIVITY | Media

The Probation Service   Go to www.criminology.uk.net

Funding

The National Probation Service is part of HM Prison and Probation Service (HMPPS), which in 2018 had an overall budget of £4.6 billion, shared between prisons and probation. This budget is provided by the government and comes from general taxation.

Ending the CRCs' contracts The community rehabilitation companies were private businesses that had a contract with the Ministry of Justice to provide probation services. They were paid for meeting rehabilitation targets agreed in their contracts. However, 19 of the 21 CRCs missed their targets for reducing re-offending and some were even supervising their offenders remotely by telephone. A report in 2018 by the House of Commons Public Accounts Committee concluded that up to £342 million had been spent on CRCs without clear benefits and by 2020 the Ministry of Justice had spent over £500m more than expected on the CRCs.

As a result the government decided to end all private sector contracts for probation work in 2020 and to reorganise the service on a regional basis. From 2022 it will be organised into 12 regions (Wales, plus 11 English regions).

Working practices

Types of criminality and offender At any one time, around 250,000 offenders are on probation. These offenders are deemed safe enough to serve their sentence in the community (or to complete it there if they are released from prison on licence).

National and local reach The NPS is a national service working to the same standards throughout the country, but delivering the service regionally and locally. The NPS is responsible for:

- preparing pre-sentence reports for the courts, to help them select the most appropriate sentence for the individual offender.
- managing approved premises for offenders whose sentence includes a residence requirement (e.g. that they must live in supervised accommodation).
- assessing prisoners to prepare them for their release on licence back into the community. At that point they come under NPS supervision.

- helping offenders serving sentences in the community to meet the requirements ordered by the courts.
- when an offender receives a prison sentence of 12 months or more for a serious violent or sexual crime, or is detained as a mental health patient, the NPS communicates with and prioritises the wellbeing of the offender's victims.

Charities and pressure groups

Unlike the police, prisons or probation service, charities and pressure groups are voluntary organisations that are independent of government control. Their aim is to promote the interests and welfare of the people they are concerned with, such as ex-offenders or victims of crime.

Charities are organisations set up to provide help to those in need, while pressure groups are organisations that campaign to achieve change. Many organisations combine the two roles. A good example is Nacro, which as a charity provides help to ex-offenders and at the same time campaigns as a pressure group to change government policies that affect them.

Nacro

Nacro stands for the National Association for the Care and Resettlement of Offenders. It was founded in 1966.

Philosophy, aims and objectives

Nacro describes itself as a social justice charity seeking to change lives, strengthen communities and prevent crime. It aims to overcome the stereotyped view of the ex-prisoner. It provides a range of services, including:

Housing Nacro houses over 3,000 tenants in its own properties, and also provides bail accommodation and support services. In 2018, over 2,600 people left custody with secure permanent accommodation.

Education In 2018, 4,900 people studied through Nacro's education services.

Resettlement advice Nacro provides support and advice about employment, education and accommodation to people with criminal records and to the professionals working with them.

Outreach projects to keep young people from offending.

ACTIVITY Research

Nacro

Go to www.criminology.uk.net

Campaigns

As well as providing services, Nacro campaigns to change laws and policies affecting ex-offenders, such as the campaign to reform the Rehabilitation of Offenders Act 1974 and criminal records checks. It is a supporter of the Ban the Box campaign. The campaign aims to enable people with convictions to compete for jobs by removing the tick-box on criminal convictions that appears unnecessarily on many job application forms.

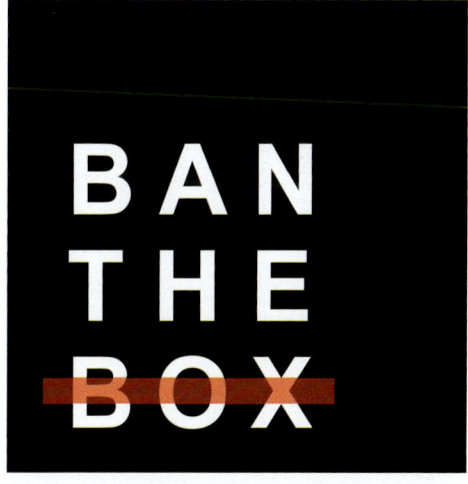

Funding

Nacro has an income of around £50m a year. Its funding comes from public donations, government grants, and contracts for providing services for ex-offenders and others.

Working practices

Types of criminality and offender Nacro works with a range of ex-offenders, including those released from prison. It also works with young people at risk of offending, such as those excluded from mainstream school. More broadly, it is concerned with the needs of disadvantaged young people and adults.

National and local reach Nacro is a national organisation with local activities and projects in around 50 different parts of England and Wales at any one time. It has a large full-time staff and many unpaid volunteers.

NOW TEST YOURSELF

Practice Question

Explain the role of the police in social control. (6 marks)

Source: WJEC Criminology Unit 4 examination 2017

Advice

Explain the police's role in upholding the law and preventing, detecting and investigating crime. Describe their powers to stop, search, arrest and question. You could note that the police's powers are a form of external social control.

Mention specialist policing (e.g. the CID, fraud squad etc.) Refer also to the police's role in protecting life and property, preserving the peace and maintaining order. Link this to the idea of policing by consent and the idea of the police as just citizens in uniform.

Remember to explain also the role of the police in working with other criminal justice agencies such as the courts, the CPS, prisons and probation service to achieve social control. For example, the police provide evidence for the CPS to build prosecution cases and officers appear as prosecution witnesses in court.

Describe the contribution of agencies to achieving social control

TOPIC 3.2

Getting Started

1. Working in a small group, imagine you are planning a new town. From what you already know about crime, make a list of features you would include in your design for the town to help prevent crime. You could think about things like the design of buildings and layout of neighbourhoods. (If you're a bit stuck, you might find pages 144-5 of *Criminology Book One* useful to get you started.)

2. Share your answer with the class. As a class, decide which design features are the most important for preventing crime.

3. What kinds of crime do you think might be reduced by suitable design? What kinds might not? Give your reasons.

Introduction

In this Topic, we look at the contribution of a range of different agencies to achieving social control, including the following:

- architects, planners and councils designing the environment of an area so as to reduce crime
- court orders such as ASBOs to control anti-social behaviour
- prisons using token economies or enforcing prison rules to modify prisoners' behaviour.

We link these approaches to some of the criminological theories that you studied in Unit 2. We also look at some of the things that make it more difficult for agencies to achieve social control, such as changes in policy that have led to budget cuts for the police and prisons.

Environmental design

Some criminologists argue that the built environment can affect the level of crime in two ways:
- by influencing potential offenders, e.g. presenting them with opportunities to commit crime
- by affecting people's ability to exercise control over their surroundings.

They argue that agencies such as architects, builders, town planners and local councils can 'design crime out' by changing the physical layout of an area.

Defensible space

The architect Oscar Newman argues that some spaces are defensible while others are indefensible.

Indefensible spaces are where crime is more likely to occur, in what he calls 'confused' areas of public space such as anonymous walkways and stairwells. They belong to no-one, are cared for by no-one, and are observed by no-one.

For example, in his study of high-rise blocks in New York, Newman found that 55% of all the crimes committed occurred in public spaces such as hallways, lifts, stairwells and lobbies, because no-one felt they 'owned' them.

Defensible spaces are areas where there are clear boundaries so it is obvious who has the right to be there. Newman argues that defensible spaces have low crime rates because of four key features: territoriality, surveillance, a safe image, and a protected location.

Territoriality

Territoriality is where the environment encourages a sense of ownership among residents – the feeling that it is their territory and they control it. Certain layouts also tell outsiders that particular areas are for the private use of residents. For example, cul-de-sacs project a 'private' image and encourage a sense of community.

Natural surveillance

Features of buildings such as easily-viewed entrance lobbies and street-level windows allow residents to identify and observe strangers. Likewise, cul-de-sacs allow residents to overlook each other's homes. By contrast, high-rise blocks often have concealed entrances that allow offenders to come and go unseen.

A safe image

Building designs should give the impression of a safe neighbourhood where residents look after each other. A negative image means the area will be stigmatised (negatively labelled) and targeted by offenders.

A safe location

Neighbourhoods located in the middle of a wider crime-free area are insulated from the outside world by a 'moat' of safety.

Crime Prevention through Environmental Design

Newman's ideas about defensible space were developed further by the American criminologist C.R. Jeffery, who introduced the approach known as Crime Prevention through Environmental Design or CPTED (pronounced *sep-ted*). Jeffery argued that the built environment can either create or deny opportunities to criminals. By altering this environment, therefore, we can reduce crime.

In the UK, Alice Coleman adopted a similar approach. She analysed 4,099 blocks of flats in two London boroughs. She concluded that the poor design of many blocks produced higher rates of crime and anti-social behaviour. She found that three design features encouraged crime: anonymity, lack of surveillance and easy escape. Her recommendations included:

- no more blocks of flats should be built
- each existing block should have its own garden or private space, so residents would look after it
- overhead walkways should be removed because they obstruct surveillance.

These ideas have been influential with planners and have led to attempts to 'design crime out'. For example:

- On the Lisson Green estate in West London, the removal of overhead walkways led to a 50% reduction in crime.
- Some police forces now employ architectural liaison officers to 'build in' crime prevention features at the design stage for new buildings.
- The 'Secured by Design' (SBD) kitemark scheme used by the building industry indicates that a new building meets crime prevention standards. Home Office research found a 30% lower burglary rate in SBD houses.

Gated lanes: an example of CPTED

Gated lanes, also called gated alleys, are an example of a CPTED tactic to 'design crime out' of an environment.

Gated lanes are lockable gates installed to prevent offenders gaining access to alleyways, such as those at the rear of many older terraced houses. They are used mainly to prevent burglaries, but may also stop fly-tipping, anti-social behaviour by youths congregating, dog fouling etc., as well as creating safe play areas for children.

Do alleyways or lanes that are not gated invite crime?

How do they work?

In a review of 43 studies, Sidebottom et al found that gates reduced burglary rates. They suggest this is for the following reasons:
- They provide a physical barrier, thus increasing the effort required to commit a crime.
- Residents taking responsibility for closing the gates increases guardianship and surveillance.
- Gates increase residents' sense of territoriality.
- Offenders can no longer use the excuse that they thought it was public space.
- Open alleys may suffer from the 'broken windows' problem of disorderly, uncared-for space that invites crime. Gating indicates it is a cared-for space that doesn't tolerate crime.
- Gating may reduce the rewards of crime. For example, it will be difficult to steal large objects if the offender has to climb over tall gates with the items.
- Cost may be an issue for residents in some areas, although Sidebottom et al found that the average cost was £728 per gate and that the average benefit was over twice the cost (£2.19 for every £1 spent).

ACTIVITY Media

Crime Prevention through Environmental Design   Go to www.criminology.uk.net

Limitations

Despite their advantages, gated lanes have several limitations as a crime prevention strategy:
- While they may decrease criminals entering from outside, they don't work against criminals who live within the gated area.
- In areas where neighbours don't know or don't trust each other, residents may be less likely to get together to install gates, or may not take responsibility for them.
- There may be difficulties installing gates if the alley is a public right of way, or if it has several owners all of whom will need to agree. There needs to be full consultation with residents to win their commitment to the scheme.
- Gated lanes can restrict access for emergency services and refuse collectors, which can be a problem.

CPTED and theory

CPTED has links with the following right realist theories and ideas:
- **Situational crime prevention (SCP)** Like SCP, CPTED involves 'target hardening' by changing the physical environment to make it harder to commit crime: e.g. barriers to prevent vehicle access to a neighbourhood will make getaways harder.
- **Felson's routine activity theory** emphasises the importance of a 'capable guardian' protecting potential crime targets. In CPTED, mutual surveillance by neighbours acts as a guardian.
- **Rational choice theory** CPTED sees offenders acting rationally. For example, if intruders fear they will be challenged by residents, they will be more likely to stay away from the area.

Criticisms of CPTED

Although CPTED has had some successes in reducing crime rates in certain areas, there are several criticisms of this approach.
- CPTED focuses on defence from outsiders who come into the area to offend, but insiders commit crime too; e.g. domestic violence.
- CPTED cannot prevent offences that don't involve physical intrusion into a neighbourhood, such as cybercrime, fraud, and white collar and corporate crime.
- Cul-de-sacs might be defensible spaces – but they might not actually be defended. For example, if the residents are all out at work all day, there is no surveillance. This highlights how social factors (such as employment patterns) can interact with environmental factors.
- Some housing estates have high crime rates because of councils' housing allocation policies rather than because of how they are designed. Some councils place 'problem families' with a history of anti-social behaviour on 'sink' estates.
- An area's reputation rather than its design may cause a high crime rate. If police regard a particular estate as crime-ridden, they will patrol it more, leading to more arrests, a higher recorded crime rate and an even worse reputation.

Prison design: the Panopticon

Another way in which the built environment can be used for social control is the way prisons are designed.

As we saw in Unit 2, Topic 2.3, Foucault argues that in modern society we are increasingly controlled through self-surveillance. He illustrates this through a description of a prison design known as the Panopticon (meaning 'all-seeing').

In the Panopticon, prisoners' cells are visible to the guards from a central viewing point such as a watchtower. However, though the guards can see the prisoners, the prisoners cannot see the guards and so they do not know whether or not they are being watched at any given moment.

Therefore, not knowing if they are being watched, the prisoners must constantly behave as if they are, just in case. In this way, surveillance turns into self-surveillance. The guards have no need to discipline the prisoners; the prisoners discipline themselves.

Surveillance theory

Foucault's surveillance theory argues that in today's society, self-surveillance has become an important way of achieving social control. We know that we might be being watched – for example by CCTV cameras – so we monitor and control our behaviour ourselves.

A 1920s Panopticon-style prison, Stateville Correctional Center, Illinois USA.

ACTIVITY | **Research**

The Panopticon today

Go to www.criminology.uk.net

Behavioural tactics

Behavioural tactics are ways in which agencies can seek to change individuals' behaviour to make them conform to social norms and laws. We shall look at two examples of behavioural tactics:

- ASBOs and Criminal Behaviour Orders
- token economies.

ASBOs and Criminal Behaviour Orders

Tony Blair's New Labour government introduced ASBOs (Anti-social Behaviour Orders) in 1998 to deal with low-level anti-social behaviour such as vandalism, graffiti, public drunkenness and youths gathering to play loud music at night.

ASBOs were civil orders, not criminal orders, and were used to restrain a person from committing actions that threatened the legal right of another person, for example, an order to stop behaving noisily outside someone's house late at night. However, breaching the conditions of an ASBO was a criminal offence, punishable by up to five years in prison.

Labelling theory and ASBOs

It gradually became clear that ASBOs were not working. For example, between 2000 and 2013, ASBOs were issued to just over 24,000 people, but 58% of them breached their ASBO's conditions, and over 10,000 orders were breached repeatedly.

Labelling theorists argue that labelling a person as a criminal or deviant can lead to a self-fulfilling prophecy. In this situation, the individual internalises the label as part of their identity and begins to live up to it, earning status and credibility from their peers. Labelling theorists suggest that ASBOs became a 'badge of honour' for some young offenders, reinforcing rather than reducing their offending behaviour and leading to repeat offending.

Criminal Behaviour Orders

As a result of criticisms of ASBOs, the Anti-social Behaviour, Crime and Policing Act 2014 replaced them with two new measures: civil injunctions and Criminal Behaviour Orders. **Injunctions** aim to deal with low-level nuisance and annoyance. Breaching an injunction can mean up to two years in prison for adults or a three-month detention order for under-18s.

Criminal Behaviour Orders (CBOs) deal with seriously anti-social individuals who cause harassment, alarm or distress to others. A CBO lasts at least two years for adults and one to two years for under-18s. Breaching a CBO can mean up to five years in prison for adults or two years' detention for under-18s.

CBOs can have both negative and positive requirements:

Negative requirements As with ASBOs, a CBO forbids a person from doing something, such as going to certain places, seeing certain people or engaging in certain activities.

Positive requirements Unlike an ASBO, a CBO can require a person to do something positive to improve their behaviour. For example, where someone has committed a drug related offence, the CBO can require them to join a drug treatment programme to address their addiction.

Token economies

Behaviour modification As we saw in *Criminology Book One*, Unit 2, Topic 4.1, a token economy is a behaviour modification programme used by some prisons, young offender institutions and psychiatric hospitals. It aims to achieve social control by re-shaping inmates' behaviour patterns so that they conform to what the institution requires.

Operant learning theory

Token economies are based on B.F. Skinner's operant learning theory (also called behaviourism) that we examined in Unit 2. The basic idea of the theory is that if a particular behaviour results in a reward of some kind, it is likely to be repeated. The reward acts as a reinforcement of the behaviour.

Social control

A token economy aims to achieve social control in the following way. The institution draws up a list of desirable behaviours, such as:

- obeying the rules
- interacting positively with staff and other inmates
- staying drug-free
- engaging in 'purposeful activity' (e.g. attending vocational training or an anger management programme).

When the prisoner behaves in the desired way, they earn a token. For example, each time a drug test shows they are clean, they receive one token. The prisoner can then exchange tokens for rewards, e.g. extra phone calls, tobacco, sweets, being allowed to have a TV in their cell or to spend more of the money they have earned. In UK prisons, the rewards can be in the form of the incentives and earned privileges (IEPs) that we saw in the previous Topic.

Through this selective reinforcement, the behaviour that the institution desires becomes more likely and undesirable behaviour less likely.

How effective are token economies?

Some studies show that token economies work while inmates are in the institution. Hobbs and Holt's study of 125 boys aged 12-15 in a correctional institution in Alabama USA found that behaviour change lasted throughout the 14-month study.

However, other studies have found that when the offender leaves prison and the reinforcement stops, the desired behaviours disappear. However, the offenders return to crime more slowly compared with those who have not undergone the programme.

Token economy programmes make prisoners more manageable while in prison, but there is a risk that their behaviour is being modified to suit the institution (e.g. to give staff a quiet life), rather than to meet the prisoners' rehabilitation needs for when they are released.

It may be that the programmes work simply because of the extra attention prisoners receive as a result, or even just that the rules are being spelled out more clearly to them – and not because of the tokens.

Institutional tactics

Institutions can use a variety of methods for reducing deviant behaviour and achieving social control. As we have just seen, institutions such as prisons and young offender institutions may use token economies as a way of encouraging desirable behaviour among inmates.

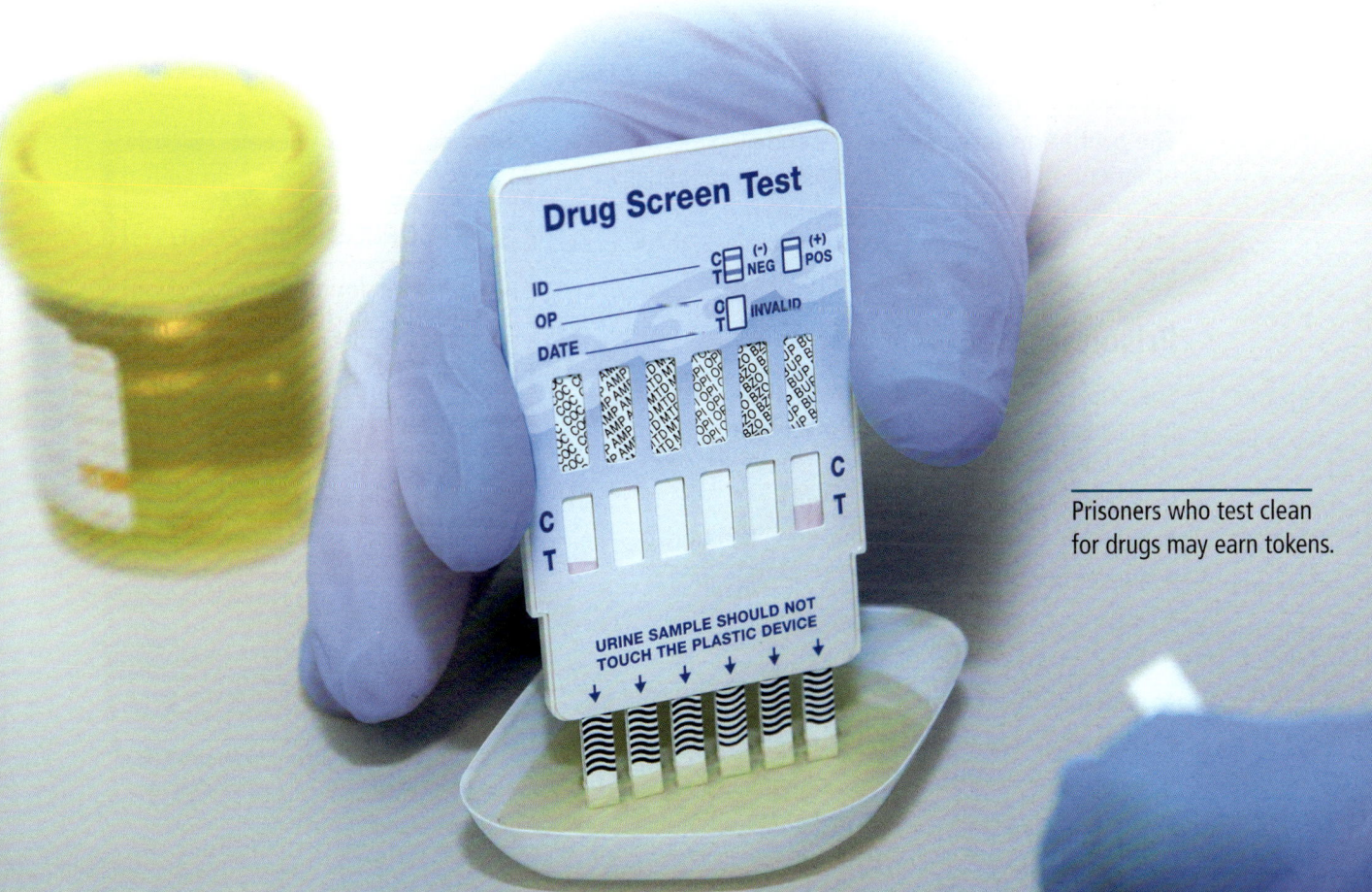

Prisoners who test clean for drugs may earn tokens.

Institutions come in many different shapes and sizes, from families to schools, workplaces to religious organisations, armies to prisons. However, all institutions have rules about how their members must behave, along with punishments for breaking them and rewards for conforming.

Sanctions

As we saw in Unit 2, Topic 1.1, rewards are also known as positive sanctions and punishments as negative sanctions. The table has some examples of rules and sanctions in different institutions.

Institutions	Rules	Sanctions
The family	Children mustn't stay out late without permission.	Withholding pocket money.
School	Students must revise for tests.	Gold star for getting full marks.
The workplace	Employees must be punctual.	Pay docked for lateness.
The army	Soldiers must obey officers' orders.	Court martial for disobedience.

> ### Questions
> 1. Which of the sanctions in the table are negative and which are positive?
> 2. For each institution, think of one other rule and a positive or negative sanction that backs up the rule.

Criminal justice institutions

Institutions or agencies in the criminal justice system have a range of tactics for enforcing obedience to their rules and achieving social control.

The courts can sentence offenders to various punishments for their offences. As we saw in Topic 2.2, this can be used to achieve both individual and general deterrence: punishment may put the convicted offender off repeating their crime and also serve as a lesson to the public in general.

The courts can also use a Community Order to require offenders to rehabilitate, for example by undergoing drug addiction treatment. The aim here is to enable them to change their problem behaviour patterns.

The probation service supervises and monitors the behaviour of offenders, whether serving a community sentence or released from prison on licence. If the offender fails to meet the requirements of their licence, they can be returned to prison or to court for re-sentencing.

Prison rules

The prison service has a set of Prison Rules that apply to all prisons. A prison governor can also add further local rules for their prison. The Prison Rules cover the following offences:

- offending, threatening or hurting someone
- preventing staff from performing their jobs
- escaping from prison
- using drugs or alcohol
- damaging the prison
- being in possession of forbidden items, e.g. a knife
- being somewhere in the prison that you shouldn't be
- not doing as staff tell you

Warning to visitors, Hydebank Wood prison, Belfast. The PSNI is the Police Service of Northern Ireland.

Breaking the rules can lead to a range of punishments. These include a caution, loss of earned privileges, cellular confinement (sometimes called solitary confinement), being prevented from working or from receiving money earned from working. Punishments are time-limited, e.g. cellular confinement can only last up to 35 days.

More serious offences can lead to having up to 42 extra days added to your sentence. Attempts to escape may also mean being moved to a higher security prison with more restrictions.

Phased discipline

Phased or staged discipline is a common way of attempting to achieve social control. A first offence, whether in prison or in wider society, is often dealt with more leniently – for example, with a loss of privileges for a few days (for prisoners), a warning, a police caution or a conditional discharge. Repeat offending, particularly if it is more serious, is likely to be met with stronger sanctions such as probation or prison in an attempt to deter future misbehaviour.

Gaps in state provision

State agencies of social control such as the police, Crown Prosecution Service, courts, prisons and probation service can achieve some degree of control over criminal and anti-social behaviour but this can never be complete. There are a number of reasons for this.

Resources

Funding of state social control agencies comes mainly from the taxes paid by the public. There are limits on how much taxpayers are willing to pay for these agencies and governments face competing demands for resources from other sectors such as the National Health Service, education, pensions, welfare benefits, local authority services and defence.

Budget cuts

Since the financial crisis of 2008, government spending cuts and re-organisations have also had an impact on state agencies, reducing their effectiveness in maintaining social control. For example, between 2010 and 2018:

- **the police budget** was cut by 19%. This led to a fall of 20,000 in police numbers.
- **the CPS budget** was cut by a quarter and the organisation lost one-third of its staff.
- **the prisons** budget fell by 16% and staff levels by 15%.

We shall examine the effect of budget cuts on the agencies of social control in Topic 3.3.

New technology

Another reason why state agencies are less able to achieve social control is the extra burden imposed on criminal investigations by digital technology. In 2018 the then head of the CPS, Alison Saunders, said that the criminal justice system was 'creaking' and unable to cope with the huge amounts of data being generated by technology. She added:

> "Take one recent rape case where they met on Tinder – it took 600 police hours to go through the digital material. You can have a judge say 'I want a download of that iPad' and it will take 15 officers working all weekend to get it."

Saunders' successor as Director of Public Prosecutions, Max Hill, has said that problems checking mobile phones for evidence have led to failures to disclose evidence and a fall in the number of rape and sexual offences charges.

The cost of using new technology such as DNA profiling also poses a limitation on the police's ability to investigate offences.

ACTIVITY / Research

New technology Go to www.criminology.uk.net

Unreported crime

Criminal justice agencies can only investigate, prosecute and convict offenders if their offence has been reported. However, as we saw in Unit 1, only about 40% of crimes are reported to the police and different kinds of crime have different reporting rates. For example:

- only about one in four rapes and attempted rapes are reported
- an estimated 2.3 million domestic abuse cases occurred in 2019-20, but not all were reported to police and only 759,000 crimes were recorded.
- white collar and corporate crime often goes unreported because people may be unaware that they have been victims, for example of fraud, over-charging or environmental pollution.

Questions
1. Suggest reasons why domestic abuse and rape are unlikely to be reported to police.
2. What kinds of crime are likely to be reported and why?

Existing laws

Social control by criminal justice agencies can only be achieved so long as there are appropriate laws in place to begin with. Sometimes, a new type of harm emerges but there is no existing law to forbid it and so state agencies are unable to bring prosecutions to control the harmful behaviour.

Social media and the law

There has been much debate about the responsibilities of social media platforms such as Facebook, Twitter and YouTube for offensive and harmful material that appears on them. For example, the right-wing terrorist who massacred 51 Muslims in mosques in Christchurch, New Zealand in 2019 was able to livestream his crimes on social media.

If such material promoting hatred and terrorism was published in a traditional way, for example as a film, book or newspaper article, the publisher could be held criminally liable. However, social media companies claim they are not publishers and in the UK they cannot currently be prosecuted for the material found on their sites.

By contrast, Germany enacted a law in 2017 requiring social media companies to quickly remove hate speech, fake news and illegal material or face fines of up to 50m euros. In April 2019, following the Christchurch massacre, Australia passed a law requiring companies to notify police or promptly remove videos depicting terrorist acts, murder, attempted murder, torture, rape or kidnap. Executives of companies who fail to comply may be liable for up to three years in jail.

NOW TEST YOURSELF

Practice Question

Describe the contribution of environmental measures such as CCTV in achieving social control. (6 marks)
    Source: WJEC Criminology Unit 4 2020

Advice

Note that this question is about environmental measures *plural*, not just CCTV, so you need to look at a number of these measures. These include examples of Crime Prevention through Environmental Design (CPTED) such as gated lanes, and the Panopticon prison design.

Be sure to use relevant key terms such as Newman's idea of defensible space (including territoriality, surveillance, a safe image, and a protected location), 'designing crime out', displacement and self-surveillance.

Describe the effect on preventing crime and increasing social control of measures such as gated lanes, removal of overhead walkways between tower blocks or creating private gardens for tower block residents.

You can link environmental measures to relevant theories such as right realism or surveillance theory. For example, gated lanes and CCTV are types of target hardening favoured by right realists because they are said to make the costs or risks of committing crime higher and the rewards lower.

You should also point out some of the limitations and criticisms of environmental measures in achieving social control. For example, gated lanes may keep out intruders but cannot prevent offenders who live inside the area from offending (e.g. domestic violence).

Also, because these measures often involve target hardening, they may just displace crime onto other areas or victims. They may also require community cooperation in areas where neighbours don't know or trust one another.

TOPIC 3.3

Examine the limitations of agencies in achieving social control

Getting Started

Working in a small group and using what you already know about prisons, complete the following:

1. What are the key aims of prison as a form of punishment?
2. Suggest as many reasons as you can why prison may not be effective in achieving its aims.
3. Share your reasons with the class.

The limits of control

Although agencies of social control such as prisons and the police seek to achieve social control, they are not always successful. For example, prisons may lack the resources and support needed to rehabilitate offenders and the police do not have unlimited powers to detain people whom they suspect are offenders.

This Topic is about the limitations that may prevent agencies from achieving social control and preventing or reducing crime.

Repeat offending

Recidivism rates

Social control measures are not always effective, as can be seen from the recidivism (repeat offending) rates. For example, in 2019, if we take all offenders who had been given a warning, fine, community sentence or suspended sentence in the previous 12 months, plus all the prisoners who were released from jail in that period, these people between them committed over half a million new offences. This is an overall recidivism rate of around 28%.

On average, those who re-offend commit a further four offences each. The average number of re-offences per offender has been gradually rising since 2009.

If we focus just on offenders released from prison, the re-offending rate rises to 36% for all prisoners and to 64% for prisoners who had received a short sentence of less than 12 months.

Around 37% of juvenile offenders (aged 10-17) re-offend within a year. For juveniles released from custody, 63% are re-convicted within a year.

The rising prison population

The prison population today is almost double what it was in 1993. Repeat offending is one reason for this increase. For example, those released from prison on licence will be recalled to serve the rest of their sentence if they commit a further offence during the licence period.

Longer sentences However, repeat offending is less important as a cause of the rising prison population than the fact that courts are now giving longer sentences. For example:

- in 2018, sentences for serious (indictable) offences were on average over 26 months longer than they had been ten years earlier
- the average minimum sentence for murder increased from 12.5 years in 2003 to 21.3 years in 2016.

Who re-offends?

- The more previous convictions someone already has, the more likely they are to re-offend. For example, in 2018 almost half (47.5%) of offenders who already had more than 10 convictions offended again.
- Offenders who served a prison sentence are more likely to re-offend than those who received a warning, fine or community sentence.
- Males are more likely to re-offend than females.
- Offenders with drug or alcohol addictions, those who are homeless, those with few qualifications and those who are unemployed are more likely to re-offend.

The dark figure of re-offending We should bear in mind that the above figures only refer to *proven* re-offending, in other words where the offender has been tried and found guilty. There is likely to be a dark figure of further offending for which they have not been caught and punished.

Theory

Right realists argue that 'prison works'. Offenders are rational actors and so the fear of being jailed acts as a deterrent to offending. However, the high rate of re-offending shows that this is not so – a fact that right realists fail to explain.

Marxists argue that it is not surprising that unemployed offenders are more likely to re-offend, since they have little chance of meeting their needs if they have to survive solely on benefits.

Civil liberties and legal barriers

Human rights abuses

In some authoritarian states (sometimes called 'police states'), social control agencies such as the police have few restrictions on their power to force citizens to behave as the state wishes them to. In such states, critics of the government may find they are not free to express their opinions and that they risk being locked up indefinitely – or worse.

For example, in 2018 the US Department of State's annual report on human rights cited the following abuses in Turkey:

> *"arbitrary killing and suspicious deaths of persons in custody; forced disappearances; torture; arbitrary arrest and detention of tens of thousands of persons, including opposition MPs, lawyers and journalists for peaceful legitimate speech; political prisoners; closure of media outlets and prosecutions for criticising government policies; blocking websites; restriction of freedoms of assembly and association; and restrictions on freedom of movement."*

What are civil liberties?

Civil liberties are basic rights and freedoms guaranteed to every individual by law. They include:

- **freedom of speech** – the right to say what you like, including freedom of the press and the media

- **freedom of assembly and freedom to associate with others**, including the right to gather together to protest peacefully
- **freedom of movement** – the right to go where you want, within the law
- **freedom from arbitrary arrest**
- **freedom from detention without trial**
- **freedom of religion and conscience**
- **the right to privacy**, especially from the state.

World Press Freedom Day protest against the Turkish government's unlawful detention of journalists.

ACTIVITY Research

Civil liberties   Go to www.criminology.uk.net

Due process

Many of these civil liberties are aspects of the due process model of justice that we examined in Topic 1.3. For example, freedom from arbitrary arrest (where the police can arrest anyone they wish) and freedom from detention without trial (where someone can be held in custody indefinitely without being brought before a court) are both important protections for the individual against the state's abuse of its power.

Clearly, the legal processes involved in due process are a barrier to the state exercising control over its citizens without good cause.

> **Question**
> What other features of the due process model can you recall? How do they limit the power of state agencies to achieve social control over individuals?

Access to resources and support

Offenders need resources and support to help them to rehabilitate and prevent them from re-offending. This is a particularly serious matter in relation to prisoners, since these are generally the people who have committed the most serious offences and/or are repeat offenders.

Resources and support inside prison

One aim of imprisonment is rehabilitation but in many cases prisons fail to rehabilitate offenders, for several reasons:

Short sentences do not give enough time to do the intensive work needed to address deep-seated problems, such as drug dependency, illiteracy and anger management. The problem is made worse by the limited number of places on appropriate courses.

Inadequate resources for education and training The 2020 report of the chief inspector of prisons said that half the prisons inspected had too few programmes of useful activity and fewer than two-fifths were delivering 'good' or 'reasonably good' activities (down from over two-thirds in 2010).

A 15% cut in the number of prison officers means there are fewer officers to supervise prisoners undertaking activities that would help their rehabilitation. Staff shortages mean that prisoners are often locked up by 6 pm, denying them access to recreational and educational facilities such as use of the prison library.

Release on temporary licence (ROTL) is intended to allow trusted prisoners out to attend training, employment and job interviews, yet very few are able to take advantage of this scheme due to shortages of staff to supervise it.

ACTIVITY / Media

Prison riot — Go to www.criminology.uk.net

Resources and support in the community

Once released on licence, prisoners serve the remainder of their sentence in the community under the supervision of the probation service. However, newly released prisoners may face difficult circumstances, including the following:

- **lack of money** Prisoners earn very little from working in prison and receive only a £46 discharge grant on their release.
- **lack of a job** Only a quarter of prisoners have a job to go to on their release.
- **homelessness** According to Nacro, one in nine prisoners has no settled accommodation to go to upon release. Prisoners lose entitlement to housing benefit if they are expected to spend more than 13 weeks in prison. This means they will usually lose any tenancy they had.

The 'End Friday releases' campaign

Over a third of all releases from prison happen on a Friday, and charities and pressure groups such as Nacro and the Howard League have supported a campaign to end Friday releases from prison. Being discharged on a Friday can mean a race against the clock to access services such as accommodation, drug medication and benefits before the weekend shutdown.

This can result in people having to sleep rough and survive on their discharge grant until services re-open on Monday. This leaves them vulnerable to re-offending – in some cases, simply to get a roof over their heads for the night. Unsurprisingly, some ex-prisoners quickly breach the conditions of their release licence and are recalled to prison as a result.

Community sentences

Some offenders serve their whole sentence in the community under the supervision of the probation service. Community sentences are more successful than prison in reducing recidivism. For example, only 34% re-offend within 12 months of starting their sentence, compared with 64% among those serving sentences of less than 12 months.

However, a significant minority do re-offend. There are several reasons for this:

- **Inadequate support for complex needs** such as drug addiction, mental health problems and homelessness. There are often too few places on specialist programmes to address such needs.
- **Inadequate supervision by probation services** There have been criticisms that the service is too lax in allowing offenders to miss supervision appointments.
- **Failures by the privatised community rehabilitation companies**, which have been criticised for failing to meet their targets and for poor supervision of offenders. As a result, the CRCs' contracts were ended in 2020.

Finance

Without adequate finance to fund their operations, agencies such as the police, prisons and CPS will be unable to achieve effective social control. However, their budgets come mainly from public funds, and as we saw in Topic 3.2, government spending cuts have had a significant impact on these agencies. This is likely to reduce their effectiveness.

The police

Between 2010 and 2018, the overall police budget was cut by 19%. (Funds from central government were cut by around 30% but some of the shortfall has been made up by extra funds from local council tax.) The cuts led to a fall of 20,000 in police numbers in the same period and there is a national shortage of detectives.

Off-duty police officers demonstrate against funding cuts.

There is evidence that police forces are dropping investigations into crimes, including sexual offences, violent attacks and arson. For example, the Metropolitan Police dropped 2.9 times as many cases on the day they were reported in 2018 as they did in 2013. The force said this was necessary to balance the books.

Police forces may be particularly tempted to drop serious cases because they take much longer to investigate. For example, rape cases take an average of 129 days to solve compared with two days for theft or criminal damage.

The Crown Prosecution Service

Between 2010 and 2018, the CPS's budget was cut by a quarter and the organisation lost one-third of its staff. The head of the CPS said in 2018 that the CPS and police were failing to investigate thousands of cases efficiently – including rape, fraud and modern slavery – and that both organisations were critically short of the skills and resources needed to combat crime.

The CPS has also been accused of downgrading charges so that it can prosecute cases in magistrates' courts, because this is quicker and therefore cheaper than taking them to Crown Court. However, this may also mean that offenders get off with lighter sentences than they deserve, because magistrates' sentencing powers are more limited.

Prisons

Between 2010 and 2018, the prisons budget fell by 16% and staff levels 15%, while many of the more experienced prison officers left the service.

Critics describe prisons as being in crisis, with rising levels of assaults, self-harm and suicides. Overcrowding and staff cuts mean that many prisoners lack opportunities for activities that would help them to rehabilitate, such as education, training and work experience. Recidivism rates are around 60% within a year of release for those serving short sentences.

Privatisation may have contributed to the crisis. In 2016, the worst UK prison riot in 25 years took place at HMP Birmingham, a prison privately run by G4S. The official report concluded that staff had become worn down by chronic staffing shortages and that prisoners 'were in effect policing themselves'. As a result, in 2020 the government took HMP Birmingham back into public control.

The probation service

In her annual report in 2019, the then chief inspector of probation Glenys Stacey highlighted a range of problems, including staff shortages, failures by the private CRCs, and a lack of confidence in the service by judges, victims, the public and offenders.

Although the probation service has since been taken back into public control, the new chief inspector Justin Russell warned in 2020 that it "must be properly funded, vacancies for probation officers must be filled and staff properly trained."

Local and national policies

Both national and local policies limit the ability of agencies such as the police to achieve social control. For example, when a new law makes a particular crime into a priority, this is likely to mean that other offences are neglected to some extent as police are instructed to focus on the new one.

National government policies

At a national level, central government introduces laws and policies affecting the work of agencies such as the police, the CPS and others. For example, in April 2019, the Home Secretary announced that he was making it easier for police officers to stop and search anyone for an offensive weapon without first having reasonable suspicion that they are carrying one. This power is available to police throughout the country under section 60 of the Criminal Justice and Public Order Act 1994.

The serious violence strategy

Increased police powers are part of a broader national serious violence strategy. This aims to involve other agencies such as youth services, the NHS, social services and education. For example, children excluded from school may be at risk of being groomed by gangs to deliver drug deals, which are a major factor in violence offences.

Local policies

Some of the priorities of the different police forces around the country are set nationally by the Home Office, but others are set locally in response to local needs. For example, in areas where knife crime is particularly high, police may respond with extra measures such as increased stop and searches.

Weapons amnesties

Knife bank outside Brixton police station.

Weapons amnesties are a good example of a local priority. From time to time local police forces hold amnesties where they will not arrest people who surrender illegal weapons. For example, a two-week guns amnesty in London in 2017 led to 350 firearms and 40,000 rounds of ammunition being handed in. Amnesties are intended to reduce the criminal use of weapons in the local area. They may also be held if new laws are being introduced which will make it an offence to possess a weapon that was not previously banned.

Moral panics

On both a local and a national level, the priorities of police and other agencies such as the CPS may be affected by media coverage and moral panics about a particular type of crime. As we saw in Unit 1, the moral panic in the press about 'dangerous dogs' led to the hasty introduction of a new law that has turned out to be largely ineffective in protecting the public.

However, one response of police forces is sometimes to de-prioritise a particular offence where they feel it is too trivial, a waste of police resources or too difficult to enforce the law.

Crime committed by those with moral imperatives

A moral imperative is an overriding sense of what is right – a sense that is so strong it compels a person to act to uphold it, even if it means breaking the law. In Unit 3, we saw several examples of people who broke the law because their conscience told them it was the morally correct thing to do.

- **Clive Ponting** broke the law by passing secret information to an MP about the sinking of the Argentinian ship the *General Belgrano* during the Falklands War. He argued that he had done so in the public interest.
- **Kay Gilderdale** broke the law by assisting the suicide of her daughter, who had been seriously ill for 17 years.
- **Rosie James and Rachel Wenham** committed criminal damage to a nuclear submarine to try to prevent it leaving port, arguing that they were acting to prevent a war crime.
- **Alan Blythe** was charged with cultivating cannabis with intent to supply. He did so in order to provide it to his terminally ill wife to relieve her pain.

In all the above cases, the defendants were either acquitted, found guilty of a lesser charge or had the charges dropped when the jury could not agree on the verdict. These cases show that it may be difficult to persuade juries to control the actions of those whom they see as acting morally.

The Suffragettes

In the early 20th century, the Suffragettes campaigned for women's right to vote in parliamentary elections. As part of their campaign of direct action and civil disobedience, they deliberately broke the law.

For example, Suffragettes set fire to post boxes, smashed the windows of public buildings, cut telegraph wires and attacked a portrait of the Duke of Wellington with an axe. When convicted, they refused to pay fines. Emily Davison died when she protested by throwing herself under the king's horse during the Derby race in 1913.

The Cat and Mouse Act

The Suffragettes' crimes were motivated by a moral imperative to force Parliament to change the law and end the injustice that women were denied the right to vote. About a thousand women were imprisoned and went on hunger strike. In 1913, the government responded by passing the Prisoners Act, commonly known as the Cat and Mouse Act because, like a cat playing with a mouse, it allowed hunger strikers to be temporarily released but then re-imprisoned them once they had recovered their health. As more and more Suffragettes refused food in prison, the authorities began force-feeding hunger strikers through a nostril or stomach tube, in many cases causing permanent health problems.

The Liberal government had introduced the Cat and Mouse Act, opposed by the Suffragettes.

The Suffragettes achieved a partial victory in 1918 when the vote was given to women aged over 30. Finally, in 1928 the voting age was equalised at 21 for both sexes.

ACTIVITY | **Media**

The Suffragettes

Go to www.criminology.uk.net

The Stansted 15

A more recent example of law-breaking as a result of a moral imperative is the case of the Stansted 15. These were 15 protestors who broke into Stansted airport's 'airside' area in 2017 to stage a non-violent protest, chaining themselves together around a plane that had been chartered by the Home Office to deport 60 people to Nigeria, Ghana and Sierra Leone. The 15 were convicted of 'endangering an aerodrome', which carries a potential life sentence. However, all 15 had their convictions quashed by the Court of Appeal in 2021.

The Stansted 15 acted to prevent the deportation of individuals some of whom were later proven to have been victims of human trafficking, and one had been raped and forced into sex work. Eleven of those due to be deported were later given leave to remain in the UK. The Stansted 15 case came in the wake of the *Windrush* scandal, in which people who had spent most of their lives in the UK were illegally deported to the Caribbean by the Home Office.

ACTIVITY | Research

The Stansted 15 Go to www.criminology.uk.net

Theory

Functionalists such as Durkheim argue that without deviance, new social values could not emerge, no change would be possible and society would stagnate. For example, the Suffragettes' law-breaking drew attention to the injustice of denying women the vote and promoted equality between the sexes as a basic value of UK society.

PREPARING FOR THE EXAM

Practice Question

Briefly explain how a lack of resources can be a limitation within prisons. (4 marks)
Source: WJEC Criminology Unit 4 2020

Answer by Chloe

> Prisoners are usually serious or repeat offenders, often because of serious problems in their lives. This means rehabilitation should be a major aim of prisons, but they often lack the necessary resources to achieve it.
>
> Many have drug dependency, causing disruption and violence, e.g. with the availability of 'Spice', but prisons lack resources for intensive rehabilitation work. Anger management is a problem for violent inmates but there are few courses.
>
> Many prisoners are poorly educated, which harms job prospects and leads to re-offending, but only half of prisons have enough training programmes.
>
> A major reason for lack of rehabilitation is staff shortages (a 15% cut since 2010), meaning no-one to supervise educational activities, library use etc. Release on temporary licence to attend training and job interviews is limited by lack of staff to supervise.
>
> Prisons are often run down and overcrowded due to lack of investment. This harms prisoner morale and overcrowding can be a source of conflict.

- Good start – links resources to rehabilitation.
- Lack of resources for drugs and anger management problems.
- Good point about training and education.
- Deals well with impact of staff shortages on rehabilitation opportunities.
- Good final point.

Overall comments

This is a very good answer. It starts well by linking resources to the aim of prisons to rehabilitate individuals with serious problems. It looks at drug dependency, anger management and lack of education, and notes the lack of resources for programmes to tackle these problems. It deals with the impact of staff shortages and makes a good point about the dilapidated and overcrowded state of prisons.

Evaluate the effectiveness of agencies in achieving social control

TOPIC 3.4

Getting started

Working in a small group, consider what you have learned so far about the police. Complete the following:

1. What are the main aims of the police?
2. What problems do the police face in seeking to meet their aims?

As a whole class, discuss how far the police are effective in achieving their aims.

This Topic examines the main agencies of social control to evaluate how effective they are in achieving their aims. We look at the police, the Crown Prosecution Service, the judiciary, the prisons and probation services, and at the work of charities and pressure groups.

The police

Social control responsibilities

The police are the main agency for the detection, investigation and prevention of crime. Their work results in a huge volume of cases being brought to trial every year, along with many out of court disposals by the police using their powers to issue fixed penalty notices, cautions and reprimands. Police forces have specialist departments, units and sections dealing with serious and complex cases, such as terrorism.

Specialist policing

The police are not the only agency responsible for investigating crime. For example, HM Revenue and Customs deals with tax evasion, the Department of Work and Pensions deals with benefit fraud and the Border Force deals with immigration offences. There are also specialist forces, such as the British Transport Police and the Civil Nuclear Constabulary, who protect nuclear installations.

Offences of public concern

In recent years, the police have made progress in prioritising some of the offences of concern to the public such as domestic abuse, where increasing numbers of cases are being reported and recorded.

For example, survey evidence from the 2017 annual report of HM Inspector of Police shows that two-thirds of domestic abuse practitioners (non-police professionals who work closely with victims) felt the police's approach had improved in the previous three years.

However, the same report shows shortcomings in the police's performance on domestic abuse:

- the arrest rate has been falling
- police are not using bail conditions to protect victims
- staff shortages are causing delays in responding to incidents, putting victims at risk
- body-worn video cameras are not always being used to gather evidence.

These shortcomings illustrate the fact that the police are not always successful in achieving social control. We shall now examine criticisms of the police's effectiveness.

Inefficiency

There have been numerous criticisms of the police's inefficiency or incompetence in investigating offences successfully. For example, the Macpherson Report noted the failure of the Metropolitan Police to gather evidence and investigate leads in the murder of Stephen Lawrence that could have led to a successful prosecution of the five leading suspects in the case.

Current trends: more crimes but fewer solved

According to the police's own statistics, crime appears to be increasing. For example, the number of offences recorded by the police rose from 4.5m in March 2016 to 5.8m in June 2020.

Knife and gun crime Police statistics for certain crimes have increased significantly. Recorded knife crimes rose from 24,000 to 35,800 between 2014 and 2020. In the same period, firearms offences rose from 4,900 to 9,800.

At the same time, police clear-up rates have been falling. In 2015, 15% of cases resulted in someone being charged with an offence, but by 2020 this had fallen to just 7%. The number of penalty notices and cautions issued by police has also fallen.

Dropped cases

As we saw in a previous Topic, there is also evidence that the police are failing to investigate large numbers of offences reported to them, including some serious ones. For example, in 2018 the Metropolitan Police Service dropped 2.9 times as many cases on the day they were reported as they had done in 2013. Over the six-year period 2013-18, the Metropolitan Police screened out a total of 525,000 crimes on the same day as they were reported.

Financial circumstances

Adequate funding is a major factor in the police achieving control over crime. From 2010, the government made major cuts in police budgets and this has been a cause of police decisions to drop investigations. With limited budgets and fewer officers, some investigations and prevention measures have had to be prioritised over others.

ACTIVITY / Research

Funding problems   Go to www.criminology.uk.net

Accuracy of the statistical evidence

The statistical evidence seems to suggest that the police are becoming less effective in achieving social control. However, police statistics need to be treated with caution, for several reasons.

Improved recording procedures

One reason for an apparent increase in the total number of crimes could simply be because the police have become better at recording them. In 2014, police recorded statistics were deemed not to meet the standards required by the Office for National Statistics. Since then, the police have made some efforts to improve crime recording, for example in the area of domestic abuse, and this has led to a greater proportion of offences now appearing in the statistics.

Counter-evidence from the CSEW

The overall number of crimes may not in fact be increasing. For example, the Crime Survey for England and Wales, a survey of victims, shows that the overall crime rate has generally been level or falling in recent years, rather than increasing as police statistics indicate. For example, in the year ending March 2020, the rate fell by 9%.

One reason for the difference between these two sets of statistics is that to some extent they deal with different crimes:

- The CSEW does not include crimes against business (such as shoplifting and fraud) or crimes against children aged under 10.
- The CSEW surveys only a sample of the population, so it under-represents some less common but more serious crimes, such as weapons offences. Police and other statistics, such as hospital admissions for knife wounds, are more accurate.
- Police statistics tend to pick up more serious crimes (they are more likely to be reported) and ones where a police crime number is needed for insurance claims (e.g. burglary and vehicle theft).

Why might hospital admissions statistics give a more accurate picture of knife crime than the CSEW?

Other criticisms of police performance

Police performance has been criticised in relation to other issues as well as clear-up rates. One area of concern is race relations.

Racism and bias

The Macpherson Report in 1999 into the murder of Stephen Lawrence found the Metropolitan Police to be institutionally racist. Since then there has been considerable interest in the relationship of the police to minority ethnic groups and concerns continue:

- **Recruitment** of officers from minority ethnic backgrounds has increased, but minority groups continue to be under-represented in the police force, including in senior ranks.
- **Stop and searches** are still disproportionately used against Black and other minority groups.
- **Tasers** are used disproportionately against people of minority backgrounds.

The basic principle of policing in Britain is said to be policing by consent. If the police fail to establish a positive relationship with all sections of the community based on consent and trust, this will hinder their ability to investigate and clear up crimes.

Media reports

There have been accusations of the police playing to the media to portray a 'crimebusters' image. For example, in 2014 South Yorkshire Police invited the BBC to film their raid on the home of Sir Cliff Richard in connection with historical child abuse allegations. No charges were eventually brought and both the police and the BBC had to pay damages to the singer.

The police have also been criticised for over-reacting to media-driven moral panics and calls for crackdowns on whatever crime the media chooses to focus on. This can draw police resources away from other areas of criminality that may be more serious or widespread.

The Crown Prosecution Service

The CPS acts as the main independent prosecutor for England and Wales. It aims to achieve social control by preparing cases and presenting them in court to secure the conviction of offenders.

Evidence of success

The CPS has had some success in achieving its aim. For example:
- in a typical three-month period, it prosecutes around 80,000 cases in Crown Court and 450,000 cases in magistrates' courts
- around 80% of the defendants that it prosecutes are convicted.

Lack of effectiveness

Despite the high proportion of convictions, the CPS to some extent fails to achieve social control by successfully prosecuting offenders.

Media reports

Media reporting of the CPS's performance has not always been favourable. For example, there has been criticism of its handling of rape cases. On 24 September 2018 *The Guardian* reported that the CPS's specialist rape prosecutors had been advised to drop a number of supposedly 'weak' cases.

The aim was to improve the CPS's overall performance by ensuring that a higher proportion of its prosecutions would succeed. One prosecutor said they were told that if they took 350 weak cases out of the system, their conviction rate would go up to 61%.

The move was criticised by experts and campaigners, who warned that it would limit victims' access to justice. For example, it could lead to cases involving younger victims, students and those with mental health problems being dropped, because these were cases where juries have been shown to be less likely to convict. The former principal legal adviser at the CPS, Alison Levitt QC, said:

> *"A system that only prosecutes safe cases is sending attackers the message that vulnerable people are open to abuse as the CPS will not prosecute."*

ACTIVITY Research

The CPS in the media Go to www.criminology.uk.net

Realistic prospect of conviction

The CPS's Full Code Test includes the evidential test. Prosecutors must be satisfied that there is a 'realistic prospect of conviction' – in other words, that the evidence would be more likely than not to convince a jury to convict. However, critics argue that the CPS should be focused less on trial outcomes and more on bringing cases to justice. The number of rapes reported rose by a third from 2016 to 2020, but the number of prosecutions actually *fell* by 60%.

Budget cuts

In recent years the CPS has suffered budget cuts of 25% and it has lost a third of its staff. The Director of Public Prosecutions, Max Hill QC, has said that the CPS cannot sustain further cuts because digital technology is imposing heavy additional workloads on its staff, with the need to analyse content of smartphones in the search for evidence and to comply with rules for its disclosure to the defence. In one case, it took 600 hours to analyse the content on one phone.

Evidence disclosure

A number of rape and other prosecutions have collapsed as a result of the CPS and police's failure to discover and disclose evidence such as text messages stored on victims' or defendants' phones. After the collapse of a rape case against Liam Allan in 2018 due to evidence being disclosed only after the trial had started, around 30 other cases that were due to go to court had to be reviewed and some halted.

Failure to build the case

In some high-profile cases, the CPS has failed to build an adequate case and this has led to the prosecution collapsing. For example, in the murder of ten-year-old Damilola Taylor, the CPS rested its case on an obviously lying witness, when proper checks would easily have established the unreliability of her evidence.

Other criticisms of the CPS

- Despite its independent status, the CPS has been criticised for being too close to the police.
- It has been criticised for being too bureaucratic, inefficient and slow in proceeding with cases. In some cases this can mean that victims and defendants have to put their lives on hold for many months.
- Failure to communicate with relevant parties. There have been examples of cases where suspects have only found out that the case against them has been dropped by reading about it in the media.

The judiciary

Media images of the judiciary

In the media, judges are often presented as old, White, upper-class males who are out of touch with modern society. They are sometimes also described as being too 'soft', handing down lenient sentences for serious offences. How accurate is this image?

Are judges biased in their judgements?

Because judges tend to come from a narrow, unrepresentative section of society, they are sometimes suspected of making biased judgements as a result.

Judges' backgrounds

- 68% of judges are male.
- More than half of judges are aged over 50. However, among judges under 40, a slight majority (51%) are female.
- Black, Asian and minority ethnic groups are under-represented: only 7% of judges are from minority backgrounds.

- They are from the higher classes. 74% of judges were privately educated and the same percentage went to Oxford or Cambridge. Two-thirds of judges are former barristers.

This may mean that judges are biased towards people from similar backgrounds to themselves, or against people who are different from themselves. However, although there are examples of male judges showing a lack of empathy for female victims of sexual assault, it is hard to demonstrate a clear pattern of bias. Likewise, most offenders are young, so it is hard to know if age makes a difference in a judge's sentencing decisions.

Evidence of gender bias

Gender bias is clearly present in certain cases. For example, in 1989 Judge James Pickles sentenced a man to probation after he was convicted of sexually assaulting a six-year-old girl. Later that year, he jailed a woman for contempt of court for refusing to give evidence against her ex-boyfriend, who had assaulted her. In 1990 he sentenced a 19-year-old single mother with a ten-week-old baby to six months on a charge of theft. He commented that getting pregnant was no reason to escape custody.

Women and ethnic minorities are under-represented among the judiciary.

Currency

While there have been cases of gender bias in the judiciary such as Pickles, these seem less common today than in the 1980s or 90s and may be less a cause of current concern. However, class bias continues to be current in some sentencing decisions, as the case study suggests.

Case study | Class bias in sentencing

In 2017, 24-year-old Lavinia Woodward was convicted of stabbing her boyfriend. Woodward was an Oxford University medical student and aspiring heart surgeon. She had attended a prestigious international school and was able to afford a top criminal lawyer.

Sentencing Woodward, Judge Ian Pringle QC told her that a jail term could damage her prospects of a medical career. Instead he gave her a suspended sentence.

The judge said that prison would be too severe a punishment because it would 'prevent this extraordinarily able young lady from following her long-held desire to enter the profession she wishes to.' He described her as having an emotionally unstable personality disorder, an eating disorder, and drug and alcohol dependence.

The journalist and barrister Afua Hirsch argues that Woodward's treatment contrasts sharply with that of other women in the criminal justice system. Like Woodward, many young women who come before the courts have similar problems, but with two differences: unlike Woodward, they usually come from deprived backgrounds and they often receive custodial sentences.

Hirsch also notes how White offending is treated differently by the media. When one Black youth stabs another, the media call it 'Black on Black crime'. Both Woodward and her victim are White, but no headlines described it as 'White on White crime'.

Are judges out of touch?

Media stereotypes of judges often portray them as out of touch with mainstream modern society and especially with the public's views on sentencing. The most notable example is perhaps Judge Pickles, who famously once asked, 'Who are the Beatles?'

The age, education and class background of judges is likely to make them somewhat atypical members of society, but whether they are 'out of touch' is harder to judge. Much more importantly, the issue is whether being out of touch makes their sentencing unreliable. Research from Australia, which has a very similar justice system to that of the UK, suggests not.

Karen Warner et al interviewed Australian jurors about judges. They found that most jurors did not think judges were out of touch with public opinion on sentencing. Even some of those who did think judges were out of touch said this was not a criticism, or said that while they thought judges in general might be out of touch, this did not apply to the judge in the trial they themselves had been involved in.

Potentially, there may be as much danger in judges being 'in touch' as being out of touch. This could mean being swayed or unduly influenced by public opinion, media outrage and moral panics. Being out of touch might just mean remaining independent.

Are judges too lenient?

Some sections of the media regard judges as too lenient in sentencing offenders. What is the evidence for this view?

The Unduly Lenient Sentences scheme

As we saw in Unit 3, Topic 3.2, the Unduly Lenient Sentences scheme allows victims, prosecutors and members of the public to apply to the Attorney General or Solicitor General (government law ministers) for a sentence to be reviewed if they feel it was unduly lenient. The scheme applies to sentences for serious offences such as murder, rape, robbery, child sex crimes and people trafficking.

If the minister agrees that the judge made a gross error in their sentencing decision, they will ask the Court of Appeal to review the sentence and if necessary increase it. If the Court of Appeal finds that the sentence is significantly below the one that the judge should have passed, they will increase it.

In fact, very few applications are made for sentences to be reviewed, and not all of these are referred to the Court of Appeal. In 2018, 140 cases were referred, of which 99 had their sentences increased. These figures need to be set against the many thousands of sentences passed each year for serious offences. This suggests that in general, judges are not being unduly lenient in their sentencing.

Unduly severe sentences

Equally, there are examples of judges and magistrates imposing what some regard as unduly severe sentences, as in many of the cases arising out of the 2011 riots, when offenders often received custodial sentences for minor theft offences.

Prisons

The prison service aims to achieve social control by punishing offenders and by rehabilitating them so that they follow a crime-free life after they are released. It also aims to exercise social control over offenders while they are inside prison so that they follow the prison's rules and behave in an orderly manner. However, the evidence suggests that prisons are not particularly effective in achieving their aims.

Social control within prisons: the evidence

Critics argue that the prison system is in crisis and that the prisons are in many cases unable to exercise effective control over their inmates. The evidence below supports this view.

Staff cuts

Between 2010 and 2018, the number of prison officers fell by 15% as a result of budget cuts. More experienced officers were more likely to leave and by 2018, a third of prison officers had less than two years' experience. This has made it harder to maintain control over inmates.

Overcrowding

The prison population has almost doubled from 43,000 in 1993 to around 80,000 in 2021. This has meant more prisoners to control as well as overcrowded conditions for many inmates: in 2018, 58% of prisons were overcrowded. In turn, overcrowding contributes to discontent and rule-breaking. Numbers are projected to reach 98,700 by 2026.

Not addressing rehabilitation needs

Increased numbers of prisoners, staff shortages and budget cuts mean that prisons are often unable to deal with the causes of prisoners' offending, including mental health needs, drug and alcohol dependency, illiteracy and lack of qualifications.

This is made worse by the fact that many prisoners are serving short sentences, so there is not enough time to address their often complex needs.

A drugs epidemic

In recent years drug use among prisoners has risen rapidly. Most of the increase has been in the use of 'new psychoactive substances' (NPS) such as Spice. These synthetically produced drugs can be 100 times more potent than natural cannabis and can cause aggression, psychosis and intense depression. Between 2013 and 2018, 117 deaths in prison were linked to NPS use. In 2016 the Psychoactive Substances Act outlawed their possession in prisons.

In 2016, the prison and probation ombudsman described these drugs as a 'game-changer' for prison safety. Despite this, the chief inspector for prisons reported that some prisons still had no strategy for reducing the supply of drugs.

The availability of drugs undermines prison discipline and control by reducing inmates' participation in rehabilitation activities, creating debt among prisoners and increasing levels of violence.

Security

The most basic requirement of prison is to hold prisoners in custody. There have been almost no escapes from closed prisons (about two a year) since 2010 and few absconders from open prisons. However, there have been numerous breaches of security, with drugs, sim cards and other forbidden items being smuggled into prisons, sometimes by the use of drones.

Safety

Incidents of assaults, self-harm and suicide have risen. In 2020 there were:

- 9,800 assaults on staff
- 32,000 assault incidents – that is, 380 assaults for every 1,000 prisoners (up from 142 in 2010)
- five homicides
- 76 suicides
- 65,000 incidents of self-harm (up from 25,000 in 2010).
- Self-harm was particularly high among women prisoners, with an average of 3.2 incidents per prisoner recorded.

Riots and disorder

Major breakdowns of order and loss of control by staff have increased. In addition to the riot at HMP Birmingham in 2016 – the worst in 25 years in a UK prison – due partly to staff shortages, there has been a series of lesser incidents. In 2018 there was serious disorder at several prisons, including The Mount, Long Lartin and Bedford. The chief inspector of prisons warned of a 'complete breakdown in order and discipline' at Bedford, described as rundown and rat-infested.

After release: the evidence on re-offending

Although rehabilitation is a primary aim of the prison system, many ex-prisoners re-offend and quickly find themselves back in the criminal justice system. For example, within one year of release:

- 36% of all ex-prisoners re-offended
- among ex-prisoners with many previous convictions (11 or more), nearly half re-offended
- 64% of those on short sentences (less than 12 months) re-offended
- around 37% of juvenile offenders re-offended.

Conclusion: the evidence on prisons

Overall, the evidence shows that the prisons are ineffective both in achieving social control over offenders while they are *in* prison, and that they are ineffective in rehabilitating them so that they lead a crime-free life after they have *left* prison.

ACTIVITY | **Research**

Does prison work? | Go to www.criminology.uk.net

December 2016. Police arriving at HMP Birmingham after rioting broke out.

Probation

The probation service has had mixed results in achieving social control through its work. In particular, there has been a difference in the performance of the public sector National Probation Service (NPS) and the privatised sector of community rehabilitation companies.

Privatisation

In 2014, the Conservative government under the then Justice Secretary Chris Grayling launched what he claimed was a 'rehabilitation revolution' aimed at reducing re-offending. A key part of the policy was the part-privatisation of the probation service.

21 private companies, called community rehabilitation companies (CRCs), were set up, each operating in a particular geographical area. The CRCs were to deal with low-risk offenders and would earn their profits on a payment-by-results basis, with targets to reduce re-offending by their clients.

Evidence

The CRCs' performance failed to live up to the government's expectations. Of the 21 companies, 19 failed to meet their targets for rehabilitating offenders and had to have an extra £342m pumped in. According to the 2018 probation service inspection report:

- offenders' housing needs were met less often: only 54% of cases supervised by CRCs, compared with 70% of NPS-supervised cases
- offenders were often supervised by telephone only
- one CRC held meetings with clients in open-plan offices, playing 'white noise' to prevent people from eavesdropping
- CRCs provided inadequate protection for victims and their children when domestic abusers were returned to the community

2014. Probation officers' union Napo protesting against privatisation and cuts in legal aid.

- probation officers in the CRCs were carrying higher caseloads than those in the public sector, because the companies were cutting staff to save money.

As a result of these failings, the government decided to terminate the CRCs' contracts early, bringing them to an end by 2020.

Bias

The political ideology of the Conservative government biased it in favour of privatisation. Conservatives see privately-owned commercial companies as the most effective means of achieving social control in the justice sector. They believe that private companies can provide both a more efficient and a more cost-effective service. For this reason the Conservative government followed a policy of privatisation in both probation and the prison service.

However, Dame Glenys Stacey, the then head of the probation service, said in 2019 that the part-privatisation was 'irredeemably flawed' and that it was difficult to see how people could have confidence in the service while it 'remains subject to the pressures of commerce'. She concluded that the core work of engaging with offenders, monitoring them and helping their rehabilitation should be in public hands.

Evaluation

The evidence from official reports strongly indicates a failure by the CRCs to achieve social control of offenders. This failure also undermines the objective of keeping the community safe, for example where domestic abusers are returned to the community without adequate supervision.

The National Probation Service

The NPS has been more successful than the CRCs in achieving social control. Overall, it has about half the rate of re-offending compared with prison. However, the service has limitations that reduce its effectiveness in achieving social control. These include:

- a critical national shortage of probation officers
- high workloads have led to professional standards being compromised
- a lack of professional leadership
- probation premises are dated, shabby and in some cases not secure
- there is no national strategy to provide enough local specialist services
- there is a shortage of places on specialist programmes to address the causes of offending.

Charities and pressure groups

Charities and pressure groups are non-governmental, voluntary organisations:

- **Charities** provide services to specific groups of people, such as ex-prisoners
- **Pressure groups** campaign for changes to government policies to benefit those whose interests they serve.

In practice, organisations such as Nacro and Women in Prison combine these two roles.

Strong commitment

Charities are sometimes better placed to reduce offending and re-offending than government agencies. This is because they have a strong commitment to one particular group or issue and specialist knowledge of people's needs. They are also strongly motivated to help and may therefore go the extra mile in a way that government or privatised agencies may not do.

Nacro

As we saw in Topic 3.3, Nacro acts as a pressure group. For example it campaigns along with other organisations to end Friday releases from prison. A third of all releases take place on a Friday, which means people have no time to access vital services and may end up sleeping rough, going without medication and re-offending.

Nacro is also a charity that provides services for ex-offenders and those in danger of offending. For example, it provides accommodation for those released from prison and supports them to find long-term accommodation. Homelessness is a major driver of re-offending and tackling it helps to achieve social control.

Women in Prison

Women in Prison (WIP) recognises that over half of women prisoners are victims of domestic or sexual violence. They face problems of homelessness, poverty, mental illness and substance misuse. WIP is committed to tackling the root causes of women's offending.

Pressure group campaigning

WIP is a pressure group that campaigns to reduce the numbers of women in prison. It presses government and criminal justice agencies to change their policies. For example:

- WIP calls for the government to drop its plans to build five new prisons for women. Instead it calls for the money to be invested in specialist women's centres and community-based solutions such as housing and mental health support that would reduce re-offending.
- WIP calls on the courts to follow the Sentencing Guidelines and use prison only as a last resort, for the most serious offences and to protect the public from harm. Yet 84% of women's prison sentences are for non-violent offences, including non-payment of council tax or TV licences.

WIP has won the support of a number of MPs as well as members of the public for its campaigns.

ACTIVITY / **Media**

Charities and pressure groups   Go to www.criminology.uk.net

Support for women in prison

As a charity, WIP provides a range of support for women in prison. This includes:

- a freephone helpline to provide support and guidance to women prisoners
- referring women to other specialist agencies
- delivering the CARE programme (Choices, Actions, Relationships, Emotions) for women in prison for violent offending who have a history of self-harm, suicide attempts, mental health problems or substance misuse.

Gaps in provision

One limitation of charities and pressure groups in achieving social control is that they are voluntary organisations. This means that they only exist where people are concerned about a particular issue or group.

For example, people may be concerned enough about victims of child sexual abuse to set up charities to support them. They may be less concerned about the abusers and less likely to set up organisations aimed at rehabilitating them. This may mean that opportunities to prevent re-offending are missed.

Media reporting plays a part in this. If a group of victims is portrayed sympathetically, this may increase support for charities that work with the group. If the media demonise a particular category of offender, it will be harder for charities that work with them to build support.

Funding is also affected by this. It is easier to persuade the public to donate funds for some groups or causes than for others that might be equally (or more) important or deserving. National and local government also fund charities to provide certain services but they too will only do so if it fits with their political and financial priorities.

NOW TEST YOURSELF

Practice Question

Evaluate the effectiveness of social control inside prisons. (9 marks)

Source: WJEC Criminology Unit 4 examination 2017

Answer by Joshua

> The social control aims of prisons are to protect the public by keeping dangerous offenders locked up, to deter offenders from re-offending by punishing them and to rehabilitate them so they lead a crime-free life when they are released.
>
> However, critics argue that as far as rehabilitation and deterrence are concerned, prisons are not very successful in achieving social control. For example, almost half re-offend within 12 months of release, and a high proportion of prisoners are serial offenders, often with many previous convictions.
>
> There are several reasons for this failure to achieve social control. Prisoners often have serious problems that underlie their offending, such as drug and alcohol addictions, mental illness, lack of education or skills, and unemployment. However, prisons often do little to tackle these problems and as a result, ex-prisoners end up re-offending and returning to jail. For example, there is a shortage of places on courses such as anger management and a lack of good quality education and skills training. Also, many prisoners are serving short sentences, which don't give enough time to address these complex needs. This makes recidivism more likely.
>
> There are other problems achieving social control inside prisons. Use of Spice and other psychoactive drugs is widespread and growing, with drones being used to smuggle drugs and other contraband into jails. There are high rates of suicide and self-harm (especially in women's prisons), and of assaults on staff and inmates. In recent years there have been serious episodes of disorder, including the worst riot in 25 years at HMP Birmingham in 2016. Overcrowding and staff cuts of 15% make it more difficult to maintain order.
>
> However, very few prisoners escape and in this sense prisons achieve the aim of controlling offenders to protect the public by temporarily incapacitating them. Also, some prisoners are serving indeterminate sentences and cannot be released if they are considered to be a danger to the public.

Annotations:
- Useful to identify the control aims of prisons.
- Uses relevant evidence to evaluate prisons' effectiveness.
- A good account of the reasons why prisons fail to rehabilitate for life outside.
- Looks at further reasons why control is not achieved.
- Points out ways in which prisons do achieve some control.

Overall comments

This is a Band Three (top band) response. Joshua sets out some key control aims of prisons (public protection, punishment and rehabilitation) and then deals with whether they do in fact rehabilitate offenders, using relevant evidence on prisoners' problems (e.g. addictions, lack of education etc.) and on lack of provision for these needs in prison. He provides good evidence on lack of control in terms of drug use, suicides, self-harm, assaults and riots, as well as staff cuts and overcrowding. He uses his evidence successfully for his evaluation that prisons are ineffective. He balances this with his final paragraph that identifies one sense in which prisons do succeed in achieving control – through incapacitation.

Preparing for the Unit 4 exam

Now that you have completed Unit 4, you need to revise and prepare for the exam. This section will help you to get ready to tackle it. It contains some advice on preparing yourself, plus two past WJEC exam questions for you to try.

There is also advice on how to answer the questions, though you might want to try doing them without looking at the advice first.

Get organised!

The first thing to do is to get your file sorted out.

1. Make a list of all ten Unit 4 Topics to give you a framework for your revision.
2. Organise your notes, activities and homework for each Topic. Use the subheadings in each Topic as a guide to how to organise them. You could work with others and share your work or fill in any gaps you have together.
3. Make a list of the main issues covered in each Topic. Using these issues, go to your notes and textbook to find the material you need in order to understand them. Make any additional notes you need.
4. From your notes and textbook, list the key ideas needed for each Topic. Link these to the issues.

Practise, practise, practise!

Once you have your file in order, the best way to prepare for the exam is by practising the skill you're going to be tested on – the skill of answering exam questions. You wouldn't think of taking a driving test without doing any driving beforehand, and it's the same with exams. Here are some ways you can practise:

Familiarise yourself with possible questions by looking at those in the *Now test yourself* sections at the end of each Topic and the ones in the practice questions on the next page.

Improve the answers you've already done. If you didn't get full marks on an assignment, re-write it, taking your teacher's comments on board, plus the advice in the *Now Test Yourself* section in the relevant Topic.

Answer any questions that you skipped earlier. You may not have done every assignment you were set. Do the ones you missed now. Your teacher might even mark them for you! If not, get a friend to give their opinion (and return the favour).

Study the student answers that appear at the end of some Topics and read the comments that go with them.

Answer past papers that you will find on the WJEC website (and while you're there, look at the mark schemes too).

End of Unit Practice Questions

Below are two questions from a past WJEC Criminology Unit 4 examination paper for you to answer. You will find advice on how to answer them on the next two pages. However, before looking at the advice, you might like to try making brief plans on how you would answer the questions. Alternatively, you can answer the questions first and then compare your answers with the advice afterwards.

QUESTION 1

Scenario

Sarah is 21 years old and is currently serving a three-year prison sentence having been found guilty of grievous bodily harm at the local Crown Court. She stabbed the victim with a knife during a fight. Her lawyer has told her she should appeal the unsafe conviction as it was investigated using the crime control model.

(a) (i) Identify who would have found Sarah guilty in the Crown Court. (1 mark)
 (ii) Identify who would have imposed the prison sentence. (1 mark)
(b) Briefly describe the crime control model of criminal justice referred to by Sarah's lawyer. (4 marks)
(c) Briefly describe **one** behavioural tactic used by prisons to achieve social control. (4 marks)
(d) Discuss the aims of the prison sentence imposed on Sarah. (6 marks)
(e) Discuss how theories of criminology have influenced the aims of sentencing. (9 marks)

Source: WJEC Criminology Unit 4 examination 2019

QUESTION 2

Scenario

A local secondary school is having a careers information evening. A police officer, a crown prosecutor and a prison governor will all be attending to inform students about their work. These guest speakers will be answering questions from students about their role in achieving social control.

(a) Briefly describe what a crown prosecutor would say about the role of the Crown Prosecution Service in the organisation of the criminal justice system. (4 marks)
(b) Discuss the role of the police service in achieving social control. (6 marks)
(c) Examine how crime committed by those with moral imperatives is a limitation in achieving social control. (6 marks)
(d) Evaluate the effectiveness of the police service and the Crown Prosecution Service in achieving social control. (9 marks)

Source: WJEC Criminology Unit 4 examination 2019

Advice on answering the practice questions

Advice on answering Question 1

(a) For (i) it is the jury who found her guilty. For (ii) the judge imposed the prison sentence.

(b) Describe some key features of the model. These include the idea that repression of crime is the key function of the justice system, because crime threatens people's freedom. It starts from a presumption of guilt: it assumes police and prosecutors are skilled at investigating, gathering evidence and identifying the guilty. It believes the system should operate like a conveyor belt, moving the guilty quickly to punishment. It emphasises rights of victims and society, rather than the suspect's. Use specialist terms in your answer. You can include an example of a relevant legal rule, e.g. extended police detention for questioning terrorist suspects.

(c) You could write about token economies, prison rules or the incentives and earned privileges scheme. If you choose token economies, include concepts like behaviour modification and selective reinforcement. Describe how a token economy works: good behaviour earns tokens that can then be exchanged for rewards such as phone calls and TVs. Prison management decides what behaviours to encourage and rewards these with tokens. This increases control by making inmates more manageable and reducing conflict. Use relevant specialist terms.

(d) Discuss aims of the sentence: deterrence, retribution, incapacitation (public protection) and rehabilitation. For example, for deterrence, discuss both individual (imprisoning Sarah to deter repeat offending for fear of going back to prison) and general deterrence (sending a message to potential offenders that they risk prison). Note that deterrence is an aim of punishment according to the Criminal Justice Act 2003. For incapacitation, as Sarah was convicted of a violent crime, she is a potential danger to others and imprisonment means she is incapable of harming the public further. Use relevant specialist terms and make reference to Sarah or to her three-year sentence.

(e) This is a synoptic question requiring you to apply knowledge of theories from Unit 2 (see also Unit 4, Topic 2.2). Discuss at least two theories and two aims. For example, you could discuss the aim of retribution. Use the concept of proportionality ('just deserts'). Link retribution to right realism, which sees criminals as rational actors who consciously choose to offend and so must suffer society's outrage for their choice. It also links to functionalism: retribution expresses society's outrage and reinforces the boundaries. Note criticisms, e.g. that offenders deserve a chance to reform, not just punishment. You could also choose deterrence, for example. Link general deterrence to social learning theory: Bandura argues that if would-be offenders see a model being punished for offending, they will be less likely to imitate the behaviour. Link individual deterrence to operant learning theory: if a particular behaviour is punished, this is likely to lead to its extinction.

Advice on answering Question 2

(a) The CPS decides the charge in all but minor offences. It decides which cases should be prosecuted, based on the evidential and public interest tests, and keeps all cases under continuous review. It advises the police on lines of enquiry and decides the appropriate charges in serious cases. It prepares and presents cases at court, using its own prosecutors or self-employed lawyers. It provides information and support to victims and prosecution witnesses. It is based on a philosophy of independence, openness, professionalism and inclusion. It is organised in 14 regional teams plus CPS Direct.

(b) The police aim to protect life and property, preserve the peace and uphold the law, and prevent, detect and investigate crime. Link this to the idea of policing by consent and working with the community. They use statutory powers to stop, search, arrest, detain and question, based largely on PACE 1984. Mention general beat teams and specialist policing (e.g. counter-terrorism). Refer to their organisation (e.g. 39 forces in England) and cooperation with other agencies e.g. CPS.

(c) Define a moral imperative as an overriding sense of what is the right thing to do, even if it means breaking the law. Those who break the law are unlikely to be rehabilitated because they believe they have done no wrong, so this limits social control. Offenders may justify their offences by arguing that they acted in the public interest (e.g. Clive Ponting and the sinking of the General Belgrano); to prevent a greater crime (e.g. Rosie James and Rachel Wenham damaging a nuclear submarine); or out of compassion (e.g. Kay Gilderdale assisting her seriously ill daughter's suicide, and Alan Blythe cultivating cannabis to provide pain relief for his terminally ill wife). Use examples and note that juries are often reluctant to convict such cases.

(d) For both the police and CPS, consider both strengths and weaknesses in achieving social control. For the police, you could refer to improvements in dealing with domestic abuse, successful counter-terrorism operations etc. Also refer to criticisms, e.g. falling arrest and clear-up rates, delays responding to incidents, increased numbers of cases dropped, inadequacies of police crime statistics, budget cuts and staff shortages, accusations of institutional racism (e.g. the Stephen Lawrence case; the use of stop and search), the Hillsborough disaster. For the CPS, note its independence in making prosecution decisions, its use of the full code test and commitment to a due process model of justice, its relatively high success rate. Discuss criticisms, e.g. dropping supposedly 'weak' rape cases so as to increase its success rate, collapse of cases due to failure to discover or disclose evidence from mobile phones (e.g. the Liam Allan case), failure to build a proper case (e.g. the Damilola Taylor case), being bureaucratic, over-centralised and too close to the police.

References

Brodsky, SL et al (2010) 'The Witness Credibility Scale: An outcome measure for expert witness research', *Behavioral Science and the Law*

Canter, D (1994) *Criminal Shadows: Inside the Mind of the Serial Killer*, HarperCollins

Canter, D (1995) 'Psychology of Offender Profiling' in Bull R and Carson D (eds) *Handbook of Psychology in Legal Contexts*, Wiley

Canter, D and Gregory, A (1994) 'Identifying the residential location of rapists', *Forensic Science Society*

Carlen, P (1988) *Women, Crime and Poverty*, Open University Press

Coleman, AM (1985) *Utopia on trial: Vision and reality in planned housing*, 2nd edn, Hilary Shipman

Ellison, L and Munro, V (2009) 'Reacting to Rape: Exploring Mock Jurors' Assessments of Complainant Credibility', *British Journal of Criminology*

Eysenck, HJ (1964) *Crime and Personality*, RKP

Felson, M. (2012) *Crime and Everyday Life*, Pine Forge Press

Foucault, M (1975; 1991) *Discipline and Punish: The Birth of the Prison*, Penguin

Gottfredson, M and Hirschi, T (1990) *A General Theory of Crime*, Stanford University Press

Hall, S et al (1978) *Policing the Crisis*, Macmillan

Heidensohn, F (1996) *Women and Crime*, Macmillan

Hirsch, A (2017) 'The Lavinia Woodward case exposes equality before the law as a myth', *The Guardian*, 27 September

Hirschi, T (1969) *Causes of Delinquency*, University of California Press

HM Chief Inspector of Prisons for England and Wales (2020) Annual Report 2019–20, Ministry of Justice

Hobbs, TR and Holt, MM (1976) 'The effects of token reinforcement on the behavior of delinquents in cottage settings', *Journal of Applied Behavior Analysis*

Kaufmann, G et al (2002) 'The importance of being earnest: displayed emotions and witness credibility', *Applied Cognitive Psychology*

Kirk, PL (1953) *Crime investigation: physical evidence and the police laboratory*, Interscience Publishers

Kuehn L (1974) 'Looking down a gun barrel: person perception and violent crime', *Perceptual and Motor Skills*

Lammy, D (2017) *The Lammy Review*, Ministry of Justice

Loftus, EF and Palmer, JC (1974) 'Reconstruction of automobile destruction: An example of the interaction between language and memory', *Journal of Verbal Learning and Verbal Behavior*

Loftus, EF et al (1987) 'Some facts about "weapon focus"', *Law and Human Behavior*

Macpherson, Sir W (1999) *The Stephen Lawrence Inquiry*, The Home Office

Newman, O (1982) *Defensible Space: People and Design in the Violent City*, Architectural Press

Newman, O (1996) *Creating Defensible Space*, Institute for Community Design Analysis, US Department of Housing and Urban Development Office of Policy Development and Research

Packer, H (1968) *The Limits of Criminal Sanction*, Stanford University Press

Plant, E and Peruche, B (2005) 'The consequences of race for police officers' responses to criminal suspects', *Psychological Science*

Prison Reform Trust (2021) *Bromley Briefings Prison Factfile Winter 2021*, Prison Reform Trust

Reckless, WC (1974) *The Crime Problem*, 5th edn, Appleton-Century-Croft

Riley, D and Shaw, M (1985) *Parental Supervision and Juvenile Delinquency*, Home Office research study no. 83

Sidebottom, A et al (2017) 'Gating Alleys to Reduce Crime: A Meta-Analysis and Realist Synthesis', *Justice Quarterly*

Skinner, BF (1953) *Science and Human Behavior*, Macmillan

Smart, C (1989) *Feminism and the Power of Law*, Routledge

Thomas, C (2010) *Are Juries Fair?* Ministry of Justice

US Department of State (2018) *Country Reports on Human Rights Practices for 2018: Turkey*, Bureau of Democracy, Human Rights and Labor

Warner, K et al (2014) 'Are Judges Out of Touch?' *Current Issues in Criminal Justice*

Wood, M et al (2015) *Re-offending by offenders on Community Orders*, Ministry of Justice Analytical Series

Index

A
abusers, 162–64, 169
accommodation, 130–31, 147, 164
accuracy, 19, 38, 54, 76, 85, 154
acquittal rates, 63
addiction, 115, 117–19, 121, 138, 140, 145, 148, 165
Adler v George, 91
admissibility, 29, 47–48, 51, 55, 85, 98–99, 101, 168
adversarial system, 54
age, 16, 29, 39, 53, 65–66, 81, 92, 124, 126, 151, 158–59
agencies of social control, 103, 141, 144, 153
aims and objectives, 123, 125, 127–29, 131, 169
aims of punishment, 107, 114, 116, 120–21, 167
Allan, Liam, 50, 157
Allende, Salvador, 72
Amnesty International, 72
analysis, 7, 9–11, 15–16, 20, 27–28, 30, 58, 77, 85
anger management, 109, 117–18, 130, 138, 143, 147, 165, 169
Anthony, Donna, 30, 54, 69, 106
anti-social behaviour, 124, 133–38, 141
Anti-social Behaviour, Crime and Policing Act, 138
appeals, 7, 11, 16, 29–30, 33–36, 41, 44–46, 56, 63–64, 66–67, 70, 74, 77–79, 82, 91, 94–95, 99–101, 111, 127, 159, 167–68
appellate courts, 44
Aram, Colette, 16
arrest, 7–8, 14, 16, 22, 27, 29, 31–34, 43, 52, 58, 61, 72, 78, 93, 95–96, 98–101, 103–4, 106, 122–24, 132, 136, 145–46, 150, 153, 167–68
arson, 10, 23, 26, 149
ASBO, 137–38
Asian, 62–63, 66, 157
assaults, 19, 25, 27–28, 34, 41, 44, 82, 101, 143, 149, 158, 160, 165, 167
Association of Chief Police Officers, 123
attachment, 104–5
Australia, 111, 142, 159

B
bail, 33–34, 40–41, 43, 46, 60, 83, 94, 96, 104, 126, 131, 153
Bail Act, 43
Ban the Box, 131
barristers, 12, 44, 52, 54–55, 59, 127, 158, 168
behaviourism, 138
behaviour modification, 138, 143
bias, 12, 37, 56, 62–64, 67, 70–73, 76, 85, 101, 109, 125, 155, 158, 163
Bingham Justices, 67, 101
biological theories, 112
Birmingham Six, 69, 78–79, 100–101
bite marks, 28
Black, 55, 63, 66, 71, 81, 155, 157–58
Black, Hugh, 78
Blair, Tony, 137
Blake, George, 64
blood, 10, 15–16, 20, 25–28, 32, 48, 80
Blythe, Alan, 81, 151

bodily fluids, 9–10, 26
bonds to society, 104
boundary maintenance, 108
British Transport Police, 13, 124, 153
Britton, Paul, 22
Brodsky, SL, 53
Brown, Robert, 82
Buckland, Robert, 15
budget cuts, see cuts
burglary, 23, 25, 41, 110–11, 117, 134–35, 155, 167

C
Cambridge, 56, 158
cannabis, 81, 151, 160
Cannings, Angela, 30, 54, 69
Canter, D, 21, 23
capitalism, 109
capital punishment, 80
CARE programme, 164
Carlen, P, 105
castration, 111–12
Cat and Mouse Act, 151
CCTV, 16–17, 25, 29, 137, 143, 168
cellular confinement, 141, 143
charities, 96, 122, 131, 147, 153, 163–65, 167, 169
child sexual exploitation, 14
Christchurch, 142
civil liberties, 16, 145–46
Civil Nuclear Constabulary, 13, 153
Clark, Sally, 11–12, 20, 30, 54, 69, 100–101
Clarke, Ken, 117
class, 5, 37, 52–53, 56, 66, 84, 87, 102, 111, 114, 122, 133, 144, 153, 157–59
clear-up rate, 154–55, 169
coercion, 104, 106
cognitive behavioural therapy, CBT, 109, 169
cognitive interview, 19
cognitive theories, 107, 109
Cohen, S, 83
Coleman, AM, 134
commitment, 104, 129, 136, 163
common law, 50, 56, 90
Community Order, 96, 112, 118, 130, 140
Community Payback, 112, 118–19, 121, 130
community rehabilitation companies, 130, 148, 162, 169
community sentence, 66, 94–95, 109, 113–14, 117–19, 121, 140, 144–45, 148
compensation, 22, 34, 45, 112–13
contribution of agencies, 133
cost, 13, 16, 39, 43, 45, 54, 63, 66, 85–86, 110, 112, 117, 125, 128, 135, 142, 163
cot death, 30, 47, 54, 69
council tax, 123, 148, 164
Court of Appeal, 29, 44–46, 56, 63, 74, 77–79, 82, 127, 159
courts of the first instance, 44
Covert Human Intelligence Sources, 17
covert surveillance, 17
CPS, 12–13, 34, 37, 40, 44, 52, 62, 67–68, 80, 85, 93–96, 103, 122, 125–26, 132, 141, 148–50, 152, 156–57, 168–69
credible, 38, 47, 49, 53, 68–69, 77, 126
Crime (Sentences) Act, 57, 83, 90, 111
crime control model, 97–99, 101, 168

Crime Prevention through Environmental Design, CPTED, 134–36, 168
crime scene analysis, 20
crime scene investigators, 7–9, 13
Crime Survey for England and Wales, CSEW, 154–55, 169
Criminal Behaviour Orders, 137–38, 169
criminal courts system, 44
criminal damage, 41, 64–65, 81, 149, 151
Criminal Injuries Compensation Authority, 34
Criminal Justice Act, 45, 49, 55, 60, 63, 80, 90, 111, 114–16
Criminal Justice and Courts Act, 60, 64
Criminal Justice and Public Order Act, 49, 150
Crimint, 14
Crown Prosecution Service, 7–8, 12–13, 35, 37–38, 40, 52, 85–86, 94–95, 122, 124–25, 141, 149, 152–53, 156
culture, 58, 103
curfew, 33, 43, 111, 118, 130
currency, 69, 76, 85, 158
custody officer, 31–32, 43, 168
cuts, 13, 42, 125, 128–29, 133, 141, 148–49, 152, 154, 157, 160, 162, 165, 169

D
Dallas, Theodora, 64
Dando, Jill, 29
Dangerous Dogs Act, 57, 90
dark figure, 145
defendant, 7, 11, 25, 29–30, 34–35, 38, 41–47, 49–50, 52, 55, 57–60, 62–71, 77, 79–81, 94–96, 98–101, 119, 121, 125, 127, 151, 156–57
defensible space, 133–34, 168
Dennis, John, 82
detectives, 8–9, 13, 124, 148
determinate sentence, 115
deterrence, 104, 106–7, 109–11, 114, 116, 120–21, 140, 165, 168
Devlin Committee, 18
digital technology, 141, 157
Director of Public Prosecutions, 73, 80, 125, 141, 157
discharge, 81–82, 94, 118, 120–21, 141, 147
discharge grant, 147
disclosure, 29–30, 49–51, 64, 85, 98, 157
disorganised crime, 21
DNA, 9–11, 14–16, 18, 24–28, 32, 53–54, 69–70, 77, 142
Dobson, Gary, 80
domestic abuse, 9, 35, 142, 153–54
Domestic Violence, Crime and Victims Act, 33
double jeopardy, 79–80, 90, 99
drugs, 9–10, 28, 31–32, 43, 48, 62, 82, 91, 95–96, 109, 111, 115–19, 124, 130, 138–40, 143, 145, 147–48, 150, 158, 160, 165, 169
drug trafficking, 111, 117
drug treatment and testing, 109, 115
Duckenfield, David, 73
due process, 97–101, 146, 167–68
Duggan, Mark, 74–75
Dunblane, 57
Dunlop, Billy, 79

Durkheim, E, 98, 108, 113, 152

E
education, 103–4, 109, 117, 129, 131, 141, 147, 149–50, 159, 165
effectiveness of agencies, 153
Ellison, L, 72
entomologists, 20, 28
entrapment, 17, 30, 48, 99–100
environmental design, 133–35
escapes, 64, 128–29, 134, 141, 158, 160, 165
European Court of Human Rights, 63
evidence, 7–12, 14–16, 18–22, 24–41, 43–44, 46–60, 62–63, 67–70, 74–81, 83, 85, 93–95, 98–101, 123–27, 132, 141, 152–54, 156–59, 161–63, 165, 168–69
evidence, admissible, 38
evidence, collecting, transferring and storing, 26, 30, 85
evidence, contaminated, 49
evidence, credible, 38
evidence, forensic, 15, 21, 68, 70, 78, 100
evidence from experts, 69
evidence, illegally obtained, 48, 98–99
evidence, impression, 27
evidence, improperly obtained, 48
evidence of bad character, 49, 99
evidence, physical, 9, 20, 25–26, 29–30, 44, 47, 85
evidence, relevance of, 47–48
evidence, reliable, 38, 47
evidence, statistical, 54, 154
evidence, testimonial, 25, 29–30, 52, 85
evidence, trace, 11, 28–29
evidence, transfer of, 85
evidential test, 37–38, 125–26, 152, 156
exclusion order, 118, 130
execution, 78, 110–11
ex-offenders, 131–32, 164
expert, 10–11, 13, 15, 18–20, 24–25, 29–30, 35, 47, 50, 52, 54–55, 59, 67–70, 78, 85, 156
expert testimony, 30, 70
expert witnesses, 11, 19–20, 25, 30, 52, 54, 69
external forms of social control, 102–3
eye witnesses, 20, 24–25, 35, 53, 68
eye-witness testimony, 18, 53, 69
Eysenck, HJ, 109

F
facts in issue, 47–48
failure to disclose, 50
failure to testify, 49
Falklands, 61, 151
fear of punishment, 104, 106
Felson, M, 136
females, 17, 22, 56, 66, 105, 145, 157–58
feminists, 49, 105
fine, 28, 44, 65, 81, 94, 106–7, 114, 118–20, 142, 144–45, 151
fingerprints, 9, 14–15, 20, 25–28, 32, 48
firearms, 9–10, 14, 31, 57, 74, 150, 154
Firearms (Amendment) Act, 57
fixed-penalty notices, 94, 124, 127, 153
forced confession, 29, 99
forensic pathology, 11, 54
forensics, 7, 15, 26–27

forensic scientists, 8, 10–11, 13, 69, 78, 85
forensic specialists, 13, 15, 20
Foucault, M, 136–37, 143
fraud, 9, 12–13, 41, 56, 62–63, 82, 124, 132, 136, 142, 149, 153, 155
freedom from arbitrary arrest, 146
freedom from detention without trial, 146
freedom of assembly, 146
freedom of movement, 145–46
freedom of religion and conscience, 146
freedom of speech, 145
freedom to associate with others, 146
Freud, 102, 106
Friday releases, 147, 164
Fugitive Slave Act, 81
Full Code Test, 37, 39–40, 94, 152, 156
functionalism, 98, 113
functionalist, 98, 108, 113, 152

G
G4S, 128, 149
Gangs Matrix, 14
gaps in provision, 141, 164, 169
Gardner, Joshua, 82
gated lanes, 135–36
gender, 31, 39, 53, 56, 65–66, 72, 158
General Belgrano, 61, 81, 151
George, Barry, 29–30, 64, 91
Germany, 142
Ghani, Mohammed, 82
Gilderdale, Kay, 62, 81, 151
glass fragments, 28
golden hour, 9
golden rule, 91
Gottfredson, M, 105
government departments, 93, 95
Grayling, Chris, 162
Green Paper, 88, 92
Gregory, A, 23
Guardian, 156
gun, 9, 20, 28–29, 36, 57, 150, 154

H
hair, 9, 15–16, 26–27, 58
Hall, S, 71
harassment, 35, 138
hate crimes, 9, 34–35, 108
hearsay, 7, 29, 38, 50–51, 68, 75, 78, 85, 99, 126
Heidensohn, F, 105
Her Majesty's Courts and Tribunals Service, 83, 94-95
Hill, Max, 125, 141, 157
Hillsborough, 73–74
Hirsch, Afua, 158
Hirschi, T, 104–5
HMP Birmingham, 128, 149, 160–61, 165
HM Prison and Probation Service, 94–95
HM Prison Service, 94–96
HM Revenue and Customs, 13, 124, 153
Hobbs, TR, 139
Hoffman, Lord, 72
Holt, MM, 139
homelessness, 119, 145–48, 164
Home Office, 11–12, 30, 78, 93, 95–96, 100, 134, 150, 152, 169
Home Secretary, 149
homicide, 11, 16, 20, 113, 160
honey trap, 22, 30, 48, 100
hospital admissions, 155

House of Commons, 87–89, 92, 130
Howard League for Penal Reform, 96, 147, 169
human rights, 17, 45, 48, 63, 72, 145
human trafficking, 35–36, 152
hunger strike, 151
Hutchinson, Paul, 16

I
ideology, 103, 163
illiteracy, 147, 160
impartiality, 62, 67, 70, 126
imprisonment for public protection, 111, 115
incapacitation, 111–12, 114, 116, 165, 168
incentives and earned privileges, 129, 139, 169
indeterminate sentence, 111, 115, 117, 165
indictable offences, 33, 41, 44, 99
individualistic theories, 109
inferior judges, 127
Innocence Project, 18, 53–54, 77
inquests, 55, 60, 73–75, 96
INQUEST, 73, 96
insects, 20, 28
institutional racism, 9, 169
institutional tactics, 139, 143
intelligence databases, 14, 24
internal forms of social control, 102, 169
internalisation, 103, 106, 169
internet, 5, 59, 64–65, 78, 84
INTERPOL, 14
interviews, 7, 18–19, 21, 24, 32, 36, 96, 123, 147, 159
investigative psychology, 20, 23–24
involvement, 39, 104

J
James, Lizzie, 22
James, Rosie, 81, 151
Jefferies, Christopher, 58, 71
Jewish tradition, 103
judge, 12, 22, 30, 33, 36, 38, 42, 44–46, 48–50, 52–53, 55–57, 60–66, 68, 70–78, 80–82, 85–86, 90–91, 93–95, 98–100, 104, 114–15, 126–27, 141, 149, 157–59, 167–68
judgements, 68, 71–72, 74–76, 85, 157
judges' backgrounds, 157
judicial bias, 56
judicial discretion, 82
judicial independence, 126
judicial oath, 126
judicial precedent, 90, 127, 168
judiciary, 52, 55, 59, 68, 85, 87, 122, 126–27, 153, 157–58
Juries Act, 60
juror infatuation, 55
jurors, 7, 38, 44–45, 53–55, 58–65, 68–69, 71–72, 78, 159, 168
jurors and the internet, 59, 64–65
jury, 7, 11, 18, 38, 44–45, 47–50, 52-56, 58–65, 67–69, 73–74, 77–78, 80–81, 85, 94, 99, 127, 151, 156, 168
jury equity, 55, 61–62, 80
juryless trials, 55–56, 99
jury nullification, 80–81
jury's role, 44, 60
jury system, 61–62
jury tampering, 45, 55–56, 63, 99, 168
just deserts, 107, 113, 116
just sentencing, 81, 83, 85

INDEX

just verdicts, 79–81, 83, 85
juvenile offenders, 144, 161

K
Kaufmann, G, 53
Kirk, PL, 25
knife crime, 36, 92, 150, 154–55
Kuehn, L, 19
Ku Klux Klan, 81

L
labelling, 98, 112–13, 121, 138, 169
Lammy, D, 63, 67
latent prints, 27
law creation, 93
Lawrence, Stephen, 9, 17, 46, 80, 90, 154–55
law reports, 68, 75–76, 85
laypeople, 7, 44, 54, 60, 65, 67, 69, 85
left realism, 98, 109
legal advice, 32, 43
legal aid, 41–44, 73, 94, 99, 162
Levitt, Alison, 156
licence, 14, 94–96, 115, 117, 121, 130, 140, 144, 147, 169
Licensing Act, 91
life sentences, 12, 57, 78, 90, 111, 115, 152
limitations of agencies, 144
literacy, 117
literal rule, 91
local and national policies, 149
Locard, E, 25–26
Loftus, E, 19, 69
Lombroso, C, 112

M
Mackrell, Graham, 73
Macpherson Report, 9, 80, 90, 154–55, 169
magistrate, 7, 33, 38, 41, 43–45, 47–48, 52–53, 55, 58, 60, 62–63, 65–68, 70, 77, 81–83, 85, 90, 94, 99, 101, 104, 106, 114, 119–20, 127, 149, 152, 156, 159, 168
males, 57, 145, 157
malpractice, 79, 101
manslaughter, 45, 60, 73, 82, 121
Marxists, 109, 145
Matrix Churchill, 57
Meadow, Sir Roy, 11, 30, 47, 54, 69
media, 7, 12, 17, 21, 25, 34, 52, 55, 57–59, 63, 68, 70–71, 73, 76, 83, 85, 90, 110, 142, 145, 150, 155–59, 164
Members of Parliament, MPs, 56, 88–89, 92, 127, 145, 164
memory, 18–19, 53, 69, 124
mental health, 29, 35, 116–19, 121, 131, 148, 156, 160, 164
Metropolitan Police, 9, 122, 124, 149, 154–55
Ming, Ann, 79, 90
Ministry of Justice, 93, 95–96, 119, 130
miscarriages of justice, 7, 11–12, 16, 20, 54, 69, 77–79, 100-1
mischief rule, 91
moral imperative, 150–51
morality, 81, 103, 169
moral panics, 55, 57, 71, 83, 90, 150, 156, 159
Mullin, Chris, 78–79
murder, 9, 11–12, 15–17, 20–22, 26, 29–30, 35, 41, 43–47, 50, 54, 57–60, 62–63, 72, 78–80, 82, 90, 100, 107, 113, 115, 128, 142, 145, 154–55, 157, 159

murderer, 21–22, 46, 107
Muslim, 103

N
Nacro, 96, 131–32, 147, 163–64, 169
Napper, Robert, 22
National DNA Database, 14, 16, 24
National Probation Service, 94–96, 129–30, 162–63, 169
New Labour, 137
Newman, O, 133–34
new technology, 141–42, 152
Nickell, Rachel, 17, 22, 100
norms, 102–4, 106, 122, 137, 167
Norris, David, 80
nullification, 80–81

O
oath of allegiance, 126
observation, 17, 24
obstacle course, 98, 101, 168
Office for National Statistics, 154
Official Secrets Act, 61, 91
operant learning theory, 103, 109, 138, 143, 169
opinion, 20–21, 30, 54, 68–69, 71, 76, 85, 104, 145, 159, 166
organised crime, 12–14, 21
overcrowding, 149, 160, 165

P
Packer, H, 97
paint, 15, 26, 28
Palmer, JC, 19
Panopticon, 136–37, 143
parole, 70, 95–96, 104, 111, 115, 143
pathologists, 8, 11–13, 20
Paul v DPP, 65
Peel, Sir Robert, 122, 124
peers, 62, 67, 87, 99, 102, 106, 110, 138
penal populism, 83
people trafficking, 13, 82, 159
Peruche, B, 71
perverse decision, 55, 63
phased discipline, 141, 169
philosophy, 122, 124–26, 128–29, 131, 169
Pickles, Judge, 158
Pinochet, Augusto, 72
Pitchfork, Colin, 15
Plant, E, 71
plastic prints, 27
plea, 33, 41–46, 55, 62–65, 81, 94, 167
plea bargaining, 41–42, 46, 55
police, 7–9, 11–24, 26–37, 40, 43, 47–50, 52, 55, 58, 63, 67–68, 71, 73–75, 78, 80, 86, 93–101, 103, 106, 122–25, 127, 130–34, 136, 140–42, 144–46, 148–50, 153–57, 161, 167–69
Police and Crime Commissioners, 124
Police and Criminal Evidence Act, 31, 123
Police Code of Ethics, 122–23
Police Community Support Officers, 124
Police National Computer, 14
Police National Database, 14
police officer, 7–9, 13–14, 17, 22, 32, 49–50, 55, 63, 67, 71, 101, 123–24, 148, 150
policing by consent, 123, 132, 155
politics, 56–57, 59
Ponting, Clive, 61, 81, 151
post mortem, 9–11, 20, 30
poverty, 109, 164

precedent, 56, 75, 90–91, 127, 168
pre-sentence reports, 130
press coverage, 63
pressure group, 73, 122, 131, 147, 153, 163–64, 167, 169
presumption of guilt, 97, 101
presumption of innocence, 98, 101, 168
pre-trial, 41, 43, 46, 58, 94
previous convictions, 39, 43, 49, 81–83, 99, 119, 145, 161, 165
Pringle, Judge, 158
prison, 16, 43–44, 60, 63–65, 70–71, 79, 81, 83, 86, 93–97, 101, 104, 106, 109–12, 114–22, 128–33, 136–41, 143–45, 147–49, 151, 153, 158–61, 163–65, 167–69
Prisoners' Earnings Act, 117
prison officers, 128–29, 147, 149, 160
prison population, 83, 112, 115, 144, 160
Prison Reform Trust, 96, 119
Prison Rules, 140
privatisation, 149, 162–63
probation, 41, 86, 93–96, 109, 115, 118, 122, 128–32, 140–41, 147–49, 153, 158, 160, 162–63, 167, 169
profiling, 7, 15–16, 20–24, 142
proportionality, 107, 113
Prosecution of Offences Act, 37, 40, 125
Psychoactive Substances Act, 160
psychologists, 19–22, 53, 69
public-interest immunity, 50, 57, 99
public interest test, 37, 39, 125–26, 152
public protection, 107, 111, 114–17, 119, 121, 168
purposeful activity, 138

R
race, 31, 71, 147, 151, 155
racial bias, 62–64, 67
racially aggravated offences, 108
racism, 9, 49, 155, 169
racist attacks, 9
Ramadan, 103, 106
rape, 11–12, 15–16, 21, 23, 26, 34, 41, 44, 49–50, 53, 56, 72, 82, 91, 113, 115, 128, 141–42, 149, 152, 156–57, 159
rational choice theory, 108, 110, 136, 168
rational ideology, 103
recidivism, 118–19, 121, 144, 148–49, 165
Reckless, WC, 105–6
recording procedures, 154
rehabilitation, 107, 109, 114, 117–19, 121, 130–31, 139, 143, 147–48, 160–63, 165, 169
Rehabilitation of Offenders Act, 131
reinforcement, 103, 138–39, 143, 169
release on temporary licence, 117, 147
relevant facts, 47–48, 77
remand in custody, 41, 43
re-offending, 86, 109, 116–19, 121, 130, 138, 141, 143–45, 147, 161–65, 169
reparation, 107, 112–14, 117–19, 121
residency requirement, 118, 130
resources, 20, 109, 141, 144, 147, 149–50, 156
restitutive justice, 113
restorative justice, 34–35, 112–13
retribution, 107–9, 113–14, 116, 118, 120–21

173

right realism, 98, 107, 110, 113
right realist, 98, 104, 108–9, 112, 136, 145
rights at the police station, 31
rights of appeal, 33, 45
rights of suspects, 7, 31, 85, 97
rights of victims, 33
rights of witnesses, 35
rights to information, 32
rights when being questioned, 32
right to legal advice, 32
right to privacy, 34, 146
right to remain silent, 32, 48–49, 99
Riley, D, 105
riot, 16, 55, 57, 71, 74, 82–83, 128, 147, 149, 159–61, 165
robbery, 14, 41, 44, 63, 82, 107, 159, 167
role of agencies, 122
routine activity theory, 136
Royal Assent, 87–89, 92
runaway slaves, 81
R v Connor and Rollock, 64
R v Kronlid, 64
R v Maginnis, 91
R v Mirza, 64
R v R, 91
R v Taylor and Taylor, 63
R v Twomey, 63

S
safe verdict, 77, 83, 85
saliva, 15, 26–28
sanctions, 102–4, 106, 140–41, 143, 169
Saunders, Alison, 125, 141
Scott, Adam, 11, 16, 70
Secured by Design, 134
selection, 60
self-harm, 149, 160, 164–65
semen, 15, 26–27
sentence, 12, 33–35, 41–42, 44–46, 55, 57, 60, 63, 66–67, 71, 78, 80–83, 90, 94–96, 99–100, 104, 108–21, 127–28, 130–31, 140–41, 144–45, 147–49, 152, 157–61, 164–65, 167–69
sentencing, 41, 44, 55, 65–66, 70, 81–83, 85, 94–96, 111, 113–14, 119, 140, 149, 158–59, 164, 168–69
Sentencing Guidelines, 55, 66, 81, 94, 119, 164
Serious and Organised Crime Agency, 13
serious violence strategy, 150
severity versus certainty, 110
sexual abuse, 164
sexual assault, 27–28, 34, 158
Sexual Offences Act, 57
sex work, 152
Shabbat, 103
Shaw, M, 105
shoeprint, 9, 15, 27–28

short sentences, 117, 144, 147, 149, 160–61, 165
Sidebottom, A, 135
situational crime prevention, 110, 136
skin flakes, 15, 26–27
Skinner, BF, 103, 109, 138, 143
Skuse, Sir Frank, 69, 78
Smart, C, 56
smartphones, 152, 157
social control, 86, 102–6, 122, 132–33, 136–46, 148–49, 152–54, 156, 159, 161–65, 167, 169
socialisation, 102–3, 105–6, 169
social learning theory, 106, 110
social media, 7, 25, 59, 68, 142
Sodexo, 128, 130
soils, 28
solitary confinement, 104, 141
special constables, 124
Spice, 160, 165
Stacey, Glenys, 149, 163
Stagg, Colin, 17, 22, 30, 48, 100
stalking, 35, 87, 169
Stansted 15, 151–52
stare decisis, 90
statute law, 56, 93
statutory interpretation, 90–91, 93, 168
stereotypes, 53, 71–72, 158
stereotyping, 53, 71
stop and search, 31, 99, 150
Suffragettes, 151–52
suicide, 16, 62, 81, 149, 151, 160, 164–65
summary offences, 41, 43
superego, 102–3, 106, 169
superior judges, 127
Supreme Court, 44, 46, 90–91, 127
surveillance, 7, 16–17, 24, 124, 134–37, 143, 168
suspended sentence, 82, 115, 144, 152, 158

T
Tabak, Vincent, 58
tabloid press, 58, 68, 71
tagging, 111
Taylor, Damilola, 12, 157
Taylor, Lord Justice, 73
Taylor sisters, 63
territoriality, 134–35, 168
terrorism, 12, 31, 33, 35, 69, 124, 128, 142, 153
Terrorism Act, 33
testimony of experts, 68
Thatcher, Margaret, 110
theft, 41, 44, 62, 80–81, 128, 149, 155, 158–59
Theft Act, 81
Thomas, C, 58, 63–64
Threshold Test, 39–40, 126
token economies, 109, 133, 137–39, 143, 169
tradition, 5, 59, 103, 106, 142, 169

training, 9, 11, 65, 109, 117, 119, 121, 124, 129, 138, 147, 149, 165
transcript, 68, 70, 75–76, 85
travel bans, 111
triable either way, 41
TV licences, 164
tyre marks, 9, 27–28

U
undercover, 17–18, 22, 48, 50
unduly lenient sentences, 82, 95, 159
unemployed, 145
unemployment, 109, 119, 165
unpaid work, 112–13, 118–19, 130
unsafe or wrongful convictions, 18, 54, 77-79
unsafe verdicts, 77

V
validity, 68–69, 71, 74, 76, 85
victim, 9, 11–12, 16, 20–21, 23, 25, 27–29, 31, 33–36, 39, 47, 49–50, 53, 56, 64, 70, 72, 74, 81–82, 85, 95–98, 100, 112–14, 117–19, 125–26, 128–29, 131, 142, 149, 152–54, 156–59, 162, 164, 169
Victim Personal Statement, 33–34
Victim Support, 34, 95–96, 169
voluntary organisations, 95–96, 122, 163–64, 167, 169

W
war crimes, 10
Warner, K, 159
weapons amnesties, 150
Wenham, Rachel, 81, 151
West Midlands Serious Crime Squad, 79, 101
White, 63, 67, 71, 81, 88, 92, 136, 142, 157–58, 162
White Paper, 88, 92
Williams, Pete, 12, 30, 53, 100, 111
Windrush, 152
Witness Care Officer, 34
Witness Charter, 35–36
witnesses, 9-12, 15, 18–20, 24–26, 29–31, 34–36, 38, 40, 43, 47, 49–50, 52–54, 59, 68–70, 78, 85, 94-95, 98, 100, 124–25, 132, 157
Witness Service, 35, 95
Women in Prison, 96, 163–64
women prisoners, 160, 164, 169
Women's Aid, 96
women's refuges, 95
Woodward, Lavinia, 158
Woolf, Lord, 65
Wrightson, Angela, 59

Y
Yeates, Joanna, 58
young offender institutions, 138–39

Z
zero tolerance policing, 98

YOUR NOTES